Lady Father

By

Susan Bowman

Patte,
God bless you
in all your
endeavors!

Susan Bowman

Aberdeen Bay
Albion - Harbin - Topeka - Washington, D.C.

Aberdeen Bay
Published by Aberdeen Bay, an imprint of Champion Writers.
www.aberdeenbay.com

PUBLISHER'S NOTE

Aberdeen Bay is not responsible for the accuracy of this
book--including but not limited to events, people, dates, and
locations.

International Standard Book Number
ISBN-13: 978-1-60830-056-3
ISBN-10: 1-60830-056-0

Printed in the United States of America.

Foreword

I was deeply honored when my friend Susan Bowman asked me to write the foreword to her forthcoming book, "Lady Father." It has been a joy and privilege to count Susan among my best friends for twenty years, and I have walked with her through many of the storms of her life as a priest. It has not been an easy journey but as her narrative attests, she is a survivor and she doesn't give up.

Susan received a call from God to be a priest in a church that just barely had gotten its mind around ordaining women. She honored that call, and did all in her power to obey it. As a result, she has experienced the ministry of the One whose priesthood she shares, her Lord Jesus Christ, and she has walked in the way of His cross. Her life has brought her many joys, but also has taken her through harrowing suffering and deeply challenging trials. It is evidence of God's faithfulness and trustworthiness that Susan continues to serve God as a priest and pastor and it gives me joy to hear her stories of how much fun she is having as pastor of Jermain United Methodist Church in White Creek, New York. Finally!

The Bible calls Jesus the "pioneer and perfector of our faith," and as His life demonstrated, being a pioneer comes with a very high price. As a woman in the priesthood of the Episcopal Church, Susan has been a pioneer. She has never waved a flag or been a mascot for a cause, other than the cause of her Savior. I believe that in the end, that Savior will receive her into His kingdom with the words, "Well done, good and faithful servant."

It is my hope that you will be inspired and emboldened, as I have been, as a result of reading these pages. And may the example of Susan's perseverance and tenacity empower you and me to stick to it as we seek to do what God calls us to do.

"Therefore, since we are surrounded by so great a cloud of witnesses, let us also lay aside every weight, and sin which clings so closely, and let us run with perseverance the race that is set before us, looking to Jesus the pioneer and perfector of our faith, who for the joy that was set before him endured the cross, despising the shame, and is seated at the right hand of the throne of God." (Hebrews 12:1-2)

Darius Mojallali
March, 2011

SUSAN BOWMAN - BIO

Susan Bowman was born and raised in Petersburg, Virginia. In 1969 she received a BA in Philosophy from the College of William Mary. She began her long and mostly self-taught journey toward computer competency, living and working around the Southeast. Through on-the-job training, Susan mastered the first automatic typewriter (MTST) and by 1971 was formatting a book on aircraft carriers using the MTSC (Magnetic Tape Selectric Composer).

Susan worked for the City of Petersburg for almost eight years before answering a call to ordained ministry in the Episcopal Church. She attended seminary at the University of the South's School of Theology and graduated with a Masters of Divinity Degree in 1984.

Following her ordination to the priesthood in 1986, Susan served as Chaplain in a girls' group home and then as Pastor for three churches until retiring in 2007. She worked as a Travel Specialist for AAA and a columnist for the AAA bi-monthly magazine, "Going Places." She leads worship and preaches at a small church in upstate New York.

In May 2010, Susan became the Senior Editor of an online magazine, Our Heritage Magazine Online. In this capacity, she writes feature articles, recurring columns, and lead stories; she edits all copy for the six online and two printed issues - http://ourheritagemagazine.com.

She has two retail websites for digital publications: http://howcanibebetter.com (self-improvement books) and http://websolutionsontheweb.com (internet marketing and affiliate products). She has written numerous eBooks, articles, and website copy for clients of her internet-based Freelance Writing business, SBUnlimited - http://gettherightwriter.com. Her finished book with an English medical doctor is awaiting publishing later this year. She can be found on Facebook and on her blog - http://ladyfather.com.

ACKNOWLEDGMENTS

Writing this book has taken a long time. I started in 1993 when I was a Fellow-in-Residence at Sewanee for two weeks. I used the seminary's computer and saved it all on a floppy disk. Some years later, I decided to finish my book, only to discover that the floppy disk was nowhere to be found. For years, I mourned its loss. Then, in 2009, I got a call from an internet guru named Hamlet Batista, who was putting together a promotional program and needed a "guinea pig." He asked me if I had ever thought of writing a book and I said, "Funny you should ask." I told him about my journey and the book I had dreamed of and he offered to help me promote the book if I would write a testimonial for his promotional program. I agreed and, 18 months later, my dream has become a reality. Many thanks to Hamlet for pushing me to keep on working and writing, and for never giving up on me.

Trying to write a book while holding down a full-time job is hard enough for a young, budding author; for a 63-year-old budding author, it's nearly impossible; so it wasn't until I took a huge leap of faith and quit my "day job," that I could write full time and finally finish my lifelong dream. I was fortunate to find the absolute best editor in the world, Lucia Zimmitti, who offered a trial editing session on the first five pages of a manuscript. I sent her six pages and, when we talked, she called my book "a memoir with a purpose." She was able to zero in on that purpose with an uncanny precision that convinced me that she was the right editor to pick my book apart and help me to put it back together into the best it could be. I was right. She not only picked up on the most meaningful parts of my story, she drew more feelings and details out of me than I thought I could ever remember. She is an editor "extraordinaire" and I am blessed to have found her.

I was also blessed with the absolute best proofreader, although she was much easier to find! After reading parts of my book, she offered! It seems that I have a tendency to write run-on sentences; she even compares me to the Apostle Paul, who was the ancient master at long and protracted sentences, some even as long as a whole paragraph. According to my proofreader, Ginny Fluet (also my sister), I hit a record – a six-line sentence – which took her the better part of an hour to dissect into three manageable pieces. Thank you, Ginny, for your patience and your unerring eye for detail; you are the queen of the commas!

I also want to thank my Book Promotion Committee for all the hard work that goes into marketing a new book. They are: Ginny Fluet, Freida Carnell, Charlotte Gordon, Mary Cole, Doris Bedell, Agnes Nawalaniec, Katie Hager, Hamlet Batista, Philippe Matthews (President, MyInternetMarketingExpert.net), Gail Harris, and Jennifer Osterhout, who helped me read my 1st galley proof.

It has been said that "friends are the jewels in the crown of God." They are one of the biggest blessings in my life and I wish I had enough pages to name every one of them. From 1975, when I became involved in the youth ministry program of the Diocese of Southern Virginia, I was blessed with the unflagging friendship and support of the Rev. David Davenport, then Diocesan Youth Ministries Director. He taught me so much about being a priest and he lived the Gospel of Jesus Christ in his ministry with the young people, giving me the model of a Christian and a priest that would help to form me into who I am today. I am eternally grateful to David for his love and trust as he allowed me to be a significant part of his ministry and his life.

There were many, many friends in the Southern Virginia family who loved me and supported me throughout my lay ministry years and who stood behind me through the agonizing process for ordination; in fact, many of them followed me and are now ordained clergy. I love you all and I thank you for everything you gave so freely.

My years in Sewanee were blessed by so many dear people: the members of the Class of 1984, who walked with me, stood beside me, held me up, and loved me through three years of struggle with the ordination process and with my own demons. I would have never made it through it all without them. There were students from other classes who loved me and supported me as well – neighbors, soul-mates, and dear friends – and who continue to be there for me whenever I reach out to them.

The Faculty of the School of Theology during the years 1981-1984 were possibly the best theological educators in the church. With its deadly but effective Core Curriculum, Sewanee managed to teach me more than I ever dreamed possible about God, the Bible, the Church, and how to be a priest. Our Interim Dean, Gireault Jones, retired Bishop of Western Louisiana, was the first one to greet our class and to assure us that he would not let us fall through the cracks in a community that was wracked with grief by the death of their beloved Dean, Terry Holmes. "The Meanwhile Dean" was true to his word and he shepherded us through the difficult first year with grace and love. I could write pages about each of the faculty members as they patiently took a middle-aged woman who hadn't been to any school in more than 13 years and who had almost totally disgraced herself as an undergraduate student, and made her into a theologian. They were the stars in the crown that is the School of Theology of the University of the South, and some are still shining on to this day. Many thanks to them all: Don Armentrout, Robert Hughes, Howard Rhys, Steven Kraftchick (sabbatical replacement), Marion Hatchett, Neil Alexander (sabbatical replacement), Bill Griffin, Edna Evans, Bill Hethcock, Craig Anderson, Jack Gessell, and our beloved Dean, John Booty. (There were other adjunct faculty members, as well as faculty spouses who taught me so much and were such good friends.)

I know the dangers of singling any one person out of such a stellar group, but I want to take this opportunity to record in this permanent venue my love and respect for Professor Donald Armentrout, who was without a doubt, the best teacher from whom I ever had the pleasure of learning anything. With his delightful, sort-of-tongue-in-cheek (although true) rantings about the "works-righteousness" of the Episcopal Church, and his adamant, podium-pounding assertions of the Lutheran "salvation-by-faith" theology, he drilled into our heads the truth of the Gospel, along with the historical timeline of our faith. He and his wife, Sue, were great friends to me and Scott. I so wanted his comments and review of this book, but his present illness makes that impossible and I pray daily for him, for Sue, and the rest of his family as they all suffer through the inevitable end of the perishable body.

There's no doubt that I would have never made it to the "Holy Mountain" without the love and support of my family. My mother and father, Belle and Howard Blount, were extraordinary parents, as they loved me and supported me, no matter what I did. They probably never totally understood what drove me into the priesthood, but just the fact that their "baby girl" wanted to be a priest was enough. They loved me and their grandson with a blind devotion that made us both feel cherished no matter how far we ventured from their home. Their heroic efforts to move us to Sewanee are but one testimony to their love for us and "Wrong-Way Howard" will live on in infamy. We both miss them terribly.

My sister Ginny and my brother David were mostly

typical annoying siblings as we were growing up; but when we finally did grow up, we came through some tough times and became the best of friends. They have been rock-solid support for me through the 25 years of my ministry and have never lost their faith in me and my dream. David's family – wife, Louise and children, Kelly and Will – have loved me through all these years and I love them, which is evidenced by the fact that I allow them, and only them, to call me Aunt Susie. Ginny's family – husband, Joe, and children (Jenny, Mark, Kris, & Katie Huber and Joe, Connie, Ben, & Jay Fluet) have been a huge support and inspiration to me. They have all allowed me to "marry" them, baptize them, and minister to them; and they have ministered to me, supported me, cared for my son during some sensitive times in his life, and been the best family anyone could hope to have in this lifetime.

There are so many more people in my life whose love and support helped to make me who I am today: the Rev. Don Porcher, Rector of St. Michael's Colonial Heights, Virginia who saw the dream in me before I did; the Rev. Don Roberts, Rector of Good Shepherd, Norfolk, Virginia who dragged the dream out of me and pushed me to follow it; the Rev. Douglas Burgoyne, Rector of St. Andrew's, Newport News and the Chair of the Commission on Ministry, who stood by me in my darkest hour and who brought light back into my life with his dream for me AND Jackson-Feild Home for Girls; the Rev. Rick Draper, who mentored me through the "Meanwhile" years, when I felt like I'd never find my way out of the oblivion of almost-not-yet; the Rev. Norm Baty, my Spiritual Director and friend, who led me on an amazing journey through my desiccated spiritual life into a rich and meaningful relationship with my Lord, Jesus; and the Rev. Darius Mojallalli, my friend of 20 years, who never failed to listen to my woes, to be my friend, and to affirm and re-affirm my worthiness as God's priest. I am deeply indebted to these clergy friends and many others who have been there for me over the years, especially those who have forgiven me my trespasses and become mentors and friends.

I give thanks to God for the faithful ministry of the Rt. Rev. David S. Ball, Bishop of the Diocese of Albany, now retired, who boldly approved my employment as the first woman to be a canonically resident priest in the Diocese. His solid support for my parish ministry as well as his courageous and successful efforts to include me in the leadership of a Diocese that was openly struggling with the issue of women's ordination, were instrumental in my growth as a priest. I thank God for him and his journey of faith that brought him to accept, ordain, and embrace women as ordained clergy.

Finally, I must pay tribute to my only child – my son and my best friend, Scott. From his relatively easy appearance in the world to this day, he has been a bright light in my life. A smart and easy-going child, he grew into a tolerable teen-ager, and then into a solid, intelligent, and loving adult. Scott was my world, as I was his, from the time he was two years old and his father and I divorced. With the blind devotion of an only child in a one-parent family, he joined me in my quest to follow God's call and in our subsequent movements all over the Eastern seaboard – from Sewanee, Tennessee to Albany, New York.

He suffered through two interminable summers as a seminarian's kid in the homes of strangers and he has survived almost a lifetime as a "PK" (Preacher's Kid). He stood by me, he ranted and raved with me, he cried with me, and he loved me through the pain of rejection, the agony of waiting, and the struggle to "keep on keeping on." To say that I would not have survived without him is a major understatement. Without him, I would have given up years ago; with him and his steadfast support and encouragement, I have risen above every challenge and overcome every obstacle. I have even found joy and fulfillment where there was little hope of anything but failure because, no matter what threatened my well-being and my happiness, I knew that my son loved me and believed in me.

When he was a not-so-wonderful teen-ager, he swore off women and marriage saying that he was NEVER going to get married and have children. I remember the day distinctly. I stopped in my tracks and whirled around to face him; I said, "You wanna bet? If you think you're going to put me through all this and then NOT give me grandchildren – think again! I will get grandchildren and don't you forget it!" Of course, I doubt seriously that he married Stacey because of that tirade; from the moment he met her, she was the one and together they have given me two precious grandchildren, Jared and Emily. They have all blessed my life immeasurably and have made it possible for me to come through the fires and deep pits of the last 10 years. They are now standing beside me and cheering for me as I have finally reached my goal and am finally living my dream.

Last, but certainly not least, I give thanks to God for all of this: my life, my son, my family, my friends, my call to youth ministry, the wonderful young people, clergy, and youth advisors of the Diocese of Southern Virginia, my call to the priesthood, two faithful Bishops, a number of mentors and Spiritual Directors, many loving and supportive parishioners, and the strength and courage to walk through it all.

Even in the moments when I felt all alone, I knew that God was with me, pulling for me to persevere, and pushing me toward the day when my ever faithful Bishop would pray, "...fill her with your Spirit and make her a priest in your church." I never gave up on God and God never gave up on me. To paraphrase the Apostle Paul, that is what faith is all about:

In everything, give thanks to God, and no matter what comes, stop, look up, and say, "OK, Lord. It's you and me."

The Rev. Susan B. Bowman
February, 2011

Dedicated to
The Rt. Rev. C. Charles Vaché
7th Bishop of the Diocese of Southern Virginia
1978 – 1991

When I first met Bishop Charles Vaché, he was the Bishop Coadjutor of the Diocese of Southern Virginia, elected to replace the retiring Bishop, David Rose. I thought he was just what a Bishop is supposed to be – stately and dignified, humble and kind, but with a powerful presence that lets everyone know that a Bishop is in the room. Bishop Vaché was all of these and more. He was a wonderful Bishop, but he was also a servant, a Pastor, and a friend. He had the strangest sense of humor, and he loved a good joke! His favorites were what he called "punny" stories and I shared his love for these "groaners"; but he also loved to make people happy.

When I was a child, my mother wore the ugliest Christmas corsage on this planet. My sister complained about it so loudly, that Mom wrapped it up and gave it to her for Christmas. Thus began the journey of the "corsage" through the female members of our family. Over the years, it was cooked in a cake, buried in a watermelon, and adorned with diamond earrings. As it became seriously dilapidated, we decided to retire it and Bishop Vaché formally blessed and retired the Blount family heirloom in a short ceremony at a

colleague's house blessing. But, alas, we couldn't live without our fun, so we found a new one, even uglier, and at Mom & Dad's 50th anniversary party, we unveiled not only a new version of the "corsage," but a local florist had reluctantly made a boutonnière to match. Bishop Vaché had graciously accepted

**The Rt. Rev. C. Charles Vaché
"The Pinning"**

my invitation to be with my family for this special celebration to surprise my parents. He hid in the basement with the other surprise guests, announced himself in a perfect "This-is-Your-Life" style, and presented my stunned parents with their new family heirlooms. I think it's safe to say that Charles Vaché may be the only Bishop in Christendom to drive two hours through winter weather to pin some atrocious-looking flowers on the parents of one of his priests. They were thrilled, my family and I were touched, and, as you can see by the picture, he had a blast!

Charles Vaché was the consummate Bishop. He was also my hero. When I began my journey, he endorsed my application to attend seminary even though he was still opposed to women in the ordained ministry. When I went back to him three months later professing a call to ordination, he nodded and said, "I knew that already." While I struggled prayerfully over my call, he courageously answered a call deep in his spirit to allow God to lead us both along the same treacherous path to the truth – Ordination is God's business.

On All Saints' Day, November 1, 2009, my beloved Bishop answered the ultimate call and joined all the saints at God's heavenly banquet. As I stood at his grave in the courtyard of Trinity Church in Portsmouth, Virginia, I gave thanks to God for this faithful and courageous man, who believed in me and who taught me to "trust the process. I wept tears of sadness for my loss and tears of joy for him, as I am certain that he was greeted at the gates of heaven by a grateful God, saying, "Well done, good and faithful servant."

LADY FATHER

THE END

It was as if someone had died. Neighbors and friends were answering the phone in hushed tones and calling my doctor while I wept uncontrollably in my bedroom. Other friends were bringing food and treats for my son as the word spread through the community. They had come when Scotty called for help after he heard my primal scream from the kitchen. I had dropped the phone and slid to the floor in a heap of despair and grief. He was only twelve years old but he knew something terrible had happened to his mother and he kept asking me, "Mom, what's wrong?"

I couldn't answer him; all I could do was cry. My world had crashed; my life was over; I was falling into a deep pit and could barely hear his panicky questions as I was screaming inside – I CAN'T BELIEVE THIS IS HAPPENING TO ME! The next thing I knew I was sitting on the edge of my bed and my neighbor was trying to calm me down enough to find out what had happened. Scotty could only tell him that I had gotten some phone call and was now hysterical.

I couldn't speak; I just sobbed as my friend, Bob, held me and my son watched in horror from the hall. Finally, I began to hear Bob's questions and somehow I managed to tell him what had happened. He was appalled at the news but he was all kindness and gentle support as he helped me get some control of myself. I realized that Scotty had come into the room and he asked me in a tremulous voice, "Mom, are you OK? Can I get you anything?" with a maturity way beyond his twelve years. I heard him but my heart hurt so badly I could not speak.

PART ONE

THE JOURNEY

The call had come just after dinner and, when I hung up, I felt as if I had been punched in the stomach and smacked in the face. My world spun out of control as I listened to the words which effectively rendered the last three years of my life null and void and probably ended my career. I felt the heat of shame and embarrassment as I heard the words the man was saying – "We're not recommending you." In my head, I heard "Reject! Reject!" I wanted to scream at the unfairness and at the frustrating finality of his last words before hanging up the phone – "we may grant you a new interview in a year."

I knew instinctively that this was it – there would be no immediate recourse to this decision. It had been made abundantly clear that this part of the process was beyond our control – whatever the Standing Committee said was sacrosanct and they would not change it. I was lost in a sea of outdated thinking and blatant gender bias against women in male-dominated roles in a church which had nurtured me, fed me, taught me, called me, and then dumped me like a misfit. I was unacceptable – a reject. The old "11th Commandment of the Episcopal Church" – that would be the one that says, "We've never done it this way" – had kicked in and kicked me right out of the ordination process.

It was late April of 1984 and I was at the pinnacle of my journey from clueless layperson to educated theologian on the way to the ordained ministry. I was preparing to graduate from the School of Theology of the University of the South in Sewanee, Tennessee after completing the requirements for a Masters of Divinity degree in preparation for ordination to the diaconate and the priesthood of the Episcopal Church. It had been a long journey and a rocky road as I navigated a system which was not prepared for me to be admitted as the first woman to the ordination process in the Diocese of Southern Virginia.

This process of discernment and formation was administered by traditional church leaders – clergy and laypeople – and, in our case, a Bishop who staunchly opposed the ordination of women. They were all fearful of the inundation they knew would come if I made it through the process and was ordained. As I heard a number of times, I was a shining light of possibility with pure motives, but I was also a blinding spotlight on this segment of the church. I was bringing attention to this diocese, which had refused to bless the godly call of women to the ordained ministry since its beginnings. In fact, they were continuing that practice even as the National Church opened the canonical doors to "anyone, regardless of race, color, and gender."

In the four years I had endured this process, I had been interviewed countless times by an ever-changing committee of clergy and laypeople, appointed by the Bishop. I had been questioned and re-questioned about issues that had little to do with my qualifications for ministry – things that never seemed to be necessary questions for my male counterparts. For instance, several times in the process, I was asked who was going to care for my son while I was working (as if I had not been supporting us for the past ten years). I was asked what I was going to do with him when I had to go out in the middle of the night to attend a dying church member. I was asked how I thought I was going to get a job without losing weight; I was informed that people in the church didn't want an overweight pastor.

I was flabbergasted at the boldness of their assumption that, as a woman, I was incapable of dealing with these issues. I had been a single working mother for most of Scotty's life and I was incensed at their insinuation that I was neglecting my parental duties by positioning myself in a line of work that could put my child in danger. I have asked many male clergy who have passed through this system and not a one of them was ever asked such questions. They had wives to take care of their children and I didn't. Also, the Episcopal Church had its share of overweight clergy and they all had ministries in the church. Of course, such interviewing techniques are illegal today, and for good reason!

But I'm getting ahead of myself. I want to tell you my story from the beginning so that you can grasp the enormity of the rejection I felt from people who professed faith in a God of unconditional love and acceptance. I want to bring to light the

unfair treatment of women that plagued the system in the 1980's
and that still pervades the parish churches in the 21st century. I want
to bring empathy to those who have suffered as I have and hope to
those who are facing the process which nearly brought me down.
I want to recall the joy and fulfillment I found as a priest in the
church of God. I want to share with you my journey and the words
of wisdom which I gained about the process of priestly formation –
simple but powerful words: Ordination is God's business and God
is the CEO in charge.

CHAPTER ONE

The Journey Begins

ST. MICHAEL'S, COLONIAL HEIGHTS, VA

It was a cold October night in 1975 and I was at a youth retreat. I was watching more than 60 teen-agers – male and female – standing shoulder-to-shoulder with adult advisors, all holding hands, and singing at the top of their lungs about peace and love and God. I had just spent two days listening to these young people talk about their faith, asking and answering questions about God, and speaking openly to a huge group of their peers about what God meant to them in their lives.

I was moved and dumbfounded. I had grown up in the same Episcopal Church but I had never been taught the things these young people already seemed to know. In fact, I honestly didn't know any of those things as a 29-year old adult. They taught me a lot that weekend, including the fact that they were hungry for spiritual truths and eager to embrace the God they had grown up with in the church. On a deep level, I resonated with that as I recalled my own days as a youth in the church.

We were members of St. Paul's Episcopal Church in downtown Petersburg, Virginia, which we attended regularly as a family and where I went to Sunday School off and on until the 6th grade. When I turned 12 and could sing in the adult choir with my parents, my Sunday School days were over. Mother and Daddy didn't attend Sunday School because they had always sung in the choir, which rehearsed at 10:30 before church. This meant they would have to leave the class early and Daddy wouldn't do that. Getting us kids to church in time for Sunday School meant they had a half-hour to kill before choir practice and then when I started singing in the choir, we just didn't do Sunday School at all. Even when I did go, I didn't get a lot from the Bible Stories. In fact, they really didn't stick with me, and at the age of 15, I was an illiterate Christian.

We had a youth group at St. Paul's but the few times I went were more than uninteresting – they were totally boring and, since I was a "county girl" (we had moved into the county so that I had attended county schools since the 4th grade), I was basically non-existent to the teens who all attended school together in the city schools. This was when I started exploring other denominations – not because I didn't like the Episcopal Church but because I craved a community where I would be accepted for who I was and not for where I went to school.

A girl who was a year behind me in school was a Baptist and I started going to Training Union with her on Wednesday nights but my mother was really unhappy about that. My father was a rabid anti-Baptist thanks to his hypocritical grandmother who claimed to be a great and faithful Christian and was the local leader of the Christian Temperance Union. However, she secretly drank herself into oblivion in a locked closet every night. My Baptist days didn't last long.

I had a Methodist boyfriend for about a year and his church had a great youth group, so I used to go with him on Sunday afternoons. They held youth retreats a few times a year and once my parents actually let me go with him on a retreat. I loved it! Most of the kids at the retreat attended county schools or they just weren't snobbish about it, so we had good friends at the retreat and I really enjoyed the retreat program about living like a Christian. I knew that I was a Christian and I knew there were things Christians were **not** supposed to do but no one had ever told me that there were things Christians **were** supposed to do. It was fascinating and I began to wish that I could go to church with these people all the time.

The closing service was in a small room so that we were all sitting close together in three rows facing a makeshift Altar where the minister had spread out the bread and wine (well, of course, it was Grape Juice – they were Methodists) for communion. I had been taking communion all of my life – on the first Sunday of every month – so this was nothing new but what **was** new was the feeling that I experienced during this service.

As we all moved up to the Altar in a line to receive communion, my boyfriend and I were being typical teenagers who are relatively uncomfortable with something – quietly giggling and poking each other. As we moved past the Altar and back into the row of chairs, I noticed that the kids who were already back at their seats were not in their seats at all. They were on their knees! I had been raised in a church where we knelt on kneelers for about half of what went on in church but I had never seen anybody kneeling on the floor like this. I knew the "Episcopal Squat" (that's where we knelt on the kneeler and leaned our butts against the seat making it slightly more comfortable) and I couldn't imagine how these kids were staying upright! Not only were they all on their knees, they were praying! They had their eyes closed and some had their hands out in front of them or up in the air and although I couldn't hear what they were saying, it was obviously aimed at God.

We didn't know what to do so we knelt down too and I tried closing my eyes but immediately started to fall over so I looked around and suddenly I noticed that the room was almost foggy. There was a mist that reminded me of a warm day when there's snow on the ground – but this had nothing to do with the weather. Even as new as all this was, I knew instinctively that this was a "God thing" – that somehow God was in the air and I felt totally out of place – like I didn't belong there because I didn't really know God. It was an awful, empty feeling and I didn't understand it at the time and I certainly didn't tell anybody about it.

We didn't talk about "the Spirit" or Jesus at home. In church the minister was the only one who spoke the name of Jesus and he always ducked his head after he said it so I grew up thinking there was something wrong with saying it in public. Also, I grew up with the Holy Ghost as the third part of the Trinity and since I decided at an early age that there was no such thing as a ghost, I wrote that dude off completely. Now, in that upper room with the real thing in residence, I knew that I had found something new – something I wanted and never had. Unfortunately, my boyfriend and I broke up that year and my membership in that youth group was ended along with our relationship. I had never again experienced anything like this until now.

All of this came flooding back to me as I experienced my first youth retreat in 15 years and I found myself wishing that there had been this type of youth activities in the Episcopal Church when I was a teenager. It was like going back in time and I left that weekend knowing that I was hungry again – eager to re-discover the same things for myself and to help more young people experience God this way.

I was suddenly on a new spiritual journey that would

transform me from a clueless cradle-Episcopalian into an educated and trained Episcopal priest – a journey that I was unaware had begun many years before. I had been on this journey for years but mostly in a semi-conscious state until it came alive on a hot Sunday morning in June 1975. I had moved back to Petersburg, Virginia with my four-year-old son who had been my entire life for the past two years. He went everywhere with me, as I couldn't afford child care and my parents were not always available to keep their grandson. They were good Episcopalians and had been gently prodding me to get back to the church-going habits they had instilled in me as a child.

      I had attended church sporadically during my years as a student at the College of William and Mary and following my marriage in 1968 to a professed agnostic. I rarely attended as my husband did not want to go to church. For five years, I was relatively content to skip church most Sundays, but I was raised in a home where Christmas and Easter were major church-going holidays and I just couldn't make myself stay home from Christmas Eve Midnight Services or Easter Morning Services, so I became a "C & E Christian."

COMING HOME

      After a divorce, I moved with my son from Atlanta back home to Petersburg where I got a job working for the city in the Engineering Division of the Department of Public Works. I couldn't have been further from my college Philosophy major but the position sounded like fun and I desperately needed a job. I worked for the City for almost eight years and it was during those years that I succumbed to the pressure from my parents and to my own desires and needs to return to the church of my childhood. My son was getting old enough for Sunday School and I wanted

St. Paul's Episcopal Church
Petersburg, Virginia

him to grow up with a strong background of faith. So one Sunday morning, we went merrily off to the church where I grew up – I was going home.

Well, the old adage that "you can never go home" came to mind as I saw the peers with whom I grew up sitting in their parents' pews with their 2.3 children, their fancy clothes, and the same snooty attitude toward me they had exhibited toward me years before. Now I was divorced, which proved them right – I was a county girl and I would never amount to much!

After several weeks of being virtually ignored, I realized that, only six blocks from my new apartment, there was an Episcopal Church, which had been "planted" by our parish in the 1960's. Since there were members of that church who had been members of St. Paul's when I was a child, I figured that I wouldn't be a total stranger. However, it still took a few weeks to get up the courage to attend. Finally, one hot Sunday morning in June, Scotty and I went to St. Michael's Episcopal Church in Colonial Heights, Virginia for our first lesson in really "going home."

I deposited Scotty in the nursery, knowing he couldn't stay still and quiet for an entire hour, and started for the sanctuary. I saw the side door and almost went in, but I instinctively knew it must enter the worship space right in front of the entire congregation. I have always hated entering a room of strangers by myself so I went around to the front entrance which would bring me into the back of the church - hopefully unnoticed.

I quickly found a seat in the back and watched as the choir processed down the center aisle. I recognized several former members of St. Paul's – people I had sung in the choir with for years. It was great to see old friends and comforting to know that I knew a few people in this group of strangers. I relaxed a little and tried to enjoy the worship. I was aware of people looking at me quizzically but it was the typical response to a newcomer in any gathered community. I was slightly uncomfortable as I had always felt so obtrusive in such situations. I was glad for the anonymity while I checked out the worship style of St. Michael's.

This all changed when I went up for communion, walking between the choir pews on the way to the Altar. Those choir members who had been former members of my church looked at me with questioning smiles that said, "Don't I know you?" When church was over, I quickly introduced myself to the Rector, the Rev. Don

Porcher, at the back door and scooted out to retrieve Scotty from the nursery. Even though I wanted to see my old friends, I started to skip the after-church reception and just go home – I really did hate going into a room full of people alone. What if they didn't really remember me? What if no one spoke to me and I ended up standing around all alone?

Finally, I decided that I couldn't hide every Sunday and, if I wanted to attend church here, I would eventually have to face it. So I took a deep breath and walked into the reception hall where Coffee Hour was in full swing. As I feared, nobody spoke to me, although a few smiled and cooed at Scotty. I felt as alone as I ever had in the church of my childhood and I couldn't wait to get out of there!

Before I could turn around, I heard a little shriek and a voice said, "Susan Blount? Is that you?" Another voice said, "I just knew that was you when I saw you in church!" These folks hadn't seen me since I was in high school but they knew me well from years spent together in choir pews. Besides, I did look exactly like my mother! They all "oohed" and "ahhhed" over my handsome son, asked about my mother and father, and demanded to know why I hadn't come and joined them in the choir.

They waved off my weak protestations, assuring me that they really needed a good Alto in the choir. I felt a sense of relief at being welcomed so warmly and I thought, "Even if I don't know anybody else, I'll feel safe in the familiarity of a choir pew where everybody knows you and you have a reserved seat every week."

I was still hesitant at the thought of just showing up on Sunday morning and not knowing where to go, which vestment to wear, or who the other choir members were. At that moment, the organist/choirmaster walked up and insisted on being introduced to the "new choir member." I couldn't believe it! They must have told him who I was as he even called me by my maiden name!

I was invited to the upcoming choir practice and when I wondered who I could get to watch Scotty, one of them said, "Don't worry about Scotty. Just bring him along. He can play with the other children." I had never heard of children at choir practice but it was a welcome innovation because it meant I didn't have to pay a sitter. I told him I'd be there.

I figured I'd better get out of there while I still felt so good about this group of almost total strangers but my friends weren't through yet. They dragged me all over the room, introducing me to everyone as "Susan Blount – she sang in the choir with us at St. Paul's in Petersburg." Well, at this point, I felt as if I had truly come home and the next Sunday I was right up in the choir where I knew I belonged.

OUR NEW CHURCH HOME

Scotty and I began attending St. Michael's regularly. One Friday afternoon in October, I came home early from work because I had the beginnings of a sinus infection and felt like a herd of elephants was stampeding through my head. I had picked up Scotty from the baby-sitter and as we walked into the house, the phone was ringing. Surprised because I'm not normally home at that hour, I grabbed the phone and was even more surprised to hear Don Porcher's voice. He didn't waste any time getting to the point: The Youth Group was scheduled to attend a weekend retreat at the Diocesan Camp but the Youth Group Advisor had called in sick. Would I consider taking them? He rushed on, "if you can't take them, they'll have to stay home and miss the retreat."

Well, what could I say? I tried telling him that I really didn't feel well either, but he countered that he knew that my car was too small for all of us so I could take his station wagon. Its heater didn't work very well, he told me, but then he went on to assure me that it wasn't far to camp. When I said I wasn't sure if I could get my folks to take care of Scotty on such short notice, he said he'd wait right by the phone while I checked with them. My folks said they were leaving soon for the lake and if I could get Scotty there within the hour, they'd be glad to take him for the weekend. And, I had to admit that suddenly I didn't feel *that* bad. For years afterward, I accused him of being a pushy arm-twisting expert, which was exactly what he was! And it worked.

So, I deposited Scotty and his suitcase on my parents' doorstep and went home to pack up my own things for an overnight in the woods of Southside Virginia. I had been warned that Camp Chanco was a summer camp and we would be staying in tents or little cabins without heat. The bathrooms were a good block away and they weren't heated, although there WAS running water. I packed warm clothes and a sleeping bag and the next morning, still sneezing and coughing, I drove my little Honda Civic over to the Rectory and exchanged it for a huge blue station wagon that was at least twice the size of my car. I hadn't driven a car this big since I used to drive my brother to the doctor's office in the family station wagon ten years before!

Don was wrong about the car's heater not working very well – it didn't work at all! So, we drove off shivering in the early October chill. By the time we got out of town, I couldn't feel my fingers or toes. Of course, the teen-agers didn't even notice; they were totally excited about the upcoming retreat. They chattered on about how wonderful Fall Weekend was and how much I would love it.

After we had been on the road for about 20 minutes, I automatically reached for my purse to get a cigarette. When I pulled one out, they all got really quiet. I looked around the car wondering what was going on. The girl in the front seat said, "Oh you smoke?" I said something appropriate about how I should quit someday but they didn't seem to care about that. A voice from the backseat asked, "Can we smoke too?" Now I could see that they had been waiting for me to light up, eager to see if I would let them smoke too. I figured that it would be rude to smoke in front of them and then say that they couldn't smoke so I thought about just not smoking at all. They must have taken my hesitation for consent because suddenly they were lighting up and rolling down the windows to let the smoke out of the car.

They began to tell me more stories about youth retreats they had attended and some of the crazy things they had done. Gradually, their voices took on a more conspiratorial tone and the stories became more secretive as they warmed up to me. They relaxed with my assurances that what happened in the car would stay in the car. By the time we arrived at Camp Chanco, we were old buddies, laughing and smoking, half-frozen from our trip in Don's rolling refrigerator. They had put me totally at ease with their openness and their trust in my discretion and I realized that I was excited and really looking forward to this new experience.

WHAT'S AN ADIRONDACK?

We registered and were escorted to "St. Luke's" wherever that was. As it turned out it was across the road – at least 150 yards into the woods. The further we walked, the colder I got because all I could see were canvas tents (I knew heaters weren't allowed in them) and tiny little huts called "Adirondacks" with very cold concrete floors and window screens but no door, so I don't have a clue what good the screens did. I looked at all of them and decided the tent might be warmer, but I didn't seem to have a vote as to our sleeping accommodations.

We had been assigned to the Adirondack, which I learned was reserved for Counselors during the summer camp sessions. I have to tell you, that knowledge didn't help a bit. This place didn't look like the premier accommodations in the area. Ah well, there wasn't anything to do but deposit my belongings on the floor, and follow the kids back to the main dining room where, fortunately, there was heat. I found myself hoping that bedtime wasn't until after midnight!

Of course, bedtime came much earlier than that. Even though I was dreading the cold night, after a long day of speeches, group discussions, singing, and praying, I was bone-weary, sneezing and coughing. However, I was totally surprised at how I felt. I was flying!

The priest who was leading the retreat was a quiet, gentle man with an obvious love for God and a remarkable story-telling ability that grabbed my heart and my spiritually deprived soul. The songs we sang were like nothing I had ever heard even after singing in church choirs all my life – they were lively and funny but still spiritually alive and touching. They were about the Holy Spirit and love and happiness and they ignited something in me that I didn't even know was there.

I just could not believe what I was seeing. Teen-agers who hugged each other and cried and prayed and sang without pretenses or embarrassment were new creatures in my Episcopal experience. I was completely discombobulated by the open atmosphere in this group of more than 200 teenagers and adults. They all seemed to have a connection with each other and with God that I have never known and that I was suddenly eager to explore.

WARMED BY THE SPIRIT

The retreat ended after lunch the next day following the most moving worship service I had ever experienced. The music was stirring, lively, and very loud. The prayers were spontaneous, a way of praying that was foreign to this cradle Episcopalian who learned to pray out of the book in unison with everyone else.

I had never experienced anything quite like it. When we gathered around the priest at the Altar as he celebrated the

Eucharist, I was blown away by the new words he was using, the
eagerness of everyone gathered there, and a palpable presence that
I knew could only be God. When I received communion, standing
in a circle, dressed in jeans, sweat shirt, and tennis shoes, with 200+
voices singing "Alleluia" in a 4-part round, I felt like it was my
first communion. It was like nothing I had ever known, but it was
something I very much wanted to do again.

We arrived back in Colonial Heights, hoarse from singing
every song at least three or four times and sharing our experiences
from each of the different groups. We still had the windows open,
but not to let out the smoke – we were too busy singing to even think
about cigarettes. We had the windows down because we wanted the
world to hear us singing about Jesus. I delivered two of the girls to
their homes and, after many hugs and tearful goodbyes, I dropped
off Don's daughters at his house. The girls raced inside to tell their
parents all about the weekend while I jumped in my car and started
it, turning the heater on high!

We hugged and said our goodbyes and I left in my blessedly
warm car to retrieve Scotty from my parent's house. I was still
singing those wonderful songs as I tried to make some sense out
of my experience. I was not really sure what had happened but I
finally decided that, whatever had actually taken place, the result
was that I had been "strangely warmed." I also realized that these
kids had something I wanted and from that moment on, I began to
bide my time until their present Youth Group Advisor would resign
and I could "move in."

It wasn't long; at the end of the following summer, Don
informed me that the advisor had called to say that she couldn't
devote time to the Youth Group anymore and asked if he could
find someone to take her place. Well, of course, he could! Within 5
minutes, I was the new Youth Group Advisor. It was September,
1976 and my journey was off and running.

WHAT **WAS** I THINKING?

As the new Youth Group Advisor, I quickly realized that I
was way out of my element. I didn't know a thing about advising a
Youth Group in the church and I told Don I seriously needed help.
Shortly after that, he received notification of a meeting with the new
Diocesan Youth Ministries Director and he suggested that I attend.
I readily agreed and I was off to my first adult "youth" meeting –

that's a meeting of adults who minister to youth and, I discovered, often acted just like the youth.

I was surprised and delighted to find that the new Youth Ministries Director was the very same priest that had led the Camp Chanco youth retreat the year before. In that short weekend, I made a handful of friends who have remained friends for 30 years. Two of them, a husband and wife team, were the new co-Advisors for the Youth Group at a church in Chester, Virginia about 10 miles north of Colonial Heights.

We struck up a rousing conversation about just how unprepared and incompetent we all felt. Within a few hours, we had convinced David Davenport, the new Youth Ministries Director, that we should stage a training retreat for people like us. Delighted with our enthusiasm, he didn't hesitate. Before the weekend was over, we had solid plans for an event we named, "Yesterday I Didn't Know What a Youth Group Advisor Was – Now I **Are** One!"

KIDS WHO LOVE JESUS

That event convinced me that I had truly found a niche for myself in the church. I became fast friends with the Rev. David Davenport; he and the advisors who had joined us formed a support group like I had never experienced in my life.

We enthusiastically planned and hosted the workshop for Youth Group Advisors at Zimmer House, a historic house-turned-Conference-Center across from Central Park in Petersburg, Virginia. Bishop Vaché was the Bishop Coadjutor, having been elected to replace the retiring Bishop David S. Rose, and until the "changing of the guard" would take place, he lived on the top floor of Zimmer House. We were please to discover that he was going to be at home during our workshop. We invited him to join us for dinner on Friday evening and to our initial session.

He gracefully accepted our invitation and we all enjoyed dinner with the Bishop. He was a gracious host and a delightful dinner companion. When we gathered for our evening session, I escorted him to a chair on my right in the circle of chairs (I had plans), and asked him to open the session with a prayer, which he did. Then I announced a fun exercise to learn each other's names; I felt him stiffen slightly and he looked at me with a "what-are-you-doing?" look on his face and whispered, "Why don't you just use name tags?"

I just pressed on, explaining how the game was played: I had a trash can in my hands. I turned to the person on my left and said, "Hi. My name is Susan and this is a trash can." That person then had to turn to the person on the left and say, "Hi, my name is Dave and Susan says that this is a trash can." The game would continue like that until everyone in the circle had introduced themselves to the person on their left. That wasn't so bad; but, the catch was that everyone had to add the name of the last person to the list of those who "said that this is a trash can." It took only three introductions, before the Bishop grabbed my arm and whispered in my ear, "This means I have to name everybody in the circle, doesn't it?" I just laughed and he didn't.

He was a good sport, though, and, when it was his turn, he tried mightily to name all of the people in the circle. With a lot of help and good-natured ribbing, he finally named everyone and then turned to me and said, "I am the Bishop and this trash can is your hat." With that, he turned the trash can upside down right on my head!

That event was the beginning of an exciting new ministry for me and for my new friends and cohorts. We helped each other plan programs and we held joint youth group meetings where the kids could bond, and we bonded as well. We all, young and old alike, learned from each other. I quickly became adept at Youth Group "advising," leading the kids in experiential community-building activities and Christian educational programs to help them grow in their faith. Of course, I found that I was learning as much as they were! During this time my own faith began to grow and I found myself completely and totally in love with a God I had barely known before. I had found a Youth Ministries community which was feeding me with more friendship and love than I had ever known.

In the spring, my journey shifted unexpectedly onto a new path when David asked me if I would consider being an adult counselor for the Senior High Camp at Camp Chanco that summer. This was the Diocesan camp where I had attended my first youth retreat, so I only hesitated long enough to check my vacation time and my parents' schedule. Everything came together perfectly and, in August, I spent a glorious week playing with some of the greatest teenagers in Southeastern Virginia, learning about God and the Church, and discovering what it really means to be a true Christian.

The adults were assigned in like pairs to a campsite where

we lived in that now very, very warm Adirondack hut! It was surrounded by tents housing a total of 16 kids who had finished the 10th-12th grades. Every night after a camp-wide bonfire and worship, we took our charges back to our campsites where we bonded with each other by sharing our life stories, our hopes and dreams, our fears and problems. We spent the entire week nurturing that bond with campsite activities and competitions with the other campsites.

I was particularly taken by one young lady who seemed to stay on the edges of everything. I was drawn to Jacqueline because she reminded me a lot of myself. She was slightly overweight and I could tell that she was very self-conscious around the slim and trim girls. I recognized the crossed arms, the over-sized t-shirts and the long shirts she wore over them even on the hottest days. She was a first-year Sr. High Camper and, like me, she was still finding her way and trying to make sense out of the "inside jokes" of the kids who had been coming to Camp Chanco every summer for years. I found myself migrating to where she was sitting during meals and in our campsite meetings. I began to draw her into the conversations, helping her to find her place while I was finding my own way in this new community.

On the last night of camp, we had sung ourselves hoarse and hugged just about every camper and counselor in the camp, and we were dragging ourselves across the road to our "home" away from home. I became aware of someone coming up beside me on the trail and was happy to find Jacqueline, laughing and out of breath from her race to catch up with me. She grabbed my hand and together we ran off together as she yelled to the others, "Last one in my tent is a toad!"

Later that night, as we all moved reluctantly out of her tent to our own beds, she grabbed my hand and almost dragged me out of the tent. We walked away from the others and she stopped, turned to me, and said, "Thank you." I was delighted, but I wanted to know more so I asked her, "For what?" She looked right at me and said, "For saving my life." I must have looked dumbstruck because she chuckled a little and said, "When I arrived here on Sunday, I hated myself. I figured everybody else hated me too because nobody ever talked to me or paid me any attention. When you came over and sat with me that night, I thought I must have done something wrong and you were going to make me move or something." I tried to say something but she said, "Let me finish or I won't ever say this."

        She went on to tell me about her parents and how they
ridiculed her for being so fat. She told me about the kids at school
and the names they called her. She said that she had no friends and
had been thinking about what it would be like to just not be there. I
was startled but she said, "I don't think about killing myself; I just
think about not being. That's the only way I can imagine not feeling
the way I do about myself."

        I couldn't resist any longer and I reached out and gathered
her into my arms and we stood hugging and crying for a minute.
Then, she leaned away, looked at me and said, "You made me feel
like a person because you talked to me and listened to me and didn't
call me names or laugh at me. It made me realize that maybe I can
be like other kids." I told her how grateful I was that she had told
me all of this and then I told her about my own painful childhood as
the butt of every fat joke there was, even from
my well-meaning but mis-directed parents.
We finally said "Good night" and went off to
bed, but it was hours before I finally slept as
I realized that what had happened to this girl
was what I always dreamed would happen to
me when I was an unhappy teenager like her.
With a full and thankful heart, I said my quiet
prayers to God and fell asleep.

        By the end of the week, I was a
seasoned camper. To say I was hooked
would be an understatement of monumental
proportions. I was already planning how I
would arrange my work schedule so I could

Susan - "the seasoned camper"

come back next summer. I was ready for a new year with my new
Youth Group at St. Michael's and had a ton of new ideas for us
to pursue in the fall. As I drove away from camp that Saturday
afternoon in August, I knew that I was on a journey I had never
expected but one that felt so right to me. I wasn't hearing voices and
it wasn't out there for anyone else to hear, but in my heart, I felt the
words, "Susan, I'm calling you."

I WANTED TO TEACH THEM WHAT I DIDN'T KNOW

        During the next year, I became more and more aware of my
keen desire to help the kids who came to Youth Group and to the

events we sponsored. I wanted to help them learn more about God and Jesus and the Church. I didn't know it then, but I discovered several years later what I really wanted was to be someone who "touched" them sacramentally; i.e., I wanted to be able to bless them, to do the Eucharist for them, counsel them, and minister to them.

As a lay person, I didn't think like that at the time, so the only thing I knew was that I wanted to learn what I needed to know to be able to teach the young people what they needed to know. I think this was partly because I was so excited about the new things I was learning and I wished I had been taught these things when I was a teenager. It was also because, I had a particularly soft spot in my heart for kids who were struggling with the same things I had suffered through. I was also finding that they were very open to the ministrations of caring adults like me.

One young man I met during a Sr. High session several years later made me very aware of how much these kids want the attention of adults and how receptive they can be when approached in the right way. He had come to camp, kicking and screaming. His mother had told me that he said that the last thing he wanted to do was spend a week with a bunch of namby-pamby religious nuts who sat around singing and talking about God.

He ended up in my discussion group and, from the beginning, he was sullen and sat outside the group looking hostile and occasionally throwing out derogatory, disruptive comments. He was verbally abusive towards a few of the kids who were really struggling with faith issues. It was at this point that I had to take him aside and speak with him about an attitude adjustment.

When we sat down to talk, he immediately launched in to the same diatribe that his mother had endured. I just let him go with it until he stopped talking and just sat there looking at me like "So what do you think about *that*?" I waited a bit to be sure he was listening and I said, "Well, Joe, it sounds like you really don't want to be here and I can understand that. When I was your age, I think I would have felt much the same way." He had opened his mouth to say something but when I actually empathized with him, he closed it and waited.

I continued very gently, "Joe, here's the thing. Whatever has made you feel this way must be something very big to cause so much anger and I know how hard it is to keep that from showing. If you can talk about it to me or maybe to Dave, you might find it easier to relax this week and even enjoy yourself."

    I fully expected another tirade so I was thrown for a loop
when he started to cry. For a moment, he couldn't speak and I
gave him time to gather his wits. As I opened my mouth to speak,
he started talking. He told me about his parents, how they were
really good to him and that he had done something awful that hurt
them. They still continued to love him and treat him well and he just
couldn't understand how they could do that when he had hurt them
so badly.

    I didn't want to ask what he had done but I didn't need to
because he continued, "I was so angry at them when they wouldn't
let me quit school and join a band that was going on the road for
a year. I'm a great musician and my dream is to be a professional
guitarist and singer. This was my big chance and they wouldn't
let me take it even though I'd only miss the last half of my Senior
year and could easily make it up the following year or get my GED.
"They wouldn't listen and they took away my guitar, my car, and
my license so that I couldn't leave and then grounded me so they
could keep an eye on me. I was so mad that all I could think of was
how to get back at them. I thought if I made them angry enough
they'd reconsider or maybe they'd just kick me out of the house and
I could catch up with the band."

    "So, what did you do Joe?" I asked. He sat for a minute
looking like he wanted to just disappear over the edge of the cliff
beside the river.

    Then he said quietly, "I went to the guidance counselor at
school and told him that my parents were abusing me and I wanted
help getting away from them." I thought, "Wow, that's big." But I
didn't say it.

    He went on, "I thought they'd just get a call from the
principal and they'd deny it and just be embarrassed. But, by the
time I got home, the police were there questioning my parents and
when I arrived they went with me to my room, helped me pack,
and within 10 minutes I was on my way to a foster home. I couldn't
believe it. They were really taking this seriously and I kept asking
the officer what was going to happen to my parents. Finally, he
told me that if my complaints were found to be true, they would be
charged with child abuse and most likely go to jail."

    Joe was having a hard time speaking but he struggled on
with his story, "I felt like I had been punched in the stomach. I

didn't have any idea that it would go that far and now I had to find a way to fix things. But the officer dropped me off without listening to me at all and I found myself in the home of a couple who had four other foster children and basically couldn't have cared less about me and my problems. They were in it for the money and all of us were a meal ticket and nothing more."

I was close to tears at the thought of this teenager cooped up with these uncaring people. He went on, "I cried all night and, in the morning, I left for school with most of my belongings stuffed into my backpack. I went directly to the principal's office and told him what I had done – that I had made up the stuff about being abused because I was mad at my parents. At first he acted like he didn't believe me and I didn't think he'd help me but finally, he realized that I was really telling the truth. He called the police department and made arrangements to take me down there to tell my story. I couldn't believe how kind and helpful he was. I know that the police would have never listened to me if he hadn't believed me and been with me. He finally convinced them that I had lied and my parents were released after spending more than 24 hours in hell."

Joe said that he had learned later that his Mom and Dad had been photographed, finger-printed, and questioned separately for hours. Once the charges were dropped, things happened quickly and he said, "Suddenly all three of us were standing on the sidewalk outside of the police station. My mother was crying and my father was holding her and telling her everything would be OK now. She finally stopped crying and I figured I would really catch it now. But do you know what my dad did?" I just shook my head as I could hardly speak over the huge lump in my throat. Joe continued with tears running down his face, "He looked at me over Mom's head and asked me if I was OK!"

Joe stopped then and wiped his eyes. I took his hand and started to say something supportive but he wasn't finished. He went on. "My Dad's words must have gotten through my mother's tears because she suddenly tore herself out of my father's arms, grabbed me, and started hugging me so hard! I could hardly breathe! And then my Dad grabbed us both and we stood there in one big family hug that made me feel like the biggest jerk in town. I couldn't believe that I had put them through such a horrible ordeal and the first thing they did was hug me and tell me they were so glad that I was OK! They didn't even ask me why I did it!"

Joe stopped again to catch his breath and I asked gently, "What did you all do then?"

"Well," he said, "None of us had a car so we started walking and that was when they asked me what had happened – what had made me say such things about them. It was the hardest thing I ever had to say, but I told them that it was just because I was mad at them for not letting me do what I wanted to do."

Joe took a deep breath and said, "You know, I fully expected one or both of them to explode at any moment and I actually think I wanted them to yell at me. I felt so guilty about what I had done that I felt like I deserved whatever they could do to me. But they weren't doing anything to me, except loving me and forgiving me and assuring me that they were fine and that it was all over now. They even said we could explore some ways that I could still join up with the band for part of the year if I kept up with my schoolwork and graduated on time! Can you believe that?" He was crying again and it took a few minutes for him to compose himself.

Then he went on with an agonizing voice, "They were being so great about this after I had put them through such an embarrassing experience. They could've gone to jail and it would've been my fault. How could they forgive me for this?" Joe finally stopped and I could see that this was the crux of the problem. He felt unforgivable because he couldn't forgive himself even while his parents were willing to forgive him. He just couldn't understand how they could still love him. He felt like he needed to be punished and since they weren't going to do it, he was punishing himself.

I pointed this out to Joe very gently and I tried to explain the concept of forgiveness as I had been learning about it myself in our program. I told him that this was just what we were learning and discussing in our group. If he could put his guilt aside long enough to hear what God means by forgiveness, it might help him to understand. The dinner bell was ringing so we made our way back to the dining hall and I watched him join up with some other kids at a table in the corner. I watched him during dinner and was pleased to see him interacting with the other kids at his table and actually looking like he was enjoying it.

The next day, Joe sat right next to me in the group and, before I could even start the discussion, Joe began to tell the other group members that he was sorry he had been such a jerk and that he wanted to be part of the group. They all graciously accepted his apology and drew him right into their circle. By the end of the session, they were all great friends and our discussions were amazing!

The rest of the week just got better and better and by the time we all left for home, I was absolutely convinced that this is what I was meant to do – help young people work through their problems in a Christ-like way. It hadn't taken long for me to discover that this Diocesan Youth Program was where God was calling me to be and I was so ready to answer the call that I jumped right in with both feet. During the next few months, I was elected as the Diocesan Youth Advisor and a member of the Youth Board.

A NEW ROLE AND A RUDE AWAKENING

It also didn't take long to get more involved at St. Michael's. I became a Lay Reader and took my turn reading the lessons at worship and the following year I was elected to the Vestry, the governing body of the parish, where I served as the Youth Ministries Chair. While females were in the vast majority among youth group leaders, women were not found in other leadership positions in the Episcopal Church prior to the 1970's, especially in the Diocese of Southern Virginia.

The Bishop had recently allowed women to serve as Lay Readers and Vestry Members so I was one of the first women to serve in those capacities at St. Michael's. I thought the whole issue about women serving in leadership positions was silly and even somewhat demeaning to women. The Bishop had the discretion to follow the "allowing" resolutions from the National Church, so he could pick and choose the roles he would allow women to fill.

I'll never forget the day that Don Porcher called me and said that he had something he wanted me to do. I figured it was some kind of busy work around the parish so I said, "Sure. What do you need?"

He said, "Well, I've been thinking about this and I want you to train as a Lay Eucharistic Minister. The Bishop has finally given us permission to allow women to serve as a LEM and I want you to be the first female to serve in that capacity in St. Michael's."

I almost dropped the phone! I had dreamed of serving the Chalice at communion but had never thought it would ever be allowed by our Bishop so I was stunned. I didn't know about the Bishop's newest actions and when Don told me that he was allowing women to be Lay Eucharistic Ministers, I asked incredulously, "Are you sure?"

He assured me that it was all legal now and he said, "Susan, you are definitely the one I want to do this. Are you game?"

Was I *game*? I was *ecstatic!* I couldn't believe it! This had been my dream ever since the youth retreat at Chanco and now I was actually going to be serving the chalice at communion! My mind was reeling but I somehow heard Don saying something about this not being such good news for everyone. I began to come down to earth as I realized that he was really concerned that some people were going to be upset about this and some might even refuse to take communion from me. Reassuringly, he said "I don't want you to get uptight about them. You just do what I train you to do and let me worry about the fallout."

I heard his words but was way too excited to worry about something that probably wouldn't happen. I knew everybody at St. Michael's and they all knew me. I couldn't wait until I was all trained and could serve all my friends the Blood of Christ and I knew that they would all be thrilled! I couldn't think of anyone who would object to me serving communion.

That Sunday finally arrived. I had learned all the theology behind the communion and practiced guiding the cup to the person's mouth and had a good feel for when to remove the cup by watching eye and head movements. I was ready for this. What I wasn't ready for was the short acolyte kneeling on the floor by the Altar. He was my first stop – my very first communicant to receive the chalice from my hand. I leaned over without tilting the cup as Don had taught me. I moved the cup in at the boy's eye level and saw him reach for the foot of the chalice to guide it. I was expecting this and was prepared for him to help move it toward his mouth. I was not prepared for the force behind his little hand. He grabbed the cup so hard that it tilted toward him before I could stop it and at least half the wine in the chalice poured out all over the front of his vestment.

I couldn't believe it! This poor boy was almost as embarrassed as I was and he ran out of the church to change and wash the wine off his face and hands. I was completely undone, but Don had seen it all as he finished distributing the bread at the other end of the Altar. He calmly walked over and picked up the other chalice and proceeded to serve those who were patiently waiting for me. Most of them had been either settling in at the rail or had their heads bowed so most people didn't even know that something had happened.

By the time the first group had all been served by Don and
departed from the rail, a second group had begun to take their
places and Don began his trip down the rail with the bread. I was
still shaking but determined not to let this mishap ruin my debut
or this holy moment for the people in front of me. I gathered up
my courage and all my training and offered the chalice to the first
man at the rail, who gently guided the cup to his mouth, took a sip,
murmured "Amen" and then winked at me!

I was overwhelmed with joy and relief – this *was* right. I
was doing the right thing in the right place at the right time and I
continued down the rail with a new confidence. It was an amazing
experience and I was so at peace with this. As the last group of
people approached the rail, I noticed that two people at the front of
the line had not moved toward my side of the rail but were standing
all the way at the other end of the rail. This was not the normal
procedure but I thought at first that maybe they were newcomers
and didn't know how we did things. As I moved toward the rail,
though, I looked again at them and realized that they were long-time
members whom I knew well.

Again I was stunned! Don had tried to warn me, but
somehow I had never really believed that anyone at St. Michael's
would object to my serving communion. After all, I figured, my
hands are no different from a man's! I just couldn't imagine anyone
being so silly or so rude but there they were, waiting at the other
end for Don to serve them from his chalice. I was so utterly shocked
that all I could think was, "How can they do this? They know me!
They're friends!"

What a rude awakening that was! Neither of them would
look at me as they hurried away from the rail and I noticed that they
left before the service was over. I was devastated by their actions
because they weren't strangers. We had known and worshiped
with each other for more than a year and I just couldn't believe that
they would do this. I tried to follow Don's advice and not take it
personally, but it still hurt. They were my friends and they had
never even mentioned how they felt about this issue.

At home later that day, I was trying to make some sense of it
all when it suddenly hit me like a ton of bricks! They were women!
Those two people who had refused my ministrations at the Altar
were not men with an anti-female agenda. They were women and
they were both highly educated professional women with good

common sense and strong ties to St. Michael's. There had been no warning in any of our conversations of any discriminatory feelings about the church's present debate over the role of women.

Even as I reeled with this new awareness, I instinctively knew that this must have been a difficult choice for them to make. I realized at that moment that this was bigger than me, bigger than St. Michael's, and bigger than any personal relationship. I was appalled and saddened as I forced myself to accept what should not have surprised me. I had suffered my first scalding by the fires of discrimination which burned brightly in the Episcopal Church in the 1970's. With that came the real truth that I had been denying in my innocent naiveté as a typical cradle Episcopalian.

We either don't notice or we refuse to believe anything bad about our church. This truth was so powerful that it nearly knocked me out of my chair. I wanted to keep denying it but here it was: my beloved Episcopal Church was being rocked by an intense and sometimes vicious controversy over the possibility that women might be allowed to enter the ordination process and become priests. Worse than that, I had to recognize that this turmoil was not only being felt on a national level. It was alive and well in the Diocese of Southern Virginia and in St. Michael's Church.

I didn't want any part of this ecclesiastical upset. I wanted to quit; I wanted to scream at the injustice of it all. But I wanted more than anything to be part of this sacred ministry. Deep inside I felt something pushy that I recognized and I knew that I wanted to do more. I wasn't clear exactly what I wanted to do but I was so overwhelmed at the thought of what awaited me as a woman in this place at this time in the history of our church that I put it all on a back burner somewhere. I just concentrated on fulfilling my new duty as a Lay Eucharistic Minister in the face of whatever local opposition there was.

I finally fell asleep that night after thanking God for this gift I had been given and asking for the courage to continue to use it to his glory. I told myself that that was all I had to do at the time and I continued to serve at St. Michael's, knowing that I was doing what God wanted me to do. I guess I should have figured it all out by then but I was still living in the same Episcopal Church as before and it just didn't occur to me at that time that I would ever be able to do more. It had occurred to God however, and even while I was unaware of it, my long journey to the ordained ministry had begun in earnest.

CHAPTER TWO

My First Steps

THE RECTOR

I quickly learned that when lay people feel the things I was feeling, the first step was to talk to the Rector of their church. I learned that from a friend I had met at a Diocesan Youth Event, the Rev. Don Roberts, then Rector of Good Shepherd Church in Norfolk, Virginia. I had brought my Youth Group to his church to have a joint event with his Youth Group and, while the kids stayed in the homes of their counterparts, Scotty and I stayed with Don and his wife.

Late that night, in a very intense conversation, they helped me to concretize the feelings I was experiencing and enabled me to be honest about them and to admit that what I really wanted was to go to seminary. Sitting on their living room floor making props for the next day's events, I experienced a defining moment in my journey – the moment when I knew that my life was about to change in very dramatic ways

Having promised Don Roberts that I would take the next step, I dutifully called my Rector, Don Porcher, the next day and we made an appointment to discuss my situation. I didn't think about it at the time, but he really didn't seem to be surprised. He just grabbed his appointment book and found a time for me. We chatted for a few moments after I arrived at his office and then I described to him how I felt. Within 10 minutes, he was grinning and reaching for his appointment book and the phone (to call the Bishop), saying "I knew it – I just knew this was what you wanted to see me about."

THE BISHOP

Well, if I thought I was nervous when I went to speak with Don, I didn't know the meaning of the word. Don had spoken with the Bishop on the phone and they agreed that the Bishop would meet with me on a Saturday morning in January of 1977 in Norfolk.

So, on Friday after work, I drove to Don Roberts' house in Norfolk so that I wouldn't have to get up so early to make my 9:30 appointment time. To say I was nervous was a gross understatement; even the word anxious didn't come close. I was terrified!

To help you understand my deep terror, let me give you a little background on our Bishop. A tall, stately, and distinguished white-haired man, the Bishop was a commanding figure in the front of the church. In person, he was often considered cold and intimidating. In my dealings with him in our Youth Group events, I had found him to be warm and congenial at times, brusque and businesslike at others.

I guess I was intimidated mostly because I knew that he held my entire future in his hands – hands which most people in the Diocese figured would never find themselves on the head of a female during an ordination ceremony. In the early 1970's he led the charge at General Convention in support of a resolution continuing a ban on women serving as Lay Readers, Vestry Members, and Lay Eucharistic Ministers. The Rt. Rev. C. Charles Vaché was well-known throughout the National Church, for his stand in favor of an all-male church leadership. While he had been elected Bishop for many reasons, chief among them were his traditional beliefs – that women should not hold positions of authority, lay or ordained, in the church.

Now, here I was in 1979, three years after the National Church voted to allow women to be ordained as priests, over loud protests by many clergy, laypeople, and our own Bishop. I was poised on the edge of a face-to-face encounter with a Bishop who had campaigned vigorously to prevent women from being ordained, who had repeatedly refused to support any woman candidate for the ordination process, nor even to sign a woman's application to attend seminary as a lay person. It was widely known that he had "slammed the door" in the face of more than one female who felt called to the priesthood; I figured I was most likely going to be the next in that long line.

By 7:00 that Friday night, I had a fever, was sick to my stomach, and had a raging headache. I was so anxious that I had literally made myself sick. When I entertained the idea of calling the Bishop to cancel, I found that Don had hidden the phones and when I complained about how bad I felt, he sent me to bed early. The next morning I was feeling better and being sternly reminded that "ordination is God's business and if he wants it to happen, it will" I left for the Bishop's office at 9:15 for the 10-minute ride to his office.

He greeted me in the hall, dressed in a plaid flannel shirt, a sweater, and tennis shoes. I was so surprised, I could hardly speak but then I realized that, since it was Saturday and the Diocesan office was not officially open, this was really his day off. While we gathered up coffee from the little kitchen, he chatted away while I composed myself and tried to imagine that we were at a Youth Event and I was the usual "Bishop Greeter and Entertainer" – a role I had played many times in the last two years.

The Bishop was unbelievably cordial and relaxed. We talked about the Youth Program in the Diocese and how successful it was in David Davenport's hands. I found myself easily telling him how I felt about Youth Ministry and what I wanted to do – that I wanted to go to seminary. I remember to this day that as I said them, I could literally hear a door slamming in my mind. (I found out later that one of the Bishop's staff who lived next door had run into his office to get his appointment book!)

I had convinced myself and him that I didn't really want to be ordained; I just wanted to go to seminary and learn enough to help the young people I loved. He said that he was concerned that I would find it hard to find a position in lay ministry if I still didn't want to be ordained after finishing seminary. Evidently, David's position was one of a few like it in the Church at that time. I very sincerely said to him that I wasn't too concerned since I would have a Master's Degree when I finished and I could get a job just about anywhere.

THE SHOCK WAVE

At that point, I figured it was over but to my utter relief, surprise (no, shock!), and delight I heard him say, "Well, if you are serious about going to seminary, you'll have to go to BACAM." I have to say, I didn't have a clue what a BACAM was but I immediately said, "No problem!" I couldn't believe it! It turns out that BACAM means the Bishop's Advisory Committee on Applicants to the Ministry and it was the first step in the discernment program for ordination. He was letting me in a door that no woman had ever darkened before. I really couldn't believe it.

Well, I wasn't alone. As I called people to let them know that the Bishop had said that I could go to BACAM, I got the same response or one like it. Basically it went, "What?!? or "Are you serious?!" or "I don't believe it!" or my favorite "NO WAY!!"

The Bishop had told me to think about it and pray on it and if I wanted to go to BACAM just to let his assistant know. Well, I didn't think about anything else for the next week. I thought and I prayed and I thought and prayed some more. I talked to several friends, both of whom surprised me by not being surprised and saying something on the order of "Yes, you should go – it's exactly what you're made to do" and "There's no doubt – God is calling you." Again, I was stunned. People who didn't even have a church connection were telling me that they always thought I should be an ordained minister – that I was a natural.

It was nice to hear stuff like that but still I hesitated, agonizing over whether God was really calling me or was it just me wanting something new and different and exciting. The following weekend was another Youth Event and I arrived on Friday afternoon to help with the set-up. I found myself easily distracted and not really "into it" even though I had been the primary impetus behind this first-ever event. It was a Youth Convention designed just like the Diocesan Convention that the adult members of the church attended once a year to consider the church's business.

We all gathered with our typical boisterous singing and crazy community building games which I usually loved and entered into enthusiastically. I had started learning to play the guitar and I loved getting up with the other guitarists and trying to keep up with them as we sang. I moved through that like a robot this time and by the time the kids were being herded off to their cabins for the night, I was in a major turmoil. I asked my friend, David if he would meet me back at the lodge after he made rounds – I really needed to talk with him. David had been a major part of my support for the feelings I had been wrestling with and I knew he would be honest.

I waited on a sofa in front of the burning fire in the hall's fireplace for about an hour. As I watched the flames eat at the log but not burn it up right away, I reflected on how God was like that – burning in you with these thoughts and desires to do ministry without destroying you. I knew that I really wanted to do this – go to seminary – it really was a burning desire. I knew that it was a huge step, especially for a woman and especially for a church member who had only been one in name for so long. I knew instinctively that the stakes were very high – what if I went off to seminary and found that God wasn't really calling me to do anything of the sort – what then? Talk about crashing and burning!! I knew that I would indeed be destroyed if that happened.

My mind went on with more such gymnastics. I had almost let the negative feelings bring me to the conclusion that God wasn't really calling me to do this, when something caught my attention out of the corner of my eye. I glanced over at the window and saw the curtains fluttering, like a breeze was coming in the window. "No wonder I'm so cold," I thought and got up to shut the window. But the window was shut tight. There was even plastic over them to keep out the draft.

Telling myself I was just so tired that I was imagining things and wondering where David was, I went back to the sofa and started praying silently to God. "Please let me know what to do – show me the way. I promise I'll do whatever you want." Suddenly I couldn't deal with the uncertainty any longer. I just had to know! Now, I hadn't had much of a prayer life up until now and I didn't really know if this was an OK thing to do but I took a deep breath and prayed out loud (actually yelled would be more accurate), "God if you want me to do this you're just going to have to give me a sign or something. I don't know what to do – you're going to have to show me." Again, my eye caught some motion at the window and I looked over. This time the curtains were not just fluttering – they were standing almost straight out like the window was wide open – the same window that was shut up tight for the winter.

I jumped up like I had been shot out of a cannon and started over to the window. This time the curtain continued to billow out into the room and when I got to the window and checked it again, it was still as tightly locked as it had been before. I thought I had finally gone over the edge as the curtain continued to flap in my face. I stood there for a moment wondering if this was really God or if I just needed a good night's sleep.

Finally I wandered back to the sofa in something of a daze and I'm not sure how long I sat there when David plopped down beside me, scaring me half out of my wits. "I didn't think those kids would ever stop running around out there! I chased 2 guys out of the girls' site at least 3 times!" He hadn't noticed my "deer-in-the-headlights" expression but then he figured something was out of kilter because I hadn't berated him for being so late. He looked at me, grabbed my hand, and asked, "Susan, what's wrong? Are you

OK?"

For about 10 seconds, I couldn't speak – my voice just wouldn't come out. Finally, I croaked, "I think I just saw God."

After he finally got the story out of me, I waited for him to say something condescending like, "Well, maybe it was God but maybe the wind was really strong!" because that's what I was still thinking in my brain, even while my heart was telling me that I had seen God. But, my dear friend David looked me right in the eye, and said, "Susan, I think you have your answer." Just then, the door opened and one of the counselors came in looking for David – seemed the boys were still running wild – so he squeezed my hand, gave me his best encouraging look and took off.

There I was in front of the fire which had just about burned that log to a cinder by now. I thought about my profound observation of several hours earlier and how maybe I was wrong about God's fire and how it worked – maybe it had just burned out. At that precise moment, the smoldering log caught fire and blazed up again and I stared at it in awe and a little fear at what had just happened and at what I now knew I was facing. I was blown away and I was scared but I had my answer.

THE MOCK ANNUAL COUNCIL

The next day was filled with activity as the participants of our first-ever Mock Annual Council worked with one of the Bishop's Assistants to learn how to craft a proper resolution. The kids worked with other Diocesan officials who helped them explore some of the issues facing the youth. They worked very hard at this and came up with some very mature resolutions about things like having young people serve on Parish Vestries and Diocesan Commissions. One group dealt with the issue of the ordination of women and the resolutions they wrote read something like this:

RESOLVED: That the Annual Council of the Diocese of Southern Virginia encourage the Commission on Ministry and the Standing Committee to consider female applicants to the ordination process and to be prepared to recommend them to the Bishop if they are qualified. The 2nd resolution called for Annual Council to encourage and even direct the Bishop to accept such recommended applicants as suitable for ordination.

These were printed out on large pieces of newsprint and we were all standing around the table reading and re-reading them to

be sure everything was spelled correctly when the door opened and
in walked the Bishop. He had agreed to chair a session of the Mock
Annual Council using the same parliamentary rules and procedures
as were used at the Diocesan Council meetings to help the young
people learn the process.

He came over to the table and we all greeted him while he
peered over my shoulder to see the newsprint on the table. "So,
what kind of resolutions are you working on?" he asked as we all
clammed up and stood like statues while he read the resolutions on
the table. I thought at that moment that if a large enough hole could
just open up in the floor, I would gladly dive into it. My brain was
working overtime figuring that the Bishop was going to see me as
some kind of major force pushing these kids to do all this to help
my cause. But, I should have known better than that. Bishop Vaché
was not a suspicious person and he had known me long enough to
know that I am not a conniving person so that was all a waste of
good angst. He looked up, smiled at my discomfort, and said, "Well,
looks like you've had some good guidance. These are perfect."

Everyone was charmed and the kids started asking him
questions about how to do this and how to say that. Before I could
turn around, it was lunch time and, as we moved toward the dining
room, the Bishop came up beside me and said, "Good job. This is a
great event for the kids." I almost fainted but managed to carry on
a normal conversation with him all through lunch, just as I had at so
many other youth events.

That night I slept better than I had in months as the answer
I had received began to settle in to my heart and become real. I
didn't have much time to think about it and so, the next day as we
gathered for the closing session, I found myself quite easily greeting
the Bishop's assistant as he came in with the news that I wanted to
attend BACAM. He grinned and said he'd send me the papers on
Monday. I turned to find the Bishop standing there grinning too,
and, as he left, he turned and gave me the "thumbs up."

CHAPTER THREE

Aspirant

THE JOURNEY CONTINUES

I was officially an Aspirant to Ministry and I was going to BACAM, regardless of the furor around the Diocese. I remember the Bishop telling me at the very beginning that there would be unhappy, even angry people in the Diocese. "But," he said, "they are not your concern. They are my problem and I will deal with them." Even though the Bishop had refused to accept several women into the Process in past months, he had agreed to license an ordained woman as an Interim Priest at a parish in Virginia Beach, an act which caused a huge turmoil among his staff and Diocesan leaders. He was still very clear about his negative feelings on the issue and he steadfastly refused to accept someone into the Process whom he knew he would not ordain. But he was weakening, people said, and the news that he was allowing me to enter the screening process was proof. This was a huge step the Bishop was taking. And he was right. There were some very excited and happy Episcopalians, but there were also many angry ones and the target of their anger was the Bishop. He was the only one who could change this eons-old policy and they wanted him to cease and desist.

I pondered all of this frequently in my newly-discovered prayer life. I had developed a routine of spending some time every morning before Scotty got up to pray about the day, those I knew who were sick, and my harrowing new journey. I hadn't learned much about prayer as a child because we didn't pray at home as a family; what I knew I had learned with the Book of Common Prayer in my hands and this is where I turned. I brought home a copy from the church and browsed through it until I found some prayers that were appropriate and helpful. I read them – but not out loud. I was still operating under the southern Episcopalian "rules of prayer." Pray only prayers from the Prayer Book. Do not make up your own. Pray silently. Pray out loud only in unison with a group. Pray to

God or the Lord and never to Jesus.

I had the wonderful memory of God's answer in the curtain but nothing like that had happened since. I prayed, but there were no more flying curtains or words from God like many of my Baptist friends talked about. So I recited generic prayers about the church, the Lord's Prayer and thought about what an ordeal this was going to be.

I knew that BACAM was a group of people appointed by the Bishop and that they must therefore be kind and generous Christians who did everything they could to put the applicants at ease. Nevertheless, just the sound of the word "BACAM" struck terror into the hearts of every aspirant to ordained ministry. I was indeed terrorized. I had heard the horror stories of men who had gone through the "wringer" as it was called. Many had come away from BACAM completely convinced that they were unsuitable for anything, much less ordained ministry. I thought about those guys and what they went through and then I realized, "They were supposed to be there – they were men. I was a woman and I was not supposed to be there." What was I thinking?

BACAM

The application form for BACAM was daunting to say the least, but I plodded through it, ignoring all the male pronouns (which made me acutely aware of being the first female to fill in its blanks). With one probing and highly personal question after another, it made me think of a mine field where the slightest misstep could be fatal. I felt like Dorothy exploring Oz as I remember muttering to myself, "lions and tigers and bears, oh my" when I turned to the last page and saw these words: "Trace your spiritual journey." It was an unbelievably thorough and personal questionnaire, requiring separate pages for many answers, but what concerned me was that this last answer wasn't going to be very long. My spiritual journey wasn't very long either so there wasn't much to be done but complete it and submit it. I mailed it off with considerable fear and trepidation because I didn't know if I was ready for the fight that would ensue. I did feel the Lord with me, giving me the courage I needed to drop it in the mailbox, and there was no doubt that I would need His presence for the rest of the journey.

When I received the packet of information from the Bishop's

Assistant about the meeting place and schedule, I could hardly contain myself. I just couldn't believe this was happening. It was my dream which had now become real. I arrived at the conference center where the interview was to be held and, as I mounted the steps, I realized that my legs were shaking and I was feeling a little queasy. Even though I had spent many fun weekends with other youth group advisors in this very building, this trip didn't promise to be fun. In fact, it held every possibility of being one of the most "un-fun" things I would ever do. In spite of my fears, I managed to appear cool and collected as I presented myself to the Bishop's Assistant, who greeted me warmly and showed me to a room upstairs where I deposited my belongings. Then I sat for a few terrifying minutes in desperate prayer that God would keep me from saying something that would scuttle my entire career and joined the others downstairs for a before-dinner social hour. It was all pleasant enough, but there was an undercurrent that was strong enough to sweep a battleship out to sea.

One of my fellow Aspirants said to me at dinner, "How did you ever manage to get here?" I looked at him like he was crazy since we were in very close proximity to the others. I saw just enough hostility in his eyes to realize that he was setting me up, so I said very calmly, "Looks like God is working overtime." He didn't respond – he just turned to the man sitting on his other side and smirked at him, "Did you hear that?" Several of the other Aspirants were also youth group advisors and we had worked together so I knew they were supportive. However, they were at other tables around the room and, at that moment, I felt like I was floating all alone in an alligator swamp and the gators were all circling!

After dinner, we met in a large plenary group to learn about the schedule for the weekend and the focus of each interview. We were cautioned to be honest and open and not to discuss the interviews with each other during the breaks. After some more general instructions and an evening prayer service, we were released for the evening. I spent a few minutes talking to my friends, who decided to retire for the night, so I followed them upstairs. No way was I staying in the swamp alone!

The next morning, after breakfast and worship, we began the interviews. Each member of BACAM interviewed each applicant in separate one-on-one sessions and then as a group (now THAT was an experience I never want to repeat on this side of heaven). I spent the weekend going from one terrifying and unnerving interview to another during which I tried desperately to be honest. All the while I was painfully aware that, as the first woman to ever be part of this process, I was an alien being and, to some, a not very welcome guest. This issue was openly addressed by several of the interviewers, but some seemed to be trying to ignore it completely. I couldn't figure out if they were in denial, if they were trying to be sensitive to my feelings, or if they were just trying to treat me like any other Aspirant. All I knew was that I didn't want to come on too strong (no one likes a pushy female!), but I did want to be absolutely clear that I was serious and committed to this process and what would follow.

My first interview was with the Priest. I knew him barely, so I didn't know how he felt about women's ordination. I felt more at ease after he said that he remembered being in my shoes and that he knew what I must be feeling. He asked me general questions about my religious background, my youth work experience and the roles I had filled in my local parish. He was somewhat sympathetic to my hesitant attempts to describe how I felt about being ordained and he shared some of his doubts during his own journey toward ordination. After an hour and a half, I moved on to my next interview with the Psychologist.

I remember very clearly his first question - "Are you aware that some people seek to enter the ministry to fulfill their own need to be needed?" I hadn't known that and I told him so, assuring him that, while I enjoyed helping people and liked being needed, I didn't believe that was what motivated me. I described my sense of calling to help young people understand more about God and themselves and my strong need to be properly educated and prepared for this ministry. That interview was much less traumatic than I had anticipated, as he was a gentle and accepting man who didn't seem to see too many shadows hiding in my past.

The next interview was with the lay person who was a member of a large parish in the diocese. She was a woman I had known from previous Diocesan events. She was clearly opposed to women's ordination, but, in our individual interview, she kept her bias in check and we just discussed the different ways I had been active at St. Michael's and how I felt about the church. The conversation was really quite mundane.

Well, she was saving her zinger for the group interview later

in the day. It was a question we all expected as it was standard fare
for any conversation about ordination. Somehow, it didn't feel like
business as usual when she jumped right in as soon as the moderator
opened the floor for questions. "So, Susan, just why is that you think
you have to go to seminary to do youth work when youth advisors
all over the Diocese do just fine without a seminary education?" I
thought, "Whew! Better step lightly!" Out loud, I said as calmly as
I could, although my heart was pumping about 90 miles an hour,
"I have a very strong pull to help teenagers learn more about the
Church and about God." As I took a breath, I could feel her getting
ready to pounce, so I continued, "I see the church's ministry to the
young people as a crucial part of their Christian formation and I
want to be certain that whatever I say to them is correct. I want to
know that what I am saying to them...." She interrupted, "There are
other ways to educate yourself. I don't see why you can't just take
EFM or something like that?" (EFM was Education for Ministry, a
4-year lay education course developed by the seminary in Sewanee.)
I opened my mouth to answer but she went on, "Just how are you
going to care for your son and do the work seminary requires at the
same time?"

I felt like I had been smacked in the face by an angry mother
who had caught me abusing my child. At that moment, I realized
that she had used our earlier session to lull me into thinking that
she was friendly so that she could catch me off guard at the right
moment – in front of the group where everyone could see me fail
miserably. I will be forever grateful to the Bishop's Assistant, who
was acting as the group moderator and who stepped in quickly and
firmly stated that this wasn't an issue for BACAM to explore. Several
others had pained looks on their faces and I knew that this woman
was going to be a force to be reckoned with during this process.

The rest of that interview remains something of a blur
as I struggled to listen to the questions and answers of the other
Aspirants. However, all I could hear was this woman's reproof
and her loud accusation of me as an unfit mother. I really wanted
to know if any of the others were asked the same question. The
issue was raised by one Aspirant but neither he nor the other youth
advisor was asked the same question I had been asked. Blessedly,
no one asked me any more questions and, at the end of the session,
we had a short break before a final worship service. It was all I
could do to stay in the building (all I wanted to do was pack up

and go home) but I knew that my future was in the hands of these
people who were watching me closely to see just what I was made
of and if I was strong enough to survive the process. I went to the
restroom, washed my face, took a few deep breaths which included
very strong pleas to God about helping me keep my mouth shut, and
joined the group for the closing service.

     As I drove away later, I found myself in tears and I just let
them flow. I cried for myself – for the humiliation, the pain, and the
ridiculous feeling that I had done something to make people reject
me or disapprove of me. I cried for my church which I now saw as a
less-than-perfect institution caught in a no-win situation. If women
became acceptable candidates for the priesthood, there would be
so much anger and bitterness that a split was almost inevitable. If
women were continually denied access to the priesthood, even after
the National Church had opened the door, there would be so much
anger and bitterness that a split was almost inevitable. I felt sad and
caught in the middle and I cried until I could finally cry no more.

     By then, I was sitting in my car in front of my parents' house
where I was picking up Scotty, and I wiped my face dry, hoping that
I didn't look too awful. I checked in the mirror over the visor and
what I saw was a cry-baby. I sat and looked at her and something
in me snapped. I shook my finger in her face and said, "You are
finished here. I don't need your tears and I don't need your self-pity.
I am going to seminary because God wants me to and you aren't
going to stop me and neither are any of the other naysayers in my
life." I slapped the mirror shut, got out, slammed the car door, and
went in to pick up my son.

THE WAITING

     Now came the waiting. The group had to compose their
findings and report to the Bishop and I had to wait to hear from him.
I had been given strict instructions not to, under any circumstances,
contact either the Bishop or his assistant. I would be notified when
the Bishop wanted to see me again. I felt like I did after a job
interview when you want so badly to call and find out if you even
have a chance, but you know if you do, you'll blow your chances
completely. Of course, I was certain that my chances were toast
anyway. All I could do was wait.

     To say the following weeks were agony would be something
of an understatement. Not only did I have to endure my own

impatience and wondering, I was inundated with questions from family and friends about the experience – what was it like, what did I think they'd say, when was I going to hear from the Bishop. Since I didn't know the answer, or even have a clue to an answer to any of those questions, my feelings of frustration were doubled. I literally went to work, fixed meals for me and Scotty, visited my folks, and went to church in a daze. I knew my whole life was hanging in the balance and, given the negative environment in our Diocese on the issue of women's ordination, I was acutely aware that the scales were precariously tilted and totally out of balance. I needed a distraction.

ANNUAL COUNCIL
There's an old saying, "Timing is everything" and I am a firm believer that success depends, in large part, on what's happening at the time and how one thing fits with another. BACAM had taken place approximately three weeks after the Mock Annual Council and, the following week, the Diocesan Annual Council met in Williamsburg. I was a delegate from St. Michael's as well as from the youth board. The youth were there in huge numbers and I could feel their excitement as the time came to present their resolutions. They did a masterful job of presenting all the resolutions, but the ones that stand out so clearly in my mind were the ones directing the Bishop, the Standing Committee, and the Commission on Ministry to abandon their long-held beliefs that only men were suitable for ordination.

I sat in the back of the auditorium and I was literally sweating because I was so nervous. The kids who were presenting the resolutions were not nearly as nervous as I was – they were just so cool as they stood up at the microphones speaking in favor of their resolutions. When the resolutions on women's ordination were presented, one young lady rose courageously and spoke to the entire Convention saying, "There are many competent and committed women whom God is calling to the priesthood, like Susan Bowman for instance. (I thought about crawling under the seat at that point.) There's no good reason for not approving her for ordination." This was a 14-year-old Jr. High School student who stood up for me with more courage than I had at that moment and I was so proud of her.

The debate that followed was lively, most of the negative comments having to do with tradition and "we've never done this

before" sentiment. Each of the three microphones set up around
the auditorium had long lines of delegates waiting to be heard.
Finally, the last person stood at the microphone in the center
aisle. I still have a vivid picture of the Rector of Christ and Grace
Episcopal Church, the Rev. Boston Lackey (whom I had known
almost all my life) coming to the microphone and standing in silence
until the Bishop said, "Boston, are you speaking for or against the
resolution?"

Boston started to speak slowly, "Well, you know, I think
there are points for and against..."

The Bishop interrupted him. "Boston, the rules of order
require that you declare to be for or against the resolution."

Again, Boston hesitated and even looked up to the
ceiling and again the Bishop prompted him. Finally, he took the
microphone in his hands, got up real close, and spoke clearly and
loudly, "Oh, what the hell, Bishop, let them in!"

The thunderous laughter and applause that followed the
momentary stunned silence even brought a tiny smile to the Bishop's
face but he quickly restored order. A vote was called for and both
resolutions passed – not resoundingly, but they passed.

FINALLY, THE ANSWER

Finally, the call came. The Bishop's Assistant called to tell
me that the Bishop wanted to see me and he asked if I could come
to Norfolk. I wanted to drop the phone, jump in the car, and take
off but I had a job and a son and, after all the waiting, I heard myself
saying to him that I couldn't get away during working hours to
make the 2-hour trip to Norfolk. Thinking it was over for sure, that I
had blown this chance, I went weak with relief when he said, "Well,
he'll be in Petersburg on Tuesday for a Lenten Service at Christ &
Grace. Could you meet him there?" Oh, yeah!

We made arrangements for me to meet with the Bishop after
the service and lunch. I arranged a long lunch hour for that day
and it was a done deal. I was going to meet with the Bishop to find
out what BACAM had recommended and what he was going to do
about it. I felt like one of those toy gyroscopes that you wind up
and wind up until you can't wind anymore and then let it go to spin
wildly across the table. I was wound up and ready to fly.

I told myself for the next week that it was all in God's
hands and that what was done was done – that the die was cast –

the Bishop already knew what he was going to say to me and all I could do was wait and wonder. Finally, the day came. I left work to attend the service, had lunch, and suddenly I was seated in the upstairs parlor of the parish house in a big comfortable wing chair with the Bishop sitting on a folding chair in front of me! (Don't ask me how that happened – it was probably because Bishop Vaché was a consummate gentleman.) This was the moment of truth and I was so relieved because there were no menacing interviewers and no intimidating figure in Bishop's regalia, there was only our very kind and supportive Bishop who started off our conversation by telling me that the members of BACAM had detected a strong call to ministry and a desire to seek a higher level of education in the church. I was on the edge of my seat – I couldn't believe what I was hearing – and then came the big "BUT." "BUT," he said, "they didn't detect a strong call to the ordained ministry."

I sat there – numb and almost in tears. It was over – this was an "ordination process" and if I wasn't on the ordination track, I was toast. Then, he sat back and smiled and said, "But, if you want to go to seminary, I'll help you get there for the first year and we'll see where it goes from there." Well, you could have knocked me out of that chair with a feather! I just stared at him, he smiled some more and proceeded to tell me that he would give me some financial support and that my next step was to apply for loans and apply to the seminaries he would approve – Virginia Seminary in Alexandria, Virginia, General Seminary in New York City (although he made it clear that wasn't his choice for me), and the School of Theology at the University of the South in Sewanee, Tennessee.

I was in total shock! This Bishop who was so clear and firm in his reasons for not ordaining women was not rejecting me as he had so many before me. I had thought the game was over but the Bishop was offering me Door #2. It was at that moment, when he informed me that he was making this historic leap with me, that Bishop Charles Vaché became my hero. In the face of many negative and hostile feelings in the Diocese, he was willing to send me off to seminary, the first woman to enter seminary with his approval and his support. I was flabbergasted, to put it mildly, so I almost didn't hear him tell me to call his Assistant if I needed anything. I came to when he got up, hugged me, said "Congratulations," and led me out the door and down the stairs.

I saw Don Porcher waiting for me at the bottom of the stairs, looking concerned and very compassionate. The Bishop gripped his hand, smiled some more, told Don that he was to be my shepherd through this process and, with another smile and a wave, he was off. I came very close to collapsing at that moment until I looked at Don and saw the look of utter shock and surprise on his face and I burst out laughing.

He was totally prepared to have to hold me up and console me following the Bishop's rejection, so it took him a few minutes to really grasp what was happening. I literally bubbled over trying to tell him everything while racing to get to my car because I was way overdue at work. The rest of the day was a total fog – I know I functioned fairly efficiently because I had a stack of envelopes to put in the mail at the end of the day but all I wanted to do was get out of that office and find someone who could appreciate what a huge thing had just happened to me. At 5:00, I ran joyfully to my car, jumped in, and sang all the way to Colonial Heights.

SHOCK WAVE #2

Again, my shock and surprise was in no way comparable to the shock wave that swept through the Diocese. There was a Youth Committee meeting that night and, when I walked in and announced to David and the others what had happened, there was total stunned silence, a chorus of "Are you serious?" and "No Way!" and then cheers and even tears. To a person, this committee had been my solid support system, convincing me that I was on the right track and that somehow God would make it all happen. Now they were sharing my joy with me.

The young lady who had presented the resolutions at Annual Council was smiling and crying at the same time, hugging me and whispering in my ear, "We did it!" I was what is known in some circles as "verklempt" so I couldn't speak, but at that moment, I realized what tremendous progress was being made toward overcoming the deeply entrenched discrimination against women in positions of authority in the Episcopal Church, at least in our little corner of it. I left that meeting singing all the way home while, at the same time, quaking inside at what lay ahead.

AND THE WAVES KEPT COMING...

For the next month, every time there was a Diocesan Committee meeting or a regional event, I would get a call from a friend who had been present to relate what had been said about me and my "situation." These reports ranged from hysterically funny to agonizingly hurtful and I usually had to pry these stories out of my friends since they wanted to protect me from the pain. However, from the time I spent with God, my clergy friends and mentors, I had learned a mantra that I repeated many times a day, especially when faced with such hurtful comments. It was simple: Ordination is God's business and God is the CEO in charge." Even when it seemed my journey would be cut short, I still repeated those words, and I let them hold me up and remind me that if God wanted me to be a priest, it would happen.

One report came from a large church's Annual Bazaar and Bake Sale. This parish was well-known as a hotbed of traditionalism on almost every issue – the Prayer Book (they still used the 1928 Prayer Book), translations of Scripture (they used only the King James Version), and women's ordination (they still had an all-male vestry and there were no women lay readers or Lay Eucharistic Ministers). My friend said she was at the Bake Sale table when the President of the Women of the Church came up to buy some brownies. She picked out the ones she wanted and, when my friend told her how much it was and held her hand out, this Christian woman ignored her and said to the other person at the table, "I'll give you my money because you don't hang around with smart-aleck women who don't know their place in the church." She tossed her money at the woman and flounced off, running into the person in line behind her. She promptly dropped her plate of brownies upside-down on the ground where the off-balance man she almost knocked to the floor stepped squarely on them. My friend said she had to excuse herself and go into the restroom, where she laughed until she cried. I only laughed about the brownies.

I literally had to drag the following story out of a friend, whom I'll call Jane. She was a member of the Commission on Ministry and had attended a meeting which took place soon after the Bishop said I could go to seminary. When the report from BACAM was relayed to the Commission on Ministry, the Bishop reported his conversation with me. Several members took issue with the Bishop for acting unilaterally without consulting the COM, which was his main source of advice on those entering the Process of Ordination. From what I was told, he made it abundantly clear that, while he appreciated and relied heavily on the COM's analysis and recommendations, he was still the Bishop and the decision to endorse someone's application to seminary was his and his alone. There was no mention in the COM's duties about dealing with those who were outside of the Process of Ordination.

That put an end to the discussion and the meeting continued. After the Bishop made an early exit from the meeting, the same person re-opened the discussion and many of the other members joined in, expressing their own concern about his actions leading to a "corruption of the process." The meeting ended and it was after the room had almost cleared that the real discussion took place, now between two members who were concerned and very angry. One woman was stuffing her papers into her bag as she loudly berated the Bishop for being "seduced by that woman from Petersburg." According to her, I was a "priest-wannabe" who was using my friendly relationship with the Bishop to get him to let me go to seminary. She called me a fraud and a sneak, assuring him that I wasn't interested in ordination but wanted "to learn more about our faith" (this with a sarcastic sneer). The other member, who was the priest in her parish, firmly agreed saying that it would be a cold day in hell before he'd vote for me to be admitted to the Process. "In fact," he said, "I'd excommunicate her for her treachery and her attempts to divide this great church if she was a member of my parish." The woman snorted and said, "She'd never be a member of our parish!"

Jane had been quietly sitting in a corner of the room waiting for a ride. She had been completely unnoticed by these two, who left the building laughing about how I would be shunned by their parish if I ever darkened their doorway. They saw me as the personification of the evil that was threatening their beloved Episcopal Church with such an abomination as a "female priest." Jane saw her ride appearing and got to the parking lot in time to hear the priest loudly proclaiming, "Don't you ever use those two words together again! There can be no such thing in this church!" He slammed his door, started up the car, and roared out of the parking lot.

Most of the reports were mixed, as there were supporters of women's ordination in many parts of the Diocese. While most were not nearly as vocal as the opponents, there were women loudly proclaiming my virtues and the Bishop's courage. These well-meaning people unfortunately did more of a disservice to the other women who aspired to ordained ministry than anything.

Bishop Vaché had told me and many others that the reason he opened the door to me was that I didn't try to knock it down. He knew that I was not "fighting a cause" and that I did not expect or demand admittance to the process because I had a right to it. The louder the banging on the door by women who demanded entrance, the more determined he was to keep that door tightly closed and even locked. I had not banged loudly; I had quietly knocked and waited.

It was because of this attitude that he really believed that I felt called to go to seminary, agreed to endorse my seminary application and make funds available for my tuition and other expenses. It became clear to me later that he also knew, even before I did, that I was indeed called to the priesthood. So when he opened the door a crack, just to let me attend seminary, he was obviously ready to open it the rest of the way. That is why he is my hero.

This was clear to many of the angry Episcopalians who never thought that the Bishop would ever open this door at all and they did not see him as their hero. They had been confident that his staunch opposition to allowing women in the priesthood would keep that door permanently locked and now they were angry. Some even called him a traitor. The Bishop once described several irate phone calls that he had received from lay people and clergy who berated him for what they considered a breach of contract.

Even though the National Church Convention of 1976 opened the way for women to be ordained, Bishops were still in charge of who was admitted to the process in their own Dioceses and whom they would ordain. The Diocese of Southern Virginia was no different than other dioceses. There were people who cheered loudly when the National Church made its historic decision and there were people who booed just as loudly. Some of those stayed and continued to voice their negative position while some left through that open door and didn't look back. Up until this moment, there was unanimity in the Diocese over one thing: our Bishop would never ordain a woman.

In one moment on one ordinary day in Lent, this cherished tradition of an all-male priesthood was suddenly being threatened as there was now a woman standing on the precipice poised to tear down that tradition. Some were appalled and some were ecstatic but, as one, the entire Diocese was watching with bated breath.

CHAPTER FOUR

The Road to Sewanee

MY JOURNEY TO SEWANEE BEGINS

My next step was applying to the seminaries of my choice. This involves filling out the school's application, writing a "spiritual journey" statement, and preparing a budget estimating your family's expenses and income for a year, including possible grants and loans.

In order to complete the application, you must also have your Bishop's endorsement. Episcopal seminaries will not admit anyone without their Bishop's signature. I had his letter of endorsement in my folder and all that remained was to take and pass the GRE's – Graduate Records Exam. I'm proud to say that after 13 years away from academia, I aced the math section! I was ready.

TIME TO MOVE ON

About a month before beginning this application process and already in the seminary student mode, I no longer had a heart for my job as the Zoning Administrator for the City of Petersburg, a position I had held for almost 4 years. I knew in my heart that I was going to be going to seminary and suddenly, I couldn't bear one more day of working at something that didn't fulfill my call to ministry. I phoned my friend David at the Diocesan office and told him how I felt and he said, "Funny, I was just going to call you and ask you if you would be interested in being my Business Manager at Camp for the summer." Oh Yeah!

I loved Camp Chanco, and I had only been able to attend one week of Senior High Week for the past 5 years. I had dreamed of being able to spend the entire summer with my friend David, working side by side with him to teach and minister to some of the finest teen-agers I had ever known. I couldn't agree fast enough although I remember David asking me if I didn't want to think about it. He named a salary figure far below what I was making as a municipal employee, but I knew it was the right move for me. I

needed to be somewhere that would allow me to prepare myself for
the journey to my new ministry that would begin that fall.

When I told my parents what I was doing, my mother was
horrified! "What if you don't get into that school? What will you do
then?" I assured her that I had faith that I would be accepted, and I
knew this was what God wanted me to do to get ready. She didn't
think it was a great idea and my father was still shaking his head
when Scotty and I packed up all our belongings, rode behind the
U-Haul truck my father was driving and moved into the Business
Manager's trailer while our possessions moved into the old dining
hall for the summer. When Mom and Dad pulled out of the Camp to
take the truck back to Petersburg, I waved and smiled so hard and so
long that I got a cramp in my face.

APPLICATIONS TO SEMINARIES

The actual task of applying to seminaries was much simpler
than I thought it would be. My first thought was to go to Virginia
Seminary, which was less than 4 hours north in the Washington
DC area. I thought how nice it would be to come home and attend
youth events and keep in touch with my church and family. The
Diocese of Virginia had been one of the first Dioceses to jump on the
women's ordination bandwagon, so it only took a phone call to get
an interview scheduled for early May. On a bright spring afternoon
before I made the move to Camp, I drove up to Alexandria, found
the seminary, made a couple of wrong turns before finding the right
building, parked, and went inside.

A very nice receptionist seemed to know who I was and
asked me to have a seat. I hadn't waited long when a tall, very
distinguished looking priest opened the door and beckoned to me
to join him. As I approached the door, he swept his hand in front
of me like a knight inviting his lady to precede him. As I went by
him, he grabbed my hand and said, "We sure are glad to see you up
here." I had fully expected to be welcome, but this seemed a very
odd thing for him to say and I almost said something unintelligible
like "Hunh?" I managed to just smile, shake his hand, and take a seat
at the table.

There were three or four other clergy at the table, which
was just a tad intimidating, but the interview went very well and
when it was completed, the Dean invited me to join the next class as
a student at Virginia Seminary. I was shocked to get an answer so

quickly and I was so excited, I almost accepted without thinking, but something was niggling at the back of my mind, so I just thanked him, assured him I would pray on it, and I would let him know after I had returned from my trip to Sewanee.

OFF TO SEWANEE

By the end of May, Scotty and I had moved to Camp Chanco to help David prepare for the summer sessions. We had several weeks before the campers began to arrive so we closed up camp for the long Memorial Day weekend and Scotty and I took off for Lake Gaston to see my parents. My interview was scheduled for Monday afternoon so we left after church on Sunday and drove more than halfway before stopping for the night. As we got closer the next day, I was remembering a trip I had made several years before to a conference center in Monteagle, Tennessee to attend a youth event called Happening. The Deacon who accompanied me and six teenagers, was a recent graduate of Sewanee and he took advantage of the trip to make a visit to his Alma Mater which was approximately six miles from the conference center.

On Sunday, we dropped him off in Sewanee and, when we rode through the stone pillars which announced that we were entering "The Domain of the University of the South," I said to the kids, "I'm coming back here some day." I knew it as well as I knew my name. Sewanee is a beautiful campus on top of the Cumberland Plateau, which made it pretty close to heaven for me with my love of the mountains. But this statement came out of much more than a desire to live on top of a mountain. I could feel the Spirit tug at me as we rode through the gates and that little voice I had heard before returned, and I felt more than I heard, "Susan, this is where I want you."

BACK TO THE DOMAIN

So, just about a year and a half later, I was riding through those same gates on a beautiful Monday morning in May and I knew I had "come home." The interview was about as different from the interview at Virginia as it could be. It was much more casual; in fact, it could be called slightly off-beat. I was interviewed by the Pastoral Theology Professor in lieu of the Theology Professor who had awakened with the stomach flu.

The Rev. Craig Anderson and I discussed my "call" as well

as my background as he periodically jumped up to chase his toddler down the hall. It seemed that, even though it was Memorial Day, his wife had to go into work that morning, so he had babysitting duty. I am quite sure that no one at any seminary or any other institution of higher learning has ever been interviewed by a Professor changing a dirty diaper on the floor of the community room.

It was a bizarre experience, but it left me with a feeling of acceptance and respect that I had not experienced in my own Diocese or at Virginia Seminary. By the way, I was so puzzled at the Virginia Seminary Professor's strange words that when I returned home, I called a recent graduate of Virginia to get his opinion as to what was meant by "we sure are glad to get you up here." He immediately laughed – more of a snort – and said, "Susan, didn't you know? You're a plum! The Diocese of Virginia (they had been ordaining women since 1976 as soon as it was allowed) would just love to steal you away. They're just waiting for our Bishop to refuse to ordain you and then they'll be in the position to step in and offer you a new home and an ordination." At that moment, I vowed not to return to Virginia as a student. I absolutely refused to be a political football between two Dioceses; I would not allow them to reduce my "call" to ministry to a cause to be won. Therefore, everything was riding on my interview with Professor Anderson and the School of Theology.

ANOTHER LONG WAIT

It was several weeks before I received a letter from the Dean's Office at the School of Theology in Sewanee. I got the letter after lunch and I started to just rip it open on the spot. Then I thought about how I would feel if it was a rejection letter. I decided I did not need to be in the middle of a large group of people, but I also did not want to be alone. So I found David, showed him the envelope and asked him to come with me to my trailer. He didn't hesitate a second; he knew what this meant to me and he knew I needed his support. We took off and in two minutes we were sitting at the table in my trailer looking at the letter. I was terrified and didn't want to open it because I was sure it was bad news. But I was excited too, because I really thought the interview went well and I just couldn't believe that God was going to bring me this far only to shut the door in my face.

So I asked David to say a quick prayer for me and he

grabbed my hands and prayed, "God, you know what is in Susan's heart and we know that this is all in your hands. Give her peace and the grace to accept whatever is in this envelope. Amen." Tears were running down my face already; the time had come. I ripped open the envelope, took out the letter, opened it and read these words, "It is our pleasure to invite you to become a student in the Class of 1984 at the School of Theology." I barely made it to the end of the sentence before my throat closed up – I couldn't speak! All I could do was jump up and down, wave the letter in David's face, and cry. He hugged me and hugged me and I finally began to calm down enough to continue reading the letter.

It went on to say what day the semester started and when I should arrive in Sewanee and then I screamed, "What?" I couldn't believe what I was reading! I turned to David and said, "You will not believe this. Listen." And I read the beginning of the next paragraph: "We are reserving you a room on the 3rd floor of St. Luke's Hall in the women's dormitory. You can find the key in a mailbox with your name on it located in the Student Mail Room on the 1st floor of St. Luke's Hall." I was again waving the letter but this time I was panicky – what were they talking about? I couldn't live in a dormitory with an 8-year-old! What if they meant to accept someone else? What if this wasn't my letter?"

All of those things and more started flooding my mind until I was shaking. David managed to calm me down by taking the letter and re-reading the part where my name and address was clear and assuring me that it was probably just a silly error. He picked up the phone and dialed the phone number on the letterhead and handed me the phone. "Just ask them," he said.

A nice sounding woman with a southern accent answered the phone and I identified myself. Before I could say another word, she said, "Oh great! I hope you're calling to accept our invitation!" I was a little surprised that the receptionist knew who I was, but I only wanted to talk to the right person to fix my living arrangements, so I told her what my letter said. She jumped right in and said that I would just love St. Luke's Hall. I let her finish and then I asked her, "What should I do with my son?" There was silence at the other end and then she said, "Oh no! You do have a son, don't you? We've made a huge mistake!" Relief surged through me while she connected me with the Seminary Housing Department. Another very nice lady with a southern accent straightened the whole thing out in three minutes and, when I hung up, I had her abject apology and my new address in Woodlands where there were apartments for students with families.

David was watching and smiling, so I thanked him profusely for being there and went back to reading my letter again. Now that it was a done deal, I was elated and terrified all at the same time. I had been accepted to do the thing I most wanted to do in my life, and I didn't have a clue how I was going to pull it off. It suddenly occurred to me with bright clarity that, by the end of the summer, I would be unemployed, with an 8-year-old boy to support, and would owe approximately $3,500 for tuition fees, housing costs, and books for the first semester, not to mention moving expenses.

I'll never forget the strange combination of feelings that flooded me at that moment – absolute certainty that I was doing the right thing, complete and total terror at the vast "unknown" that both my son and I would be facing, as well as an unholy fear that the day would come for me to move to Sewanee and I wouldn't have enough money to even make the trip. It took about an hour with David, listening to his words of encouragement, a long conversation with the Bishop who assured me that "writing letters and asking for money is how a seminarian earns a living," and many hours of prayer before I was able to relax a little and get somewhat excited about my future.

CHAPTER FIVE

Summer 1981

CAMP CHANCO

Scotty and I were both excited to be spending the summer at Camp Chanco. Scotty was finally old enough to be a real camper and stay in a campsite and he was beside himself with joy and anticipation. David let him attend two sessions, even though he was a year younger than the campers in Session #2. He had spent so much time at Camp over the years and he was mature beyond his years, so he was considered to be a "camper extraordinaire."

The summer passed quickly as I kept the camp's records, ran all over southeastern Virginia buying supplies for the programs and the out-trips, and assisting the Director in any way I could. Whenever teenagers are involved, there are always issues, and I became a chaplain to the staff, many of whom would spend hours in my trailer talking, crying, laughing, and singing. I also became a favorite target for the smoke bomb Brigade – a clandestine group of male counselors whose claim to fame was that they had bombed both my trailer and the Director's house without getting caught.

THE POOF CLUB

Since they obviously were enjoying getting away with their smelly pranks, I was instrumental in instigating a movement by the female counselors to retaliate. I didn't have access to cherry bombs, and we wanted to make a completely female statement, so we devised a new kind of bomb – a Poof Bomb. This device was a partially inflated balloon half-filled with baby powder. It was simple to use, but the real trick was to sneak up on the guys without being detected, get close enough to hold the Poof Bomb over their heads, stick a pin in it, and yell "Poof" while running away quickly enough to avoid getting covered with powder. The Director wasn't particularly pleased with my role in all that – but he loved the image of his tormentors staggering to the bathhouse in the middle of the night covered with baby powder!

There were many special teenagers there that summer and one of them – the female staff member in charge of the waterfront became one of my favorites. She had a crazy sense of humor and we could talk for hours about anything. She came to rely on me as a confidant and, consequently, she spent a lot of time in my trailer. One hot day, she was working in the kitchen after dinner when she slipped on a wet spot and fell hard on the concrete floor, hitting the side of her head on the counter as she went down. I heard the commotion and came running as one of the kids yelled at me, "Come quick! Linda's hurt!"

She was on the floor in the kitchen, her face as white as a sheet and her eyes somewhat glazed over, but she looked at me and said clearly, "I fell down." This calm and concise statement was so out of character for her that we all became alarmed, and I went to the nurse's office to call her father, a medical doctor in nearby Suffolk. He said to bring her to the emergency room right away and he would meet us there. Someone drove us while I was busy trying to make heads or tails out of the gibberish coming out of the young lady lying across my lap in the back seat.

DR. BOWMAN?

I was so glad to finally arrive at the hospital where her father could take charge, which of course, he did. Linda was x-rayed all over, and by the time they were finished, she was relatively awake and coherent. It appears that she had just a mild concussion. I thought, "Whew! Thank God she's all right!" I also thought it was over, but my role in this scenario had only just begun. I had assumed that she would go home for the night, but, as her father began to give me instructions for caring for her in the coming hours, I realized that she had managed to talk him into letting her return to camp. My first thought was to brain her again, but her father was looking at me very seriously and telling me, "Now, here's the really important thing. You cannot let her sleep more than two hours at a time. She's going to be sleepy, and she needs to sleep some, but you MUST wake her up every two hours, walk her around, and be sure that she's awake, coherent, and able to take nourishment before she goes back to sleep."

I must have looked like an idiot standing there with my mouth gaping because he said, "Susan did you get all of that? Do you want me to go through it again?" I nodded dumbly, certain that I had heard him wrong. He couldn't be sending his daughter back to camp after this! How could he bear to let her out of his sight, and was he completely nuts turning her over to me when it was so obvious that this injury was really serious? I listened again as he went through the instructions firmly and clearly, making it abundantly clear that she was not to be allowed to sleep more than two hours at a time. The tone of his voice and his very specific words made it clear to me that I was responsible for this young lady's well-being, if not her actual survival.

When he finished his second explanation, he asked if I got it, and I said I did, but I did ask him if he was sure she was OK to go back to camp. "You know how crazy it is there," I reminded him, "and you know how she is. Do you think she'll do what she's supposed to do?"

He looked at me with great kindness and complete trust and said, "That's why I'm putting you in charge." Well, I was honored that he would trust me with his daughter's health, but I was also scared to death. All the way back to camp, I kept thinking, "What if something awful happens? What if I can't wake her up? It'll be my fault if something happens to her." Besides, I suddenly realized that it was only 9 pm so it was clear that I was looking at an all-nighter!

We arrived back at camp, and everyone gathered around as we half carried the very sleepy Linda into my trailer. I tucked her into the bunk across from mine, and every member of the staff came in to kiss and hug her and let her know how glad they were that she was alive. David then came in and said a heartfelt prayer of thanks for her survival, asking God to continue the healing process during the night. I was touched when he added, "and keep Susan awake so she can take care of her." It was at that moment that it really dawned on me what a heavy responsibility I had been given. I sat on the edge of the bunk watching Linda sleep and said a few of my own prayers. Then I set the alarm clock to go off in two hours and thought I'd try and get some sleep.

WHAT IF SHE DIES?

There was way too much going on outside my trailer to allow anyone who had not been bonked on the head to sleep, so I gave up and joined in the nightly camp worship around the fire only a little ways from my trailer. I kept looking toward the trailer and imagining all sorts of awful things that could happen to Linda while I was out there, so I finally gave up and went back to my vigil on the edge of my bunk. Linda slept on, and I watched her easy breathing thinking surely she must be OK if she can sleep this well. With that thought just leaving my brain, I became aware of the sudden quiet in the trailer. She wasn't breathing! I shook her arm and screamed, "Linda! Linda! Wake up!" One of the counselors passing by the trailer heard me and he was beside me in an instant. The two of us were patting her cheeks (actually we were slapping them) and yelling at her to please wake up! Suddenly, her eyes popped open and she said, "Would you please stop hitting me? I'm awake." I fell back on my bunk as my knees gave way in relief. I heard her saying, "How can a girl get any sleep around here?" so I knew she was OK, but it took me a few moments before I could even speak.

I looked at her and, trying to keep my panic from showing said, "Sorry, but you wouldn't wake up. Your father said that I had to wake you up!" She was already falling back to sleep and I figured since she hadn't been asleep two hours, it was OK. So, I ushered out the frightened counselor, assured him that she was fine, and went back to my bunk. I told myself I couldn't take my eyes off of her for the rest of the night, except to visit the bathroom and reset the alarm clock. I was still awake when it went off at 11:30 pm. I gently shook her awake, made her get up and walk outside to get some fresh air. She drank some orange juice and ate a cracker, but they didn't stay down long, so I walked her around some more knowing that this wasn't a good sign. I thought about calling her father, but she insisted that she was better and so, against my better judgment, I got her back in bed and set the alarm clock for 2 am.

It took about two minutes after she fell asleep for me to pick up the phone and call her father who answered on the first ring. I described to him what had happened, thinking that he would insist that we bring her back to the hospital, something I was eager to do, but he said that these things were normal with a slight concussion and, as long as I didn't let her sleep more than two hours at a time, she would be fine. He said he thought she'd get better faster with us because she loved camp and me and the rest of the staff so he was glad that I was there to take care of her. Sounding way more confident than I felt, he hung up and I'm sure he went right back to sleep.

I didn't think there was much chance of me doing that, but

at some point in the next two hours, I dozed off. The alarm brought me out of the bed like I'd been shot out of a cannon, and I almost fell on poor Linda who didn't even hear the thing which had scared me half out of my wits! I had to shake her for a few minutes before she began to stir and I realized with absolute clarity why it was so important to keep someone from sleeping too long after a head injury. I'm certain that if I hadn't kept waking her up, she would not have been able to wake up on her own. The thought made my blood run cold again and I looked closely at the alarm clock to see if there was some way to make it louder!

At 4 am, I again shot out of the bed, but this time, Linda was also waking up. Gratified that I didn't have to go through the anxious process of waking her, I greeted her with a huge hug, got her up and to the restroom, and we went to the dining hall to find some hot chocolate. We sat on the counter where she had hit her head some 10 hours before and talked about the dangers of wet floors. I took the opportunity to remind her that she had been wearing "flip-flops" (which were prohibited) when her feet slid on the floor, and they probably kept her from being able to maintain her footing. She looked very sheepish and said that she knew it was her fault. Suddenly she was crying and apologizing for causing so much trouble, and I hugged her and assured her that I loved getting up every two hours all night long!

She laughed weakly, and we finished our hot chocolate and headed for another two-hour nap. By 10 am, we had survived three more rude awakenings by the alarm clock, made several trips around the dining hall to get her blood flowing, and even gotten some breakfast in her. Shortly after that, her father appeared in camp to check her out. I was so glad to see him! I wanted desperately for him to tell me that the danger was over and that Linda was going to be just fine. I paced outside of the trailer while he examined her, and then watched as he put her through some paces on the level ground in front of the dining hall.

SHE LIVES!

By then, counselors and campers were gathering to watch and cheer her on. She was obviously enjoying the attention as she was cracking jokes and even had her old rosy complexion back. I was again weak with relief when her father pronounced her well on the road to recovery, handed me a sheet of much less stringent instructions for her care, hugged and thanked me for keeping her safe, and drove, waving, out of the driveway. Linda spent another few days in my trailer as we all watched her carefully according to her father's instructions and it was a real wrench to let her go when she finally moved back to her own quarters. We had bonded during those three days when I had her life in my hands and that bond has remained strong almost 30 years later thanks to communication on Facebook and email!

It was a grand summer, as I thoroughly enjoyed my job as the Business Manager. One of my duties was to gather the camp's program supplies, and this gave me outings to the surrounding towns where there were stores larger than the corner gas station in Surry. After the end of the 2nd session, when Scotty was not participating as a camper, he accompanied me on many of these trips and our favorite ones took us across the ferry to Williamsburg. Having attended college there a dozen years before, I loved going back to my old haunts for lunch, and I even tracked down a few sorority sisters who were now living in the area. Scotty enjoyed the Toy Shoppe and other sights in the area, but we usually didn't have too much time for sight-seeing.

Another of my regular duties was to meet the out-trips at their half-way point with new supplies for the return trip. These were mostly bicycle trips that left camp on the 2nd day and returned on the next-to-the-last day in time for closing ceremonies. My favorite trip to meet was the Tangier Island trip that went through the Northern Neck of Virginia to Reidsville on the eastern shore of Virginia where the Rappahannock River meets the Chesapeake Bay. From there, a boat takes visitors and residents to Tangier Island, a small piece of mosquito-infested land right in the middle of the Bay. It is a small island, approximately five miles square, with humans inhabiting only about one square mile; the rest was ruled solely by huge swarms of mosquitoes which made enough forays into the human world to make Deep Woods Off an absolute necessity.

There are no vehicles on the island, except for bicycles, so we walked from the boat to the cute little shops on our way to the restaurant for lunch. To say it was good was a gross understatement! We sat at family-style tables heaped high with standard Chesapeake Bay fare – Crab Cakes, Fried Fish, Oysters, Cole Slaw, and Mashed Potatoes. It was a feast fit for a king, and we left for the boat feeling like overstuffed pigs. I'm not sure about anybody else, but I slept all

the way back to our van and didn't even wake up when we passed
the smelliest fishery on the East Coast!

PLAYING BISHOP

The in-camp program that was so ably planned and
executed by our Program Staff was different every session, but each
one celebrated its own Big Day in the middle of the week. This was a
day totally devoted to one theme, and the whole camp got involved
making costumes and preparing for a huge play before lunch.
During one session, the theme was Camelot, and there was much
excitement as the kids vied for the coveted parts of King Arthur,
Lancelot, and Maid Marion. The Program Director came to me on
Tuesday morning that week and asked me if I would be willing to
help out with the play. There was a hint of something going on, so
I said that I would consider it. I wanted to know exactly what this
group was planning before I got in the middle of it!

This kid looked at me with a huge grin and said, "We want
you to play the Archbishop of Canterbury." My first reaction was
"No way!", but then I thought, "This will, most likely, be my only
opportunity to wear a Bishop's miter," so I agreed. It was a simple
part; I only had to crown the king and I only had one line. The
kids made me a miter and a grand robe to wear, so when Big Day
dawned, I was ready for my debut as the lordly head of all Anglicans
in Medieval England.

The play went on as I stood in the back hall awaiting my
cue to enter and put an end to the huge debate going on about who
was going to be the King of England. Just as I recognized my cue,
I looked toward the main door of the dining hall to see the last
person in the entire world I wanted to see at that moment. Bishop
Vaché had picked this day and this moment to make one of his few
appearances at camp. The Program Director saw him at the same
moment and told him what was going on, and I saw him nod, grin,
and sit down at a table by the door to watch.

I could not believe this was happening! Of all days in this
entire summer for him to visit, this had to be the worst! Here I
was, dressed up like a Bishop – no, not just any Bishop, but the
Archbishop of Canterbury, for crying out loud! It was all I could do
to keep from running out the back door, but I had promised these
kids I would do this…. "Wait a minute!" my brain screamed. "Did
they set this up?" I looked around and, sure enough, most of the

staff were trying desperately to keep from laughing as I watched the
Bishop settle down to watch me make an utter fool of myself.
    The battle going on in my brain was fierce – do I get
suddenly sick and take off out the back door – do I throw down
my miter and refuse to be the butt of their joke – or do I suck it up
and be a good sport and hope that the Bishop's sense of humor is
intact and working. It was close, but the coward in me lost out and
I marched out right on cue to crown Arthur the King of England. I
was cool and everything was fine until I opened my mouth to speak
my one line. Then, it hit me square between the eyes that the words
I had to say were not words I wanted this Bishop to hear. There was
nothing to do, though, but persevere so I took a deep breath and
shouted my one line, "Cease! Quiet! I am the Bishop. I have seen
Sir Arthur release Excalibur from its stony home. He is the rightful
King of England." The other characters started arguing again, and I
slammed down my staff on the floor and bellowed, "I am the Bishop
and this is your King." With that I placed the crown on Arthur's
head and the play was over. I mustered up every ounce of dignity I
had left, marched right out the back door, and collapsed in the hall
knowing in my heart that my dreams of going to seminary were as
good as over. I just knew the Bishop was going to see me as a pushy
female trying to make a point with these kids. I even convinced
myself that he would think I had known he would be there and had
planned the whole thing.
    As I got up from the floor, my son ran up to me and said,
"Cool Mom!" and at that moment, I also realized that the Bishop
would not appreciate his nickname for the week – "Son of a Bish." I
knew I was doomed. I also knew that I couldn't hide any longer, so
I deposited my costume in the back room, and tried to get to a lunch
table as far away from the Bishop as I could, but alas! There he was,
waiting for me, grinning from ear to ear, and reaching out to shake
my hand. "So, Bish," he said, "You were in good voice today!"
    I almost fainted. Not only was he amused, he really seemed
to appreciate my part in the kids' little dramatic joke, which he had
figured out was aimed at us both. He was being a much better sport
than I was since I had already glared at several staff members and
muttered something like, "You'll pay for this." Unlike me, he was
enjoying every minute of their fun **and** my embarrassed discomfort.
I was even more amazed when David asked him to say the blessing,
as was traditional when the Bishop visited camp for a meal, and he

graciously turned to me and said, "Let's have the **real** Bishop say it."
I was so flabbergasted, I could hardly speak, but I managed to repeat
our traditional family blessing thanking my Dad and God, in that
order, for all the years those words had been seared into my brain.
They came out automatically and I sat down in relief that I could
finally put something in my mouth besides my foot.

MY OTHER SUMMER JOB
        Camp Chanco was a busy place, and my duties kept me
hopping, but in the midst of it all, I was also busy trying to raise the
necessary funds for my first year in seminary. The Diocese would
provide financial assistance, but it wasn't nearly enough, so I had to
look for other resources. I found three or four foundations which
had grants available every year for seminarians attending Episcopal
schools, and I worked hard at the applications, my requests, and
estimated expenses until I had a well-written letter and a tight
budget. I mailed them off and then waited. I was scared to death.
What if I didn't get enough money? Why should these people want
to give me money and what if they did but there wasn't enough?
There were some funds only available to men going to seminary,
but I was surprised to find one grant for women students from
a foundation somewhere in California. I was also surprised and
appalled to find that the Episcopal Women's Educational Fund,
administered by the Diocesan women's organization, would not
supply funds for seminary education. Their rules only allowed
grants to be paid to students attending undergraduate schools
and trade schools, such as nursing programs. My request for an
exception was swiftly and tersely denied.

MONEY FROM HOME
        I applied to all the organizations I could find, and the
waiting was agony, but slowly and surely, the responses began to
come in. I was completely shocked to receive promises for $500 per
semester from one and $1,000 per semester from another one. There
were a few other small awards with offers to pay for books, but it
was still not looking like enough to me. Then I received a letter
from my mother's cousin in Fayetteville, North Carolina where
my mother was raised. I had written to our family members about
my plans to attend seminary. Cousin Mary Coit remembered that
another cousin had set up a fund at St. John's Episcopal Church in

Fayetteville, where my mother and I were both baptized. It was intended for assisting seminarians and she thought I'd have a good chance to get a grant from it. She offered to write a recommendation for me. So I wrote her back asking her to do that, and then I wrote to the Rector, introducing myself, explaining my situation and asking if there was a possibility of receiving a grant for my education.

I received the most gracious letter from him explaining that the fund I was asking about had been set up according to our cousin's will. It stated that the money was only to be used "to support the seminary education of worthy young men seeking ordained ministry." My heart sank as I read that and I could feel the anger rising in me, but the next sentence brought me right up straight in my chair.

He went on to say that he was certain that the Vestry, with his gentle persuasion, would look favorably on finding a way to help me. I had no idea what that meant, but I had faith that this gentle sounding man meant what he said. I filled out the papers exactly as he instructed, put in my request for $500 a semester and thought, "Well, that's probably a waste of time." I just couldn't see a group of Southern men (now there's a prejudicial statement!) going against the will of another of the good old boys to help a girl who had not darkened the door of their church since she was two months old.

Imagine my surprise when I received a long letter from the Rector of St. John's telling me that he had spoken with my Bishop. Furthermore, he said that he and the Vestry had worked hard to devise a way to help me without "breaking the will" or going against the spirit of the man's bequest. What they came up with was brilliant! They would send a donation to my Bishop's discretionary fund along with a request that the Bishop make that money available to a worthy seminarian, namely me. "Oh, and by the way," he went on, "we don't think $500 a semester is enough, so we're going to give you $1,000 each semester instead." They asked that I report to them at the end of each year. He relayed the wish of each of those men (whom I had sorely misjudged) that I would work hard to excel in seminary and make them all proud. David was with me in the trailer when I opened it. I read this rare and amazing testament to how God was at work in the midst of the stubborn resistance I was experiencing in so many other places. We gave thanks, and then he held me while I wept.

TIME TO GO

When the day arrived that I had to pack my belongings into another U-Haul, I couldn't believe that it was time to go. The day my parents came to camp to pick us up, many of the summer staff were still there, and they loaded the truck in record time. This was a mere half hour after they had all stuffed themselves into my red Mustang, on which I had just made the last payment. All 18 of them stayed packed in my car long enough for the Chaplain to lay a huge blessing on my vehicle, which finally belonged to me. The timing was perfect as I left to embark on my new journey without one penny of debt and enough promises of grants and loans to support us for the first semester. I didn't even think beyond that. After watching the acceptance letters come in with promises of more money than I had asked for, I was secure in the knowledge that God was indeed in charge of this operation.

The send-off from Camp Chanco was both exhilarating and tearful. Scotty and I were leaving not only family, but dear friends we had known for some six years. We had spent almost three months with some of them for 24 hours a day, seven days a week, living in very close proximity. I was leaving my best friend and the youth program that had transformed me and it was indeed gut-wrenching.

With tears in our eyes, Scotty and I hugged them all while my parents watched. Suddenly, I began to be aware of loud giggling coming from behind me. I turned to find two guys strapping the huge archery target (filled with wet smelly hay) to the top of my shiny red Mustang – "so God could keep better track of me." As other staff members began running for buckets and the water spigot, we all sprinted for the vehicles.

Scotty jumped into the truck with his grandfather, whom he thought was relatively safe from attack, and my brave mother joined me in the car. I took off in a spray of dirt and pine needles, struggling to see from underneath the huge target hanging over my windshield. Mom and I tore at the ropes, which thankfully had been tied hurriedly. With some effort, we loosened it and as I sped off down the road, we let it slide backwards into the road amid cheers from those whom I loved and would miss terribly in the months to come.

THE TRIP
            I cried most of the way to Petersburg where we were picking
up their car, while my Mother tried in vain to cheer me up. She knew
how much I cared for the friends I had just left behind but she didn't
seem to grasp the depth of my connection with Camp Chanco and
the entire youth program. In the past five years, I had been rescued
from the depths of a dry spiritual hole and discovered a faith I had
never known before. I had heard people talk about Jesus being their
friend when I was growing up, but the Episcopal position on this
was clear in our part of the church so I learned at an early age that
anyone who claimed to talk with Jesus was highly suspect. Now, I
had friends who said they talked with God every day, and I knew
a whole bunch of Episcopalians who were very clear about their
relationship with Jesus – he was their friend!
            I was beginning to see that my 30-some years as an
Episcopalian had been in name only, and suddenly, I was faced
with a whole new reality about what I had previously thought of
as "going to church." Now, I was learning that there was so much
more to the Christian faith than I had ever suspected. I felt like the
disciples must have felt when they found themselves in the middle
of a storm on the usually safe and familiar Sea of Galilee. Part of my
world was in an upheaval, as every day brought new and unsettling
ideas about God and prayer. My safe Episcopal world now felt
anything but safe.
            I didn't know how to talk to other people about God – I'm
sure that I had only said the name of Jesus a dozen times in my
life outside of worship, and now I was going off to a place where
everybody talked about Jesus all the time, openly and joyfully. I
didn't quite know how I was going to deal with that. Already, my
new efforts at a more personal prayer life were weak and sporadic,
since I didn't really have anything to go on and I had no one to
guide me. No way was I going to ask anybody – how could I even be
thinking about going to seminary if I didn't know how to pray?
            I was in a real dilemma, because I really thought I knew
how to pray – I was an Episcopalian, knew where everything was
in the prayer book, and knew most of the important stuff by heart!
This was how we prayed, so I thought I was good at it. Now, I was
finding out that I didn't have a clue how to pray. I desperately
wanted to "talk" to God like a friend, and I just didn't know how
to do that. I finally decided that I just had to jump in with both feet.

I just had to try it. I figured the worst that could happen was that I would feel like an idiot. Since I already felt that way, I had nothing to lose. Besides, who was going to know except me? Well, God would, but I had it on good authority that God was very forgiving and understanding. Surely, God already knew that I was not doing this very well; maybe I'd make a good impression by trying to get better.

So, here I was in the car with my Mother, who was trying so hard to be cheerful. I was trying to stop crying, but I also had this huge urge to pray – out loud! I wanted to tell God that I was so sad to be leaving my friends and so scared about what was ahead. However, I knew that, if I suddenly broke out in a heartfelt prayer, my Mother would finally be convinced that I was certifiable! So I prayed to myself between sobs, "God, I'm so, so sad to be leaving here. You gave me all these wonderful people and this wonderful place, and now I have to leave it all behind. My heart hurts and I've been crying so hard, my head hurts. Can you help me stop crying before Mother jumps out of the car?"

My next thought was, "Good grief, Susan! What kind of prayer was that?" Whatever it was, it worked. My tears stopped, I could breathe without gulping for air, and after a few moments, I could even talk. Mother was asking about the archery target, and I found myself telling her stories about camp. By the time we pulled into the gas station to hitch my Mustang to the U-Haul, we were laughing. I felt better and Mother was beginning to understand why I had been so sad.

WRONG WAY HOWARD

When I played basketball in high school, girls were still only playing one-half of the floor. The forwards stayed at their end when the ball went to the other team, and the defense remained at their end when the offense had the ball. Of course, the boys ran up and down the whole court, which could get confusing in the heat of a close game. One of our boys, whenever he saw a clear court to the basket, would take off down the court. He was fast, so, most of the time, he had reached the other end of the court and made an easy lay-up before he realized that everyone was yelling, "Wrong way Robert! Wrong way Robert!" Knowing my own capacity for that kind of confusion, I was eternally grateful that I never was in danger of getting turned around and going the wrong way.

I can't say the same for my father, although he was a good driver in those days. I was so grateful to have him driving the truck with my Mustang hanging off the back. I had never mastered the art of backing up a towed vehicle since I had enough trouble turning the wheel in the correct direction when parallel parking; there was no way I would ever be able to turn the wheel in the opposite direction to get a towed vehicle to go where you wanted it to go. I was driving their car and happy to be behind the wheel of a single vehicle. We followed the U-Haul towing the Mustang, so I could adjust my speed to match its slower speed without constantly looking back to see how far behind they were.

We spent the night in Petersburg after picking up the car, and we got a very early start in the morning. By the time we got on I-81 South, we were starved and decided to look for a place to eat our picnic lunch. We wanted a nice spot to eat outside where we could stretch our legs as well as eat our own food. We got off at an exit with a sign for a state park, and we hit the jackpot. It was a small park about two miles off the interstate, and we were able to drive right up to the edge of a beautiful lake with picnic tables and even a bathroom! We had our lunch, used the facilities, and took off our shoes and socks to wade in the cool, clean water. Well, Mother and I did. Daddy was chomping at the bit to get back on the road and, in his haste, he backed up too quickly so that the car and the truck did a little jackknife. As he got ready to pull away, I saw a wire hanging off the back of the truck. When I got him to stop, we discovered that it was the wire that controlled the trailer's brake lights. He couldn't fix it, so he decided to go on without us and stop at the gas station at the interstate and get it fixed. We'd catch up with them since they couldn't go much over 45 or 50, and we could travel much faster. Mother and I waved at them as they rode off, and we wandered back into the water.

After awhile, we packed up and got back on the road. We had masterfully calculated that it should take us about an hour to catch up with them. When the hour passed and we hadn't found them yet, we figured that we had done something wrong so we recalculated. We still came up with the same answer: we should have overtaken them within an hour, an hour and 20 minutes, at the latest. We kept going, and every mile that passed brought us closer and closer to the Tennessee state line and to a state of panic. Finally, we saw the Welcome Center, and we knew that they couldn't possibly be ahead of us. We pulled off the interstate and went to the building to find a phone.

Just as we got to the door, it occurred to me that if they were behind us, they could sail right by the Welcome Center and never know we were there. So, Mother stayed outside watching the cars pass by while I went in to make the call. This was way before any of us had cell phones, so I had to be content with calling the State Police to see if there had been any accidents involving a U-Haul truck towing a red Mustang. It was a long shot, since they would have had to have pulled off the interstate and then gotten into trouble or we would have seen them.

The Virginia and the Tennessee State Police dispatchers told me that there had been no accidents or anything involving a U-Haul; now I was really worried. I reported the news to Mother, and, while we were relieved, the feeling quickly turned into panic as we realized that we had no way of finding them. All we could do was wait. Since the police knew where we had called from, we decided to stay there. We were standing behind the car watching the traffic on the interstate when I thought, "What if they go by and we're standing way up here? They couldn't see us from the road even if they knew we were here."

In two minutes, my Mother and I were sitting on the hill in front of the Welcome Center where we could see every vehicle that came down the road. We were close enough to the road that, if we saw that big orange truck, we could get to the exit ramp before they passed by. Then, we could jump up and down and wave them into the exit. After twenty minutes of anxious pacing and jumping up every time we saw any kind of truck, we finally spied the beautiful orange and black "U-Haul" barreling down the road toward us.

We took off for the exit ramp, wildly waving our arms and yelling at the top of our lungs. We knew that they couldn't hear us, but we didn't care; we just needed to yell! Of course, they saw us (who wouldn't see us out there?) and they turned off onto the exit ramp. We jumped in the car and moved to where the U-Haul could park in a pull-through space. Pulling up beside them, I hardly had the car in park before Mother was out of the car running, and I was right behind her. The two guys jumped down from the truck, and we were all hugging and kissing and crying (not my Dad of course). It took some time for us to tell our story and get the anxiety and frustration out of our system; then I looked at Daddy and said, "So, where have you two been?"

Scotty looked at his grandfather and must have decided to keep quiet, because there was a silence before Daddy said, "Well, we went to get the wire fixed, and I had to back the truck around several times so that the guy could get to it. Then we had to test it out before he would let us get back on the road." Finally, it passed inspection and they took off as fast as Daddy could move. Needless to say, Daddy was anxious to get on the road; when he was on a trip, he never wanted to stop more than five minutes for anything, and, by this time, he had been off the road for more than an hour!

So they jumped back on the road. They began to watch for us, and when we didn't catch up within an hour, they began to get as worried as we did. He finally decided to get off the interstate and try to track us down. As they pulled up to the stop sign at the exit, they could plainly see the sign pointing to the re-entry ramp leading to I-81 **North**. Yes, it's true. They went the wrong way. Somehow in all the backing up and turning around, he had gotten himself turned around and, when they got to the first interstate entrance, they merrily got on – and Daddy drove on in the wrong direction for about 40 miles.

They had no way to let us know where they were, so they got back on I-81 **South** hoping that they would catch up sooner rather than later. Of course it was later, and by the time we were reunited, we were all exhausted from worry. So, after we had been on the road for less than an hour, we started looking for a place to stay for the night. We found a nice Holiday Inn, checked in, had an early supper and by 9:00, most of us were sound asleep. I was not.

I couldn't sleep, because every time I closed my eyes, I could see the truck heading North. At first, I was just so grateful and relieved that I kept thanking God (silently of course) for keeping my father and my son safe. After I got all that out of my system, I suddenly saw them going North again, and I wondered, "Is this a sign? Is God trying to tell me to go back home? Am I going the wrong way? Does God want me to turn around?"

After about an hour, I finally got up and went outside to get some air. I sat on the hood of my car and looked at all the stuff that was packed in it. Suddenly, I saw in my mind the picture of 18 Camp Chanco staff members stuffed into the car and all of them chanting, "Take us with you! Take us with you!" I remembered David's last words to me, "You're going to love seminary. God go with you." In a flash, I remembered my Bishop's encouraging words as he sent me off to seminary with his blessing, "I'll help you out for the first year and we'll see what happens." Surely, God would not want me to turn my back on **that** after all it took to bring Bishop Vaché that far. Suddenly, my eyes wouldn't stay open another minute. Now that my mind was at ease, my body was crying for sleep. I let myself back into the room and fell on the bed; I'm sure I was asleep before my head hit the pillow.

THE HOLY MOUNTAIN
    My friend, who had attended Sewanee, had explained to me that Sewanee was the name of the town situated just off I-24 between Chattanooga and Nashville. As we drove through Chattanooga, Mother and I were fascinated with the strange names for the attractions close by – Ruby Falls, Lookout Mountain, and the Incline Railway. Of course, we were dying to stop at the Chattanooga Choo-Choo, but we didn't have the time or the energy. So, we cruised on, and 45 minutes later, we were climbing the east side of the Cumberland Plateau. The interstate went right up the side of the mountain at a steep incline. When we arrived at the

The Holy Mountain
Monteagle Mountain, Cumberland Plateau, Tennessee

top, the road flattened out so abruptly that it felt like we were on one of those log flume rides where the log car chugs and chugs up the steep incline very slowly. Just when you're sure that the car is going to slide backwards, it reaches the top, the nose comes down, and the car plops down in the water and sits flat until it starts roaring down the flume. The Cumberland Plateau was something like that, although there were about six miles between the spot where our car plopped down on the flat top of the mountain and the spot where the highway plunged down the west side.
    The exit to Sewanee is the last one before the edge where the highway starts down the west side. It is also the exit for Monteagle,

Tennessee where I had attended the Happening two years before. When we got off and came up to the stop sign, I recognized everything and remembered exactly how to get to Sewanee. Of course, it wasn't hard – we just turned left, drove six miles and there were the two stone pillars again. Each one bore a large bronze plaque identifying the property as the Domain of the University of the South, and I recalled the thrill I felt the other two times I drove through the gates. This time, though, I was so far past thrilled that I was having trouble breathing and felt as if I might hyperventilate. As we entered the campus proper, I heard Mother gasp. I looked over and saw her staring at the huge trees lining the wide, gently curving road between spectacular stone buildings. "Beautiful, isn't it?" I managed. All she could do was nod. All I could do was pinch myself to make sure this was real. I had made it back to Sewanee, but this time I wasn't visiting – I was here to stay.

CHAPTER SIX

Seminary

SEWANEE: THE UNIVERSITY OF THE SOUTH

From the shores of the James River in Southside Virginia, Mother, Daddy, Scotty and I had journeyed more than 600 miles to what was reverently called "The Holy Mountain" by its inhabitants. Sewanee is a small town that is surrounded on the west and the south by exquisite scenery as it sits on the edge of the plateau with spectacular late afternoon sunsets. The view on the southern end of Tennessee Avenue is breathtaking. Standing beneath the huge 70' high cross, a memorial to those who gave their lives in American wars, and looking out over the valley floor never failed to fill me with awe. I thought that this was going to be my favorite spot until several days later when Scotty and I were exploring the famous Hammer's Department Store in Winchester. As we started our approach to the "Mountain," I looked up to see if we could really see the memorial cross as we'd been told, and I came very close to running off the road. The cross was indeed visible; in fact, it was sparkling so brightly in the setting sun that I had to pull over since all I could see was the bright light of that cross. In the three years that I lived in Sewanee, the sight of that cross never failed to bring tears to my eyes.

Sewanee is the ultimate "college town" as almost 100% of the town property belongs to the University. Local residents who "own" their homes actually have a "lease for life" with the University. When school is in session, the population is approximately 2,500; during the summer, that number drops to approximately 800. The Seminary is officially called The School of Theology of the University of the South as it is the only post-graduate department, which gives the college its university status. The undergraduate school is top-notch and the seminary, also known as St. Luke's, is ranked near the top of the 11 seminaries in the U.S.

A SOUTHERN WELCOME
    I had heard of the big cross and other landmarks and really
wanted to explore more of the Domain, but we were all tired and
still had to unload the truck and two cars before we could rest
again. Reluctantly, I handed the directions to Mother, and she
began to read off the turns to me. It was simple and not very far to
Woodlands where we had been assigned to a 2-bedroom duplex
apartment. The residences in Woodlands had each been financed
by one of the owning Dioceses of the University of the South, and
we were heading for the "South Carolina" house. It was actually a
duplex much like the one in which we had lived in Colonial Heights.
    We made the last turn and headed down the hill to "South
Carolina", which sat at the bottom of the hill on a curve in the road.
There was a single-family house on one side, a wide open field on
the other side and one across the street. Another duplex stood next
to the corner lot and then more space between that building and
the houses at the top of the hill. The street was narrow and lined
with trees, and brightly colored flowers, dogs, and children were
everywhere.
    We drove carefully down the street, dodging the dogs and
the kids, and pulled up in front of our new home. By the time we
had cut off the engine and gotten out of the car, the doors were
opening and people were pouring out of both sides of the duplex.
Before we could take a step, we were surrounded by excited men
and women, all talking at once. They were introducing themselves
and welcoming us to "the Mountain;" some hugged us and others
shook our hands eagerly. It was obvious that they were really
happy to see us, and it quickly became clear that they weren't just a
welcoming party; they were a moving crew.
    It was a hot August afternoon, and we had dreaded
unpacking in the heat, but with the help of our new neighbors, the
truck was unpacked in less than an hour. By dinner time, most of
the boxes were empty and our little 2-bedroom duplex apartment
had become our home for the next three years. We were side-by-
side neighbors with an upcoming Senior and his wife, who would
become dear friends, along with most of the students living in the
area. The homes, duplexes, and quadruplexes were all built by the
different owning Dioceses in the 1950's. The University maintained
them and leased them to the students for a reasonable amount; many
of them had just been renovated, including ours.

It wasn't a large apartment, but it was large enough; in fact, our belongings looked lost in these rooms which were more spacious than our former apartment. We had just said good-byes and thank-yous to our movers, and we were beginning to think about going back to the inn and restaurant we had seen

The Bowman's Side

South Carolina House
Woodlands - Sewanee, TN

in Monteagle when the doorbell rang, and the second shift arrived. This was the "dinner crew" and they came bearing all sorts of scrumptious looking dishes. There was even hot bread, a gorgeous chocolate cake, a cooler full of cold Cokes and beer, and a pitcher of Kool-Aid for the kids. They had dinner set up and our plates served before we could turn around and say that we were going out and why didn't they all join us!

Dinner was delicious and the company was exhilarating as we were regaled with story after story about life on the "Mountain." By the time it was getting dark, the kitchen was clean, left-overs were in the refrigerator, and we were sprawled out in the living room thinking we may never move again, even to get to the beds.

THIS WAS REAL

The next morning I was making coffee in the kitchen when Mother came in looking for Daddy. I don't know why she asked, because my father was a creature of habit, and if he didn't have a morning newspaper, he could barely get through the morning, much less the rest of the day. I told her that he had gone out about 30 minutes ago to get his paper, and I was beginning to wonder if I'd ever see him again. He had refused to let me give him the map so he could find the store. It was just as well, because he would have gone looking for a "short-cut" anyway like he always did. He hated stop signs and stop lights and would go to great lengths to avoid them. There were two stop signs and a yield sign on the way to the store, so I figured he had gone looking for another way, and there was no telling where he was at that moment. She laughed, agreed, and said she just may have to stay in Sewanee with us.

Just then, the door flew open, and there he stood with a newspaper for himself and a cup of steaming coffee for his wife. He was beaming! "I found a short-cut to the store! You'll miss one stop sign and that yield sign!" There are some things in this world that are "constants," that you can count on without fail. My father was one of them. You could set your clock by his arrival at the paper box outside their house, his opening the door of his tiny little accounting office in Gasburg (yes, there is a town in Virginia named Gasburg!), and his nightly raid on the freezer for his 9:30 pm bowl of ice cream. He was as faithful as the day is long and I looked at Mother and said, "What did I tell you!"

It was Saturday, and I couldn't wait to find out more about school and what it was like, but I knew that Daddy was itching to get on the road. He was an early riser and liked to start out on a long trip as early as possible. I was able to convince him to have breakfast and a short tour of the Domain before they started home. So we ate some pancakes, which he insisted on cooking, and piled in their car for our grand tour. We went out Tennessee Avenue to the cross and oohed and ahhed over the view. We drove out past the golf course to the western overlook and oohed and ahhed over the view. We drove around Morgan's Steep and oohed and ahhed over the view. There was a definite pattern forming; everywhere we went there was a gorgeous view of the Cumberland Valley and by the time we returned to Woodlands, I was head over heels in love with Sewanee.

The Memorial Cross
Sewanee, Tennessee

ANOTHER PAINFUL GOOD-BYE

We had put it off as long as we could, and finally it was time to say good-bye to my dear parents. They were as supportive as I could have ever hoped for, even though I don't think they were

quite sure what I was doing and why. What they did know was
that this was what I wanted to do, and they were always supportive
of me regardless of whether they understood it or agreed with it.
Since I had returned to Virginia as a new divorcee, they had been
there for me at every turn. They had taken us in while I looked for
a place to live and work, they had helped me rent a lovely house in
town, they found the necessary home furnishings and moved us in,
even helping with the rent at first. They had been there every time I
needed a babysitter, and they had cheered mightily when we started
going to church. When I announced to them that I was going to go to
seminary, they didn't seem too surprised; Mother just looked at me
and asked, "Why?"

They weren't quite as excited when they realized that this
meant we'd be moving, and I know it pained them that I was taking
their only grandchild 600 miles away. They had watched from afar
as I prepared for the move from Camp, and, now, they were leaving
us in a strange place. However, Mother did say that she was glad
to see my apartment so that she could at least picture us when we
called. She was also glad to meet so many of my new neighbors and
I know they felt comfortable knowing that we would have so much
support in our new home.

As we went out to the car, which Daddy had packed after
breakfast, I felt the tears prickling at my eyes. I looked at Mother,
who was already dabbing at her eyes with a tissue, and I knew that
this would not be a clean getaway. We hugged and hugged again,
and it seemed to take forever to let go. Mother went back inside for
one last pit stop, and then she had to go back to get her purse that
she had left in the bathroom. Daddy was in the car with the engine
running, just as he always was when it was time for them to go
somewhere. He called Mother a "piddler" because she never just
got ready, went out the door, and got in the car; she "piddled." She
picked up the newspaper, she checked the oven, she spread up the
bed; in fact, Daddy always said that she could find more things to
do between the time he left the house and the time he arrived at the
front door with the car running than he could in a lifetime!

Finally, she was through, and she got in the car, wiping her
now streaming eyes. Scotty and I hugged her through the window
one last time just as Daddy slipped the car into gear and backed
out of the drive. We both waved until the car disappeared over
the hill, and we cried. Holding each other up, we turned and went

inside to begin our new lives together on the "Holy Mountain."

SETTLING IN
        It was during the moving in that we discovered that tragedy
had struck less than a month before. The Very Rev. Urban (Terry)
Holmes, beloved Dean of the School of Theology, had suffered a
stroke while returning from a 6-month sabbatical. He had been
taken to an Atlanta hospital, where he died on August 6th. The
University was in shock, but the seminary was paralyzed by grief.
        Most of those who had helped us move in were incoming
members of my class, and they had quickly explained to us what
had happened, so we were actually surprised at how many of the
returning students showed up to welcome us. They all had loved
their Dean, and his sudden death had plunged the entire student
body, as well as the faculty and staff, into a state of shock that was
just beginning to wear off when we arrived three weeks later.
        Most of our class had never met Terry Holmes since he
had been away during the interview process. However, we soon
discovered that the Rt. Rev. Gireault Jones, retired Bishop of Western
Louisiana, had been named the Interim Dean and had the daunting
task of holding the Seminary together, while welcoming an incoming
class. Bishop Jones was a graduate of Sewanee and he loved the
"Mountain." So when he retired, he and his wife Kathleen had
bought a house located between the main campus and Woodlands,
which they had lovingly named "Meanwhile."
        Bishop Jones was a small man with the kindest face I have
ever seen, and we all fell in love with him the moment he walked
in to our classroom on our first morning as seminarians. He smiled
at us all, and said very simply, "Good morning, I am your Dean."
He went on to describe for us the horrible moment when they were
informed that Dean Holmes had died. He gently brought us into
that moment and led us through the ensuing days and weeks during
which they all tried to come to grips with this totally unexpected
situation.
        He told us about the phone call that he had received asking
him to serve as the Interim Dean for the upcoming year, and he
spoke honestly about his reluctance to "come out of retirement,"
which he was enjoying more than he had ever anticipated. He
spoke of his brief, but intense, struggle, and how he quickly came
to the realization that, not only was God calling him, not only did

his seminary need him, but **we** needed him. He said that it became
clear to him that the Class of 1984 would quickly become lost in the
grief that had gripped this community unless there was someone to
prevent that. He stopped for a moment, and then, with a twinkle in
his eye, he went on, "Has anyone seen my house?" We all looked
around wondering if this was something we should have done
by then. He smiled and continued, "You know, of course, that
it's named "Meanwhile." Well, of course, we didn't know that,
so we all looked rather ignorant, but he was undaunted. "So," he
asked, "doesn't anyone want to know why we named our home
"Meanwhile?"

We may
have been new, but
we weren't stupid,
so we responded,
almost in unison,
"Yes!" It quickly
became obvious that
he loved to be asked
this question, because
he looked around
and said, "Then will
someone please ask!"

"Meanwhile"

A brave soul in the front row took the cue and said, "So, Bishop, why
did you name your house 'Meanwhile?'" He grinned and said in
that southern drawl we'd all soon come to love, "Well, I'm glad you
asked. You see, for many years, we lived in New Orleans. In a few
years, we'll live in heaven. But, *meanwhile*, we're living in Sewanee!"
And so, he told us, he was the "Meanwhile Dean" and we loved him
instantly.

He put us at ease with his soft southern accent and his gentle
voice, but his words gave us a much needed sense of security and
hope. He said, "In the months to come, this community will do its
best to welcome you and help you to become part of the community.
The reality is that they will not be able to do this as they have in past
years. I want to assure you that you will not be forgotten – you will
not be left adrift in this new and scary place we call the Junior year.
As of this moment, I am **your** Dean. Come see me any time, day or
night; call me with your questions; my door is open to you."

Over the next few months, his words became reality, as the

staff and faculty were understandably in their own world. They were
in their offices and in front of their classes, but were naturally pre-
occupied with their personal grief. They were cruelly burdened with
the task of re-ordering themselves to function without their Dean
and to begin the search process for a new leader.

Of course, we were all struggling with our own grief over
leaving behind our homes, families, and friends, as well as with the
newness of life in a tiny community where most of our daily living
needs were not met by local retailers. In fact, there were only two
"grocery stores" – one a convenience store out on the bypass, where
everything was over-priced, and the University Market, where we
had the privilege of charging purchases to our University account,
but not a whole lot of choices to buy. The majority of the members
of our class were working on their second careers, so most of us had
been out of school for years. There were a few "youngsters" fresh out
of college, but they agreed that the level of courses we were taking
were challenging, to say the least. Personally, I was having my own
struggles with post-graduate level work 13 years after receiving my
undergraduate degree. I quickly became grateful that I had been
assigned to a tutorial group for the "killer" Old Testament course
taught by the legendary Professor, the Rev. William Griffin.

When I say, "I struggled," I am understating the reality. I
was in a panic, as I realized that I was way out of my league. I had
squeaked through William and Mary, majoring in Philosophy, which
should have afforded me a strong foundation for seminary studies.
The truth is, I had chosen that major because it required only 27
hours of concentrated study, and I really wanted a liberal arts
degree; actually I was majoring in "getting out and getting married"
(not in that order as it turned out), and I have to admit, not much
stuck.

Sewanee was in the forefront of the Episcopal seminary
system with its "Core Curriculum," which provided 10 hours a week
of Old Testament instruction in the 1st semester followed by 10 hours
a week of New Testament instruction in the 2nd semester. I had read
about this in the catalog during the application process, and I was
excited, but terrified at the same time. I thought I could handle most
of the courses, but I thought I would be thrilled if I could just skip
Theology and Homiletics (that's a fancy word for preaching). Just
the word "Theology" struck terror into my theologically ignorant
brain, and I had never been able to get up in front of people to

speak or sing or do anything without a serious case of the stomach butterflies. I had almost perished at my graduation when I had to give the Valedictory address; I couldn't imagine how I would survive preaching a real sermon from a pulpit!

I quaked with fear before every Theology class for at least the first month, but it quickly became my favorite course, as I began to learn so much about God and my faith that I didn't know or even imagine. Slowly, I found myself becoming more comfortable actually talking about God, and the more I learned, the more I loved it. I began to think that maybe I'd actually make it through the next three years and that I might even pass.

Homiletics was another case altogether, since I was facing a "double whammy" – not only did I have to get up in front of others to speak, but I didn't know what I was talking about. Besides, most of them knew way more than I did. In our first semester, we preached to each other in class, and I was so scared that I got sick the day of my first sermon in chapel. But I had a great Homiletics teacher, Edna Evans, who taught two things: confidence and one-sentence sermons. Her honest feedback not only taught us the basics of homiletics, but her encouragement even in the face of an abysmal first try, gave us the confidence to keep trying until we got it right.

ME? A PREACHER?

My first sermon in class was a disaster. Not only was I sick to my stomach, but I was very unsure of my "one sentence." It was a new concept to me, and, while I had worked hard on it, I was not very confident about my conclusions. I found a wonderful quote by a noted Theologian, William Barclay, who was on our suggested reference list, and built my sermon around it. It was the first time I had ever done anything remotely like this, so I approached the podium with trembling knees. Edna had taught us to always pray before stepping into the pulpit, and I said my short, "O God, please get up there with me and make these words be the right ones," and there I was, standing in front of a dozen other would-be preachers and a well-educated critic.

I started a little weakly, but I concentrated on throwing my voice to the spot on the back wall that Edna had pointed out to us, while working hard not to just read the words in front of me. About half way through, I mentioned my "killer quote," and named my source, and, in the next instant, I heard a loud noise like a shot. I saw one of my male classmates throw down his pen in disgust, while making some derogatory remark that I couldn't hear, but that I could feel down to my core. I had no idea what had set him off, and I came very close to running out of the room, but Edna had already shut him up with her famous glare that said, "Shut up! Save it until later". Then she turned to me with a nod and an encouraging smile as if to say, "Go on."

I finished, but I was devastated. I couldn't look at any member of the class, much less this man who had completely destroyed my first attempt at preaching God's word. Not knowing what had perpetrated such rudeness, I was at a loss to know how to respond. Edna took care of that for me almost before I got back to my seat. She quickly reminded the class of the rules of feedback, one of which had been most rudely broken. She made it clear that she would not tolerate such violations in her class, and, if anyone had a criticism of any student's sermon content or delivery, it was to be noted as she had instructed and offered at the appropriate time. She also went over the rules for the preacher, making it clear that she expected me to bide my time and let her feedback method take its proven course.

With that stern reminder, she opened the floor for feedback, looking intentionally at a student on the opposite side of the room from where the outburst had come. The feedback was reasonable and encouraging but everyone was on edge and eager to get to the really "loud" feedback. Finally, it was his turn, and I noticed that he had calmed down somewhat, but he still had a dark look on his face. I couldn't imagine what I had said that would elicit such an angry response. Well, he tried mightily to control himself, but it was no use. He picked up his pen and pointed it at me and snarled, "Anyone who would quote that lamebrain shouldn't be allowed in a pulpit!" God bless Edna Evans! She jumped in immediately, demanding first that he calm down and apologize to me for his angry words and inappropriate feedback. He tried, but it didn't come off very sincerely, and when she made him apologize to the whole class for his misuse of feedback, he could barely be heard. Then she told him that if he could control his anger, she would let him share his opinion of the content of my sermon. It took him a moment, but he finally calmed down and gave a civilized, but totally biased, argument why Mr. Barclay's biblical commentary was, at best, useless and, at worst, just plain wrong.

I was still shaking by the time class was over, so I stayed behind while everyone else left the classroom. I just could not understand why this classmate had reacted so strongly. He was a rather harsh critic in class, but he had never attacked any other preacher, and some of them had even offended him. As I got up to leave, Edna came over and said, "Susan, don't let him get to you. It may be the worst reaction you'll ever get to a sermon, but don't count on it. You'll never please everyone who hears you preach, so you have to toughen up. You're going to be a great preacher, so put this out of your mind and concentrate on what you do well." I was flabbergasted – "I was going to be a great preacher," she said. Oh my! I felt weak in the knees again, but this time with relief and joy. Just maybe, I could do this after all

My real nemesis in the first semester was a course called Critical Study of Religion. I had hardly read the Bible growing up, much less heard about reading it "critically." It had never occurred to me that you could do such a thing as be critical of biblical writings or any writing for that matter. I was taught to read the material, learn it, and spit it back. I was never encouraged to question anything I read, so when this man started talking about "dialoguing with the book" and being critical of what we read, I was at a loss. It took the first month of the course to grasp what he meant by "critical." I knew that he didn't mean being negative, but that it meant being analytical. It meant studying the people who wrote the book, including the Bible, learning why they wrote what they did, and reading learned theologians who became famous with their astute commentaries on Scripture. The papers we had to write about these great thinkers almost wiped me out; however, Old Testament was a piece of cake compared to Rudolf Bultmann!

Our New Testament professor, Steven Kraftchick, was a non-denominational minister from a seminary in Atlanta who was filling in for the professor who was on sabbatical. He had patiently explained over and over what my assignments were, and, after much struggling with my first exegesis (a critical analysis of a passage of Scripture), he graciously gave it a C. Then, he introduced us to the German theologian, Rudolf Bultmann and his controversial method of Biblical form criticism called, "demythologizing Scripture." He claimed that modern scientific analysis of the text is required to separate the genuine from the miraculous claims, thereby revealing the true message.

We had to read a whole book on this very un-Episcopal method of reading and studying the Bible, and one of my clearest memories of my first semester in seminary was sitting in my armchair trying to read this awful book! I had read it once and written a paper, which the professor returned to me filled with red marks. He painstakingly went through my disaster of a paper, patiently explaining how to read critically and write about what I learned. I had two days to re-write my paper.

I started reading but after a few hours, I dropped the book on the floor and said, "God, I cannot do this." I started to cry, but, after a few minutes, I remembered the words of Steven Kraftchick: "Critical Study of Religion is just taking the words you read and asking the author what he meant by that. Just dialogue with the book." I thought to myself, "If I can't get past this book, I might as well as go home." So I picked it up, took a deep breath and started at page one. This time, I took notes. I wrote down questions I had, and, when I would find an answer later in the book, I'd go back and write it down. It took me most of the night, but I not only made it through "Kerygma and Myth," I had a great outline for a paper.

After class the next day, I re-wrote my paper, typed it up and, with fear and trembling, put it in Steve's mailbox in St. Luke's Hall. It was on time, and I was so tired that I went home and slept for two hours! After class two days later, Steve stuck his head out of his office door as I walked by his office and asked me if I had time to talk about my paper. I was so nervous, I could hardly answer him. I went in and sat down with the butterflies roaring so loud I thought he could probably hear them. He turned around in his chair with a huge grin on his face and said, "Susan, you got it!" I must have looked like I'd seen a ghost because he burst out laughing and handed me my paper. All I could see was a huge red A- in the top right corner and I almost fainted! I grabbed the paper, looking quickly through the three pages and found only one red penned note in the margin. It said, "Good question!"

I left his office on a cloud and as I look back on that first year, there is no doubt that he was solely responsible for teaching me how to read with a critical eye. He re-taught me how to read books, how to study, and how **not** to take everything at face value and just spit it back the same way. I learned to read thoughtfully and intelligently, something I was not taught in high school, college or anywhere else. I credit him with my 3.75 GPA at the end of three

years (which was a far cry from the 2.4 GPA I had earned at William
and Mary some 12 years earlier).

The New Testament Professor, the Rev. Howard Rhys,
returned for the 2nd semester, and we had all been anticipating this
with varying degrees of fear and trembling mixed with curiosity.
Dr. Rhys had been teaching New Testament for many years and his
dramatic flair was legendary as was his depth of Biblical knowledge.
He was definitely of the "old school," but he was a breath of fresh air
with his off-beat interpretations, which left us in hysterics but also
got his point across. His most famous was an explanation for how
the Gospel of John was put together: "John was sitting at his desk
with the completed pages strewn all over it. It was a hot day and
his Filipino houseboy started up the large fan, which blew all of the
pages into the air and they settled on the floor in random order. John
jumped up from the desk, gathered the pages together and when he
saw them, he was so upset, he flung himself out the window!" With
that, Dr. Rhys actually flung himself out of the window. Well, he
didn't really mean to go that far, but in his flamboyant gesturing, he
tripped and really did fall out of the window!

He was unhurt but my sides ached from laughing – and I
got the point. John's Gospel is ordered significantly different from
the other three. This demonstrative lecture style was his stock and
trade and we all had been warned. We also knew of his opposition
to the ordination of women, so I expected there to be a significant
difference in how he treated us. Most of the time, there was no
discernible difference but it was also in the backs of our minds that
when the time came for the faculty to make its recommendation
about each student, he never voted against a woman just because
she was a woman – he just didn't vote at all. That way, he knew
that it would not be his inability to endorse the church's new policy
that kept a woman from being ordained. He may have been old-
fashioned and stubborn about some things, but he was much loved
by everyone and highly regarded for his integrity.

GETTING "IT"

Even with the many hours I spent in academic pursuits, I
also discovered that seminary is not just an educational experience.
It is an institution of "priestly formation." 99.9% of the student
body enter seminary with the intention of being ordained upon
graduation and Sewanee was no different. Although there were a

few students in our class who were studying for an STM Degree (Masters in Theological Studies), I was the only one in the Masters of Divinity program who was not a Postulant for Holy Orders (the first official step toward ordination in the Episcopal Church).

As we got to know each other, I found that most of my fellow classmates had struggled with their sense of call and were now solidly on the ordination track. I was still struggling with just what God was calling me to do and be. I had been very clear at BACAM and with the Bishop that I wanted to attend seminary and learn as much about the Bible and the faith of the church as I could, so that I could be well prepared for a career in youth ministry in the Church. I had entertained the thought of being an ordained priest, but I had dismissed it as a stumbling block to the Bishop's endorsement of my application to seminary. I figured as long as I wasn't threatening his position on the ordination of women, he would be more inclined to support me, and that was exactly what happened.

So here I was, a seminarian with the Bishop's sincere blessing, but I still felt somewhat precarious. Why would I want to muck things up by bringing up ordination? Besides, wouldn't everyone think I was trying to slip in the back door or something? Then, there was the reality that the ordained ministry was a life that was so far removed from anything I had ever experienced, that I couldn't even imagine it. Not only that, but I was poised on the precipice of a very difficult and scary journey. If I were to pursue ordination, there was the beast called "The Process," a complicated and delicate path through the steps in the journey, which had to be successfully navigated and completed. As if that wasn't a big enough deterrent, entry was firmly closed to females. I definitely wasn't considering being the one to push the door open any more than the tiny crack I had walked through to get to Sewanee.

I did enjoy the opportunity to mix with a segment of the Episcopal Church that was mostly favorable towards the ordination of women. There were a few faculty members who weren't on board yet, but they were fair in their grading. For the most part, I found myself being treated just like all the other students, with respect for who I was and not what I was. It was a pleasant change.

From the beginning, the other women in my class talked with me at length about their own calling and their experiences with Bishops and committees. They were fortunate to come from

Dioceses where women's ordination was widely accepted, especially by their Bishops and the Diocesan leadership. They commiserated sympathetically with me over my situation, but when I declined to join the "Women's Group" on campus, I realized that they hadn't quite grasped my reality.

I knew in my heart that if my Bishop found out that I was associating with a group that had a reputation for "cause-fighting," my credibility with him would be shot. Of all the things I needed most at that time, the Bishop's approval was at the top of the list! I refused to do anything to upset that apple cart, even though I know my female classmates thought me a coward. I actually felt a little brave standing up to them for what I knew was the right thing for me to do.

TRP WOKE ME UP!

TRP stands for Theological Reflection Practicum, where we spent the better part of three hours once a week reflecting on a piece of Scripture and how it affected our own lives. We began the semester by "getting to know each other," and, as I listened to the stories of how my classmates had experienced their calls to ministry, I began to get nervous about sharing my own story. It was so inconsequential sounding next to their stories, and there was the lingering, half-buried idea that I just didn't want to address.

Finally, the day came, and it was my turn to tell my story. It didn't take long for my classmates to zero in on the truth, when I got to the point where BACAM reported to the Bishop that I didn't feel called to ordination. One guy said, "What! They must not have been listening!" I was surprised at that, because I had told them exactly what I told BACAM – that I didn't feel called to ordination, that I just wanted a seminary education. Suddenly there were three people talking at once, and the moderator had to call for some order. "Let's speak one at a time," he said. Another student asked to go first; he leaned over toward me and said very gently, "Susan, you may have fooled them, and you may have fooled yourself, but you aren't fooling any of us. We have all been where you are, and we know how we felt and what it looks like to hover on the edge of this decision. You are right there, and, I don't know about the rest of this group, but I know which way you want to jump."

There were nods and smiles all around the room, as they all agreed that my chosen "non-ordination track" just didn't square with what they saw and heard from me. One woman said, "I know we aren't supposed to say that we know exactly how another person feels, but I really do know how you feel." She waved off the moderator with a "Let me finish, OK?" She continued "I had to struggle with the exact same thing. I didn't want to admit to anyone how I felt because I thought nobody would approve, and nobody would accept me as a priest. I was terrified, and it took a long time and a lot of encouragement before I was able to admit to myself and others that I really felt called to be ordained. This is not a small decision that you are facing and that we have all faced. It's our whole lives – all of us." She was spent, and the moderator suggested that it was time to draw things to a close. He suggested that someone lead a prayer for my discernment and that everyone keep praying during the coming weeks.

One of the students was ready, for he quickly said, "The Lord be with you" like a good Episcopalian. We all responded, as good Episcopalians do, "And also with you." He began, "Lord, we are gathered today with our sister Susan, and we all know, as you do, what she's going through trying to make sense of her feelings and what she thinks is your call to her. We pray that you will bring her clarity about what you are calling her to do, that you will give her the openness to hear it, and the strength and courage to face what it brings. Amen."

I just sat there. I was still trying to deal with the fact that everyone thought they knew what I wanted to do, when I didn't think I knew myself. Everyone seemed to sense my need to be alone, because the room emptied out, and suddenly I was all by myself in the room. I desperately wanted to jump up and run after them, saying, "You're right! I do want to be ordained! I don't know what I was thinking!" But I just wasn't ready – there was a huge lump that kept the words in my throat and a weight on my body that kept me in the chair. It just wasn't time yet.

The next few weeks passed so slowly that I thought I was in some parallel universe somewhere. Every day, I tried to concentrate on my classes and spend some time with Scotty, but all I could think about was the upcoming TRP session. What would I say, if anyone asked me if I had made a decision? I tried to pray and to ask God to let me know for sure like he did with the curtain but the words wouldn't come at first and when they finally did, there was silence. It seemed that God had backed off and was letting me deal with this one on my own. I got angry at that – how could God bring me up here, and just dump me when I needed him most? If I was supposed to be on the ordination track, why didn't I know it? The rest of my class seemed to know it, and I just couldn't figure out how they could be so sure.

The following week in TRP, I was relieved that the moderator didn't say a word to me, but just went on to the next life story. I knew that it would re-surface, but that it was up to me to determine the right time. It came a few weeks later, when a fellow student described attending church as a child and watching in awe as the priest baptized his baby brother. He told us, "I couldn't take my eyes off of this priest and what he was doing," and when it was over, he turned to his mother, and said, "I want to do that when I grow up." She, of course, was ecstatic as any self-respecting mother would be. He went merrily on with his life, until, at age 26, she reminded him that he wanted to be a priest.

As he described the Baptism scene for us, I began to feel warm, and I felt the tell-tale lump in my throat and the butterflies that let me know that something was happening. Suddenly it was like a movie screen opened up, and I could see myself at the age of five sitting in the pew with my grandmother. I watched as the procession passed by, wishing that I was a boy, so that I could carry the cross down the aisle. When it was time for discussion, I told the group about this scene, and several of the young students looked perplexed, until I reminded them that girls weren't allowed to be acolytes in the 1950's!

I was telling them about the low church of my childhood, and we were laughing about the Altar Guild ladies in their white gloves being the only ones allowed inside the chancel rail besides the minister. Suddenly I knew – it wasn't that I wanted to be a boy, so that I could be an Acolyte. I wanted to be a boy, so that I could grow up to be a man. Then I could do what the minister was doing. I didn't really want to tell anyone, but it must have been obvious that something had just happened because they began to bombard me with all the questions they had been holding on to until I was ready to finish the discussion.

At that moment, I heard a quiet voice, as plain as day, and I knew that it wasn't any of my classmates. To be sure, I asked them later, and they all were adamant that they hadn't said a thing. It could only have been God, with that quirky divine humor, saying,

"Give it up Susan!" So it all came out – the reasons why I had hidden my true sense of calling from the Bishop and BACAM. I admitted that my fear of the "hostile" process in my Diocese had influenced my responses to the Bishop and BACAM as to my true intentions for wanting to go to seminary. One student astutely said, "Susan, we've all been there and gotten past it – what's really holding you back?"

I didn't know how I was going to say what it was, for I knew. I guess I had known all along, but I couldn't admit it, even to myself. It was clear to me at that moment that the time was now. I had to come clean. I had to admit to my own prejudices about women being ordained as priests. I was completely embarrassed to even say the words to this group, but I plunged in. I had thought a lot about being a priest, and I had even tried to imagine myself in a priest's vestments, but it had felt utterly foreign. It even filled me with a deep sense of inappropriateness when I thought about being an ordained priest. It just didn't *feel* right – a woman in a clerical collar or a woman wearing a stole just looked strange.

I thought that everybody would laugh at me but they all just nodded. It seems I wasn't the only one who struggled with such feelings but one of them wisely pointed out that what I was describing was merely the "outward and visible sign" of a priest. This led us into a deep discussion about the sacraments of the church and why there was such resistance to a woman being a priest. Although many in the church claimed that it wasn't Biblical and that if Jesus had meant for women to be priests, he would have had women apostles, for most of us in that room it wasn't a theological bias. We all agreed that Jesus would have been the first to ordain a woman if there had been any such ceremony in the 1st century. He had always treated women as equals. So what was in the way?

At this point, the moderator had us all stop and get quiet. After a few moments of deep breathing and centering, we heard him asking, "When you close your eyes envision yourself as a priest. Picture yourself in an alb and a stole standing behind the Altar. What do you look like? What does it feel like?" After a few moments of silence, he said, "Now let a woman into your vision. She is dressed in the same vestments, an alb and a stole, but she also has on a chasuble because she'll be celebrating the Eucharist." More silence. "Now," he said, "make it more specific. Imagine that Susan is celebrating the Eucharist. How does it feel to think of a woman you know actually performing priestly functions?"

There were tears running down my face, as I realized that
the vision of a woman celebrating the Eucharist was so foreign to
me that it actually turned me off. I kept seeing myself in an alb
draped with a priest's stole, and it just looked so weird. This became
the question for the day – a pertinent issue which we always took
with us to reflect on during the week: "How does it feel to think
of a woman actually performing priestly functions?" Even before
the end of the class, I knew that I had my own bias against women
"dressed up like a priest." I knew that I had to come to grips with
and get past that emotional response in order to find my true calling.

The following weeks were intense, as I struggled with my
feelings and my fears. Over coffee in the lounge, in between classes,
I talked with classmates who listened and commiserated. Most of
them, however, had supportive Bishops and were not faced with
the possibility of not being ordained at the end of seminary. I spent
hours praying that God would change my heart and make me as
certain as they were about their call. I waited in vain for a "sign"
and finally, after several weeks, I called a friend in Virginia for
some advice. He had been so excited for me when I was accepted
at Sewanee and was one of my most ardent supporters outside
the church. When I had first spoken to him about wanting to be a
youth minister, his first response had been "Perfect! You will be
great at that!" When I had expressed my reluctance to consider the
ordination track, he had been supportive of my decision, but had
been disappointed. "You're a natural! You would be a great priest!"

When I reached him on the phone and described my
dilemma, his first response was, "Are you still in denial?" I had been
expecting something like that from him, so I just pretended he had
said something like, "Gee, it's great to hear from you, Susan!" We
got past the pleasantries and my brief description of Sewanee, my
classes, Scotty's school, and I asked him if we could talk seriously.
He assured me that he was absolutely there for me, and I shared
with him my struggles over the issue of ordination. Finally, I said,
"So what do you think? Am I crazy or what?"

He promptly replied, "Of course, you are, but not because
you want to be ordained."

I thought, "He must not have been listening," and I asked
him, "What makes you think I want to be ordained? I said I was
afraid and unsure, but I don't know if I want to be ordained or not."

He laughed. "Susan, you are a great friend, and I'm very

proud of you for following your dream, but you aren't listening to yourself! Everything you have done for the past year, everything you have just said to me screams one thing loud and clear. You want to be a priest. Why don't you just do it?"

I took a deep breath and started to explain how I had prayed and just wasn't getting the answer I needed but he interrupted me at that point and asked, "Why did you call me?"

I was surprised at his question, so it took a few seconds to reply. "Well," I said, "I was praying about this and, when I didn't get an answer, I decided I needed to talk to someone who would talk back to me. I picked up my address book and opened it, and there you were – right on the page in front of me – so I called you."

As I said it, I thought how silly that sounded, but he didn't miss a beat. "Susan, there's your answer. I can see it and I'm not even religious like you! You called me, because I have the answer you need."

I was stunned. "You mean, you think God was telling me to call you?"

He laughed. "Well, I don't know if I'd go quite that far, but it's very simple to me. You needed an answer. You called me, asked me, and I answered. Be a priest. You're a natural, and, if there is a God directing all this, it's obvious that he sent you to me for the right answer." I broke out in goosebumps; I had never heard him speak about God at all and suddenly he was God's messenger! When I didn't answer (because I couldn't find the words), he said gently, "Susan, stop all this anguishing over the inevitable. You're stressing yourself out for no reason, and you're keeping me up past my bedtime. Go. Be a priest." He hung up.

I sat with the phone in my lap until I must have fallen asleep because, the next thing I knew, the alarm was going off. I had slept soundly all night for the first time in weeks. I got Scotty in the shower, fixed a cup of coffee and started to say my morning prayers. In that instant, I knew in my heart what I was going to do. I knew in that defining moment that God was calling me out of my own prejudices and fears to be his priest.

BACK TO THE BISHOP

It was an exhilarating moment, but that feeling didn't last too long, as I quickly realized that, since my intentions as an Aspirant were now different, I had to meet with the Bishop again, face-to-face. Even though in my mind, it could have been a simple matter to just change my status from Aspirant to Postulant, I knew that was wishful thinking. The Bishop had a process in place and he wasn't known for taking short-cuts, so I was sure that he would require another interview with BACAM. Besides, this step I wanted to take now was huge, because, if BACAM recommended me, the Bishop would then be faced with the decision whether to fling open the door to the ordination process or lock it up tight again.

I had a few moments of serious terror, as I imagined myself telling the Bishop, whom I had convinced that I didn't want to be ordained, that I was indeed called to ordination, and I now wanted to be in that process. In that instant, I came very close to backing out. I had been gripping my coffee cup so hard that it slipped out of my hands and skittered across the table, coming to rest against the telephone without spilling a drop. "Well," I thought, "OK Lord. It's you and me again – you and me and the Bishop."

It was still early, so I got Scotty off to school, went to Chapel and, on the way to class, I started to tell several of my classmates about my big decision. I actually opened my mouth to say "Guess what?" but my fears were still in control enough to keep my decision to myself for the time being. It was not beyond the realm of possibility that the Bishop would refuse to even consider the possibility of admitting me to the ordination process. After all my private and public struggle to come to this point, there was no way I was going to tell a soul of my earth-shattering decision until I knew that there was a chance that it could make a difference in my status.

So I got through the morning without sharing my big news, and by the time I got home for lunch, I was ready to explode. I had to tell someone, and I knew who that someone was. I sat down with the phone in my lap, but all I could do was look at it. I was terrified – again. I was reminded of my first meeting with Bishop Vaché, as I realized that I was nauseous and had a roaring headache. Finally, after much sweating and whining to myself, I said, "Get a grip, Susan, he's just a bishop." After a quick prayer that God would give me the right words, I picked up the phone and called his office, only to find out he was out of the country. I couldn't believe it! After all that angst, I couldn't even speak to him, and I'd have to wait until he returned to ask him if he would meet with me. He'd have to find a time, and he'd be so busy after just returning from a long trip.

I was about to thank his secretary and hang up when I

heard her ask, "So, what did you want to see the Bishop about? Is everything all right down there?" Well, this scenario had not occurred to me, and, for a moment, I was speechless. "Susan, are you there?"

I jumped and then heard myself saying, "I'd like to talk to him about the ordination process."

"Ah," she said like it was exactly what she had expected me to say and wondered what had taken me so long! "Why don't we go ahead and make an appointment for a day while you're home for Christmas break?" I was weak with relief! She didn't think I was wasting my time! In a minute, we had set up a time on December 20th and, with that, she was gone. It was done. I had an appointment with my destiny and, thank God, I now had more time to get ready. I was on the right track and I could wait.

Figuring that an application for Holy Orders involved another lengthy, detailed form, as well as another spiritual journey, I spent some time in the following weeks trying to revise my original application to BACAM. While most of the first part would be the same, with the addition of my 5-year-old child's dream, I ended up chucking most of the recent part of my journey. So much had changed in my life, including how I related to God and how I viewed my journey so far, that I had to totally re-write it. I now had to approach new people to act as references, so I asked several of my professors to write a letter of reference for me, and I called my friend David asking him to be my third reference. I knew there would be a physical exam and a psychological evaluation by the Diocesan psychiatrist, so I made an appointment with my doctor in Sewanee for the day before semester break. There were papers to finish for the end of the semester and a killer Old Testament exam to survive, but by the time Scotty and I started the trip north, I was as ready as I could be in case the Bishop agreed to let me attend BACAM.

The difficult part of this meeting for me was that I now had to retract my assurance to the Bishop that I was not seeking ordination. I had been afraid at our first meeting, thinking that if I admitted my true feelings, this Bishop, who did not, and would not, ordain women would shut the door on me, as he had when other women had spoken of their desire to be ordained. Now it was a year later, and I was just as afraid, if not more so, because it was even more likely that he would not only shut that door, but slam it hard. If he thought I had "pretended" I wasn't interested in ordination, so that when I did admit my true intentions, I would already be in the "back-door," I was a goner.

The big difference for me now was that I had a support system in Sewanee, and so I had people who, not only helped me "practice" for my encounter with the Bishop, but they encouraged me and gave me their phone numbers to call for last minute pep talks. I had just gotten off the phone with one of my classmates, who reminded me again of how I had arrived at this point and how right this was for me and for the church. I went off to the Bishop's office from my friend Don's home, with his final words about who was really in charge of this whole process, so that, by the time I pulled into the parking lot in front of the Diocesan Office, I was ready.

Our meeting was pleasant, since we had an easy relationship largely due to the time I had spent with him on youth retreats. We both loved a good pun, and we had developed a unique correspondence which included sending long jokes (he called them "stories") back and forth in the mail (his secretary absolutely hated them!) and sharing "groaners" whenever we saw each other. He had managed to find a few new "stories" overseas, and we groaned and laughed over them until we had to get serious.

I was wondering just how to start, when the Bishop said, "So, Wendy tells me that you now think you might want to be a priest." It was such shock to hear those words come out of his mouth that I couldn't speak for a moment. I thought maybe I had heard him wrong, but he said, "So, you know you'll have to go back to BACAM." I was nodding dumbly at this point, not daring to believe what I was experiencing with this man who was calmly speaking about this as if it were an everyday occurrence – as if I were a man.

I finally said, "I figured I would have to do that. Is that possible?" He assured me that there was one scheduled in early February, and he would put my name on the list if that's what I wanted to do.

"You'll have to fill out all the papers and have the medical exams again, but you should have time before then to return everything to us." It suddenly dawned on me what was actually happening, and that he was not only serious, but seemed pleased at my decision. What was going on here? Had someone exchanged Bishops on me? But then he said, "Oh, have you heard about the two tankers carrying paint across the Atlantic? I shook my head slightly and said, "No, Bishop. I didn't." I knew what was coming. He went on with a twinkle in his eye, "One was hauling red paint, and one was carrying blue paint, and they got their signals mixed and collided in the middle of the ocean. Do you know what happened to the sailors?" I said with a groan, "No." He smiled and said, "They were marooned!"

With that, he jumped up, said he had an appointment and that he would ask Wendy to get the forms I needed and make me an appointment with the Diocesan Psychiatrist. I was still laughing at his awful joke but I managed to tell him that I had already had my physical exam in Sewanee and had a copy of the report. He clapped me on the back and said, "Good. Sounds like you're on your way." I stood there, not moving for the door because one huge question had entered my already reeling brain. What if I did get past BACAM and what if I did get into the ordination process, what then? I was trying to figure out how to ask this very tricky question when he said, "Susan, let's take this one step at a time. After BACAM, go back to school and I'll call you when I get their recommendation." The interview was over.

BACK TO BACAM

Suddenly my life was on a fast track. I had tons of paper work to fill out, the appointment with the Psychiatrist and I had to get blood work done before I left to return to Sewanee. It was only a few days before Christmas so all the arrangements were made for the following week and I went home to Lake Gaston to spend Christmas with my family. I had received the best Christmas present ever so most of the packages I opened were anti-climatic. Our traditional celebration included the Christmas Eve service where I got to sing in the choir I had grown up with, including the dear Jewish woman (our paid Alto soloist) who had sung at my wedding. It was just like it used to be: we processed up the aisle to "O come, all ye faithful," sang "Silent Night" on our knees in the dark, and then marched joyfully out of the church singing "Joy to the World." As the minister said the final prayer at the back of the church, I looked in at the stately old church where I had been raised and nurtured, and I couldn't resist a trip back to my grandmother's pew where it all started. While people were filing out of the church, I moved against the flow, speaking to people I had known my whole life who had no clue why there were tears in my eyes.

I moved into the pew and over to the divider where I had always sat with my grandmother on my left so she could pay attention to the service and watch me at the same time. I stood there for a moment, and then I sat right in that same spot. This was where it had begun – my yearnings to be a priest. I was lost somewhere in 1952 wondering if God had been speaking to me even then, when I heard my Dad say, "You gonna wear that vestment home?" I laughed and said, "No." I got up, and he said, "Well let's go, it's Christmas already." I hugged him and went downstairs to return my borrowed choir robe, and, in 20 minutes, we were sipping hot chocolate by the Christmas tree and waiting for "Santa."

We returned to Sewanee for the 2nd semester, and, several weeks later, I was on the road again. I left Scotty with a classmate and his family and left for the long drive back to Virginia. I had been busy trying to get ahead in my classes while preparing for my interview with BACAM. This time I had so much help with proofreading my spiritual journey and other papers, practice interviews, and just good old pep talks. My classmates and other students were incredibly supportive, and everyone wished me well, when I left the seminary building that morning after Chapel. There was a special prayer for my safe travel and a successful BACAM session, and I left the "Mountain" knowing that I was not traveling alone.

Having already experienced the ordeal of BACAM once, I was fully prepared for the pressure and the sly comments by those who didn't share the Bishop's new intention to allow women to explore the road to ordination. As I drove north, I thanked God over and over for my "Peanut Gallery" back in Sewanee, who were encouraging me even as I got further away every minute. Many hours of Theological Reflection Practicum had put all of us in the mindset that, as I would hear many, many times in the next few years, "Ordination is God's business." I was developing a new-found faith in the ordination process as one that may be administered by humans, but was, in reality, under God's control. It had also become abundantly clear to all of us, especially to the women, that God was not prejudiced against women or biased towards men when it came to calling priests to his church.

I was also well aware that many people in my Diocese did not share that conclusion; in fact, there were many who called women's ordination an abomination against God's royal priesthood. Some of those people served on the Commission on Ministry, the Standing Committee, and BACAM. I knew that I would have to face those people again, but this time, I had a newly formulated strategy firmly planted in my heart. It was a simple mantra: God wanted me to be a priest, so God would take care of anything in the way of that plan. I repeated it so many times as I drove to the conference center, that by the time I arrived in Petersburg, I was calm and peaceful. I felt the support of my community in Sewanee, the support of my family and friends in Virginia; but most of all, I felt God's call so strongly that, this time when I was asked if I felt called to the priesthood, I was able to answer clearly and sincerely, "Yes."

It wasn't "a walk in the park," but, at the end of the weekend, I felt confident that I had represented myself and God's plans for me with grace and confidence. I have to say that some of that confidence resulted from the fact that none of the former "naysayers" were present on the committee this time. That confidence was proven to be well-placed, as several days after I returned to Sewanee, I received a cheerful call from the Bishop himself with the results of my 2nd BACAM experience.

He started the conversation by telling me a new "story" he had heard, so I had a good feeling about what was coming. After a good laugh, he said, "Susan, I got the report from BACAM, and they unanimously recommended that you be considered by me and the Commission on Ministry to enter the ordination process. They detected a strong call to ordination, and I am considering their positive recommendation." I could hardly breathe, as I waited for what was coming next. BACAM's approval was great news, but it was only half the battle. The Bishop now had to approve my entrance into the ordination process. This was only granted to those that he felt had the necessary qualities for priesthood and to those whom he would be willing to ordain at completion of the process. I didn't fool myself that I fit into that second square hole.

Imagine my total shock, when he ended the conversation with an invitation to apply for Postulancy. He said "Wendy will send you the forms, and you should fill them out as soon as you can. Send everything to the Chair of the Commission on Ministry, who will let you know the date, time, and place of the next meeting for Postulancy interviews." I wanted to ask when that would be, but I just could not say a word. I was in shock.

Then I actually heard him say these words: **"Susan, I cannot ordain you myself, but, all things being equal, if you pass through the process successfully, I will not stand in your way and I will find someone to come here and ordain you."** Thank God for his efficient secretary who sent me all these instructions in writing, because I don't think I heard a thing he said between **"apply for Postulancy"** and **"ordain you."**

I feel sure he heard the wild cheer that erupted from our classroom the next morning when I announced the news. They certainly heard it in the other two classrooms and soon there was cake and sparkling grape juice all around, as my fellow seminarians celebrated with me. What a moment of joy that was, and it was one that had to last me for a long time.

PART TWO

Postulant for Holy Orders

OVERVIEW

If you ask any priest over the age of 75 how he became a priest, you'd hear something like this: "Well, my minister asked me if I had ever thought about being a minister (they weren't called "priests" in Virginia in those days), and I said I hadn't, and he said I should. The next week, we were sitting in the Bishop's office, he patted me on the back, and said he thought I'd be a fine priest, and told me to apply to Virginia Seminary." That was the "good ole boy" system.

The process that was in place in the Diocese of Southern Virginia in the early 80's, was a far cry from the simple "non-process" of the past.* It was well-structured, with a number of levels and steps to navigate, and it was known as simply "The Process."

1. **Postulant for Holy Orders** – the first official step towards ordination
2. **Candidate for Holy Orders** – the second step leading towards ordination
3. **Deacon** – a transitional ordination for those called to the priesthood
4. **Priest** – final ordination

The Process was only accessible to those who were approved by the Bishop after the screening interview by BACAM (Bishop's Advisory Commission on Aspirants to the Ministry). This was a weekend-long interview by a group of people, hand-picked by the Bishop, each of whom was an expert in a certain area. There was a Psychologist, an Educator, an Ordained Priest, a Lay Member of an Episcopal Church, and the Bishop's Assistant. This Commission conducted an in-depth interview, collected and considered the findings of the group, and forwarded them to the Bishop with their recommendations. The Bishop took these recommendations very seriously, but it was still his decision to accept or not accept a person into The Process. Whatever the verdict, it was the Bishop himself who contacted the Aspirant with the news, good or bad.

If the Bishop had no compelling reasons to disagree with BACAM's positive recommendation, he then set the whole Process into motion. This Process was administered by the Commission on Ministry, a committee of lay and clergy of the Diocese, who were appointed by the Bishop. This Commission was the first official stop in the Process, after the Bishop received a positive recommendation from BACAM. With an official phone call and a formal letter, the recommended Aspirant was then invited by the Bishop to an official interview with the COM.

The interview was conducted in a large group composed of the COM and members of the Standing Committee, a committee of lay and clergy elected by the Annual Council of the Diocese. This Committee was charged with making the final recommendation to the Bishop after the last three steps were completed, and, when one is not recommended by this group, it is the President who gets to make the career-ending phone call. The Bishop, as an ex-officio member of the COM, attended most meetings to assure that he would get to know those in the process before having to make a decision on their suitability for ordained ministry. Interviews before this combined group of powerful and influential Diocesan leaders were understandably terrifying. If the Aspirant survived the interview, and if the COM also sent a positive recommendation to the Bishop, he usually accepted the Aspirant into the Process. The Aspirant then became a Postulant for Holy Orders and an official participant in the Process of Ordination.

Prior to 1980, no female in our Diocese had even gotten close to being an official Aspirant interviewed by the COM/Standing Committee, much less a Postulant for Holy Orders. Therefore, the invitation to a female to get anywhere close to this Process was a momentous moment in the life of the Bishop, the Diocesan leadership, its lay people and clergy. When the news spread in the early days of 1982, that the Bishop had opened those sacred doors to a woman, the reverberations were palpable. The phone lines were ringing – some with the Hallelujah Chorus and others with songs of sorrow and impending doom.

*The Process as I have described it in this book has since been changed by the Diocese of Southern Virginia, which now welcomes women in every level of ministry, lay and ordained. BACAM no longer exists.

CHAPTER SEVEN

Postulant for Holy Orders

THE COMMISSION ON MINISTRY

Among those who were watching the Bishop the closest were the people around him. They would now have the task of evaluating the first woman that the Bishop had allowed anywhere near the process for ordination. Some were eager to get me into a clerical collar. Others were somewhat anxious about what was surely to be a rancorous process, while still others didn't want any part of what they considered to be a sham. Several members resigned, but a significant number stayed on, determined to preserve the Process as they knew it.

This was the alligator swamp that I was about to swim in, and I was terrified one moment and excited the next. I knew it was going to be tricky to keep from being eaten alive, but I was quickly allowing myself to be lulled into a sense of security by those around me. They were convinced, and had convinced me, that God was at work in the Bishop and in the Diocese. I believed that, and I grabbed at their confidence and support like any desperate swimmer in an alligator swamp. They became my strong and secure boat, keeping the alligators at bay and keeping me safe as I moved toward the Process.

POSTULANCY AT LAST

My introduction to the Commission on Ministry was a dreaded event, even though I knew some of the members of the Commission from my Diocesan activities, and several were staunch supporters of me and my journey. I wanted to relax but I kept hearing a little voice in my head reminding me that the COM had never considered a woman for postulancy and that the air in the Diocese was still thick with resistance to that ever happening. Besides, it was a process aimed at preparing priests of the church; therefore, it was a tough road, not a stroll in the garden. It started with the paperwork.

Following the Bishop's invitation to an interview with the COM, I had to struggle with yet another hefty application, an update to the spiritual journey, and examinations by a physician (one of the Diocese's choosing) and the Diocesan Psychiatrist. By the end of the semester, I had all the paper work completed and submitted. When I arrived back in Virginia, there were appointments set up for my medical examinations, in time for my interview, which was scheduled for early August.

During the summer months after the first year of seminary, all students in the ordination track were required to participate in Clinical Pastoral Education (CPE) at an approved facility. CPE is an 8-week course, which provides "on-the-job" training for pastoral ministry in a hospital or other social ministry venue. It was also a psychological/emotional experience that is equal to about five years of intensive work with a professional therapist. This was another of the many dreaded events in the life of a seminarian. It was, and still is, almost universally feared, endured, and complained about loudly by seminarians in every denomination.

This is mostly because of the intense time spent in small groups called IPR, InterPersonal Relationships. Need I say more? Our sessions were intense and highly personal, as we poured over each other's "Verbatims," the painstakingly written narratives of our visits with patients in the hospital, and assessed each other's pastoral skills and "interpersonal foibles." There were ground rules for this program, which included strict confidentiality, absolute honesty, and professional courtesy, but the one rule which caused the most angst among group members was the one that required complete openness. So, when we discussed each other's skills and non-skills, it was a "no-holds-barred" event.

This made IPR sessions difficult, and even painful at times, but I have to say that I learned a lot about myself, and it was refreshing to be in an environment where women were readily accepted as equals. There was a lot of "unhelpful stuff" (a nice way of describing the garbage of other people's baggage) that we were forced to hear and endure as well. For instance, when we prepared our self-evaluations at the mid-point of the program, we also had to prepare an evaluation of everyone in our IPR groups.

One woman in our group was a Baptist, young and idealistic, as well as a pleasant car pool companion, who wrote this about me: "Susan is a nice person, but I am uncomfortable around her because she reminds me of my sister." This came after four weeks of riding back and forth to the hospital with her every day, eating lunch with her most days, and sharing many coffee breaks on the hospital floors. Needless to say, I was crushed, but I was helped back to some resemblance of self-esteem by a dear friend. When I shared my evaluation with him, he reminded me that "CPE is a valuable experience only if you take the worthwhile parts and discard the rest in the toilet where they belong." He used much stronger language than that, but you get the picture.

One of the issues I had to deal with during this course was my upcoming interview for Postulancy and my anxieties about the interview itself as well as my developing relationship with "the process" and the Commission on Ministry. The other students in my IPR were not Episcopalians, and our group leader was an ordained Baptist minister. They all had various protocols to follow, but none were as stringent as the Diocese of Southern Virginia's ordination process. When I received the Commission on Ministry's official notification of the date, time, and location of the interview, I found that it was being held on a weekday, which meant that I would be absent from CPE on that day.

Total participation was required for completion of a CPE course, so any absence had to be approved by the program director and the student's IPR group. So, I dutifully put in my request for a day off, and, at the next session, our group leader brought it up before the group. It was one of the most difficult experiences of my entire CPE course, as every member weighed in with their own questions and comments about this "summons" I had received. The group leader asked, "Why are they requiring you to interrupt your CPE training to come to a meeting? Tell them that you don't get "days off" from CPE."

I was horrified at his suggestion that I "tell" the Commission on Ministry anything of the sort and I said, "My attendance at this meeting is not an option. It is a requirement of the program. I have to go. I don't want to but I have to."

He came right back at me, "Why? Why do you **have** to go?"

"Listen," I said, "this is not something I'm looking forward to; in fact, this is an intimidating group and I'm scared to death!"

When I said that, one member of the group asked, almost angrily, "Then why are you going? If you don't want to go, why are you letting them push you around?" I was dumbfounded. I couldn't believe these people were giving me such a hard time about this although I shouldn't have been so surprised. Most of the Protestant denominations didn't have such discernment processes in place since they were ordained by an individual congregation; therefore, the process I was entering was foreign to them.

So I explained in some detail how our process worked and when I finished, the group leader asked me, "So why do you have to go on the date they suggested? Why don't you just tell them that you're busy that day?"

I looked at him stupidly and it was all I could do to keep my voice calm as I said, "Because I can't."

The group leader acted like he hadn't even heard me. He said, "Susan, you are giving these people way too much power over me."

I had to take a really deep breath to calm the butterflies in my stomach and the angry words that threatened to pop out of my mouth and then I said simply, "I am not giving these people any power over me; they already have it."

He threw up his hands, "Why do you think they have power over you without you giving them permission? Nobody can have power over you unless you give it to them."

I knew they were trying to make me admit that I was giving up my own power out of some sense of unworthiness, but I refused to play their game. I tried to explain to them that this was not a power play to see if was serious. I said as patiently as I could, "This is a process that is set up to screen and monitor people who want to be ordained. When you apply to enter the process, you accept the rules and one of the rules is 'when the Commission on Ministry tells you to be at an interview on a certain date, you go.' Unless there are dire circumstances, you are expected to be there."

One man asked me, "Why are these people even involved in your ordination? I only have to report to my Pastor and if he and the Board of Deacons need to speak with me in person, he calls me and asks me when I can be available? Who are these people and how can they push you around like this?"

I was getting annoyed by now, but I continued my patient explanation of our Episcopal beliefs about ordination and the philosophy behind the discernment and monitoring process which was canonically (legally) given to the Bishop and all boards and commissions he appoints or the Diocese elects. I felt like I was talking to a thick wall which I had no hope of penetrating with reasonable explanations.

The next question convinced me that I was wasting my breath. It came from the group leader, "Well, I'm curious to know why you are putting yourself in this position. These people are using their 'process' to force you into giving up your power to choose your own destiny and this is a power play, pure and simple, whether you believe it or not. See, here's what's really going on: they think that if they can push you hard enough, you'll quit trying to get into their process which, by the way, isn't even open to women. So, again my question is, 'Why are you putting yourself in this position?'"

I was so frustrated by that time that I came very close to telling them all to get off my back and then walking out. I felt like a child being chastised for just being a child and I finally said to them, "I don't think we'll ever see eye to eye on this issue and, while I appreciate your concern for me, I have to do what I have to do. So, I will not be here on Friday. I will be in Norfolk at the Commission on Ministry for the most important interview of my life and I will appreciate your prayers for me on Friday." I left the session that day, still shaking my head at their refusal to accept the reality of my situation as an Aspirant in the Diocese of Southern Virginia – a situation that allowed me no possibility of turning down this invitation.

On the day of the interview, I was as ready as I could ever be and I entertained myself as I waited my turn by imagining the COM's response to some of the suggested statements of my CPE group. I was rather enjoying the prospects, when the man who had just been interviewed came out of the meeting room and his face looked as if he had been struck by lightning; his face was pale and he was on the verge of tears. It was obvious that his interview had not gone well and I smiled a little and said, "Tough, huh?" He looked at me and nodded, unable to stop his tears. "What did they tell you? I asked gently, but he rushed past me, leaving me with a sense of panic as I realized that he was a male! I was in serious trouble.

I expected the first question but it still gave me that "butterflies-in-the-stomach" feeling when I heard, "Why can't you do the ministry you feel called to do as a lay person? Why do you have to be ordained?" I had answered that question during the BACAM interviews and I had talked this over many times with my classmates, all of whom had dealt with the same questions themselves. But, I still felt the twinge of something like fear when I looked around and saw the look on several faces that said to me, "there's no right answer to this question – nothing you can say will convince me that you need to be ordained."

I took my deep-breath-with-a-prayer that I had perfected and said as calmly as I could, "I know that lay people can certainly do youth ministry, but I feel a strong pull to help young people understand and experience their faith on a deep level and I feel unprepared for that. I want to be able to minister to them sacramentally – to be able to bring them God's grace through God's forgiveness and in the Eucharist." I was pleasantly surprised at how easily my answer came out and how well it seemed to be received.

One man asked, "what do you mean by 'sacramentally'?"

I was a little taken aback by the question and I wondered if he was being snide but I couldn't afford to get into game playing with them, so I simply said, "I mean 'in the sacraments' – baptism, confession and absolution, and the Eucharist. I want to be able to baptize them, help them bring their sins to God and experience his forgiveness through absolution and, above all, I want to bring God's saving grace to them in the Body and Blood of Christ." I stopped and thought, "Wow! That was good!" but instantly knew that what I thought didn't mean a thing in this room.

I was relieved when the man nodded and said, "Thank you for your answer." I felt like I had really connected with him and the others seemed impressed with what I had said. So I relaxed a little as the interview turned toward my ability to do the academic work.

The Chairman said, "Your GRE scores were impressive and your grades are good so far. Do you think you are capable of handling the more advanced courses?"

I almost laughed out loud at the idea that there could be anything more difficult for me than Critical Studies of Religion, but I controlled myself, and said, "Absolutely. I love the curriculum at Sewanee and think it is perfect for my learning style. I can't wait to get into Church History and Theology next year."

The Chairman also reviewed the positive recommendations from my professors and there were several positive comments from members of the Commission. The Bishop made it clear that he was pleased with this recommendation and I must have visibly relaxed because he smiled at me and moved on to ask about Scotty and how he was adjusting to seminary life. I was even animated as I described life on the "Mountain." I said, "It was hard moving so far away from home but we both love Sewanee and I'm convinced that this is where God wants me to be. We have made good friends and feel very at home in the seminary community."

The interview ended as the Chairman said, "Susan, thank you for your time and your honest answers. You will be hearing from us soon. Have a safe trip back to Sewanee." I got up and almost tripped over my own feet in my haste to get out of the room before someone decided to ask one more question and destroy the moment.

I left feeling very positive and when I reported back to CPE on Monday morning, I was ebullient. I started out describing the sour look on some of the faces around the table and how I reduced them to drawings on the wall as I had been coached to do by a classmate. Then I regaled them with all of the positive comments I could remember. Finally I told them, "I was scared, but I knew that this was a place I had to be and something I had to do and as long as I kept that in front of me, I stayed calm and actually answered their questions very well."

Someone said, "Well, good. When will you get an answer?"

I said, "I don't know, a week maybe."

The leader asked me, "Can you call in a few days and see if there's word?"

I was horrified. "No way!" I said, "I have to wait for them to let me know the results." I could see him starting up again so I said, "Listen, I've thought a lot about our conversation on Friday and here's the bottom line for me. I did give them power over my future because I had to in order to be admitted to this process. It's simple: 'No process, no ordination."

I was still anxious though as I reminded myself that no woman had ever been where I had been and no woman had even been considered to be where I wanted to be. I still waited with bated breath for the call to come, and, as the days passed, I grew more and more anxious. I called my friend David in the Diocesan office to see if he had any idea what was happening, and he reminded me that the Bishop had left on vacation before the COM meeting was over, that he was still on vacation, and wouldn't return until after Labor Day. Resigned to a long wait, I returned to my final days of CPE, a week with family, and the long trip back to the "Mountain."

It was indeed after Labor Day – a whole week in fact – when

I finally received the call from the Chairman. He was a dear man, who was one of my biggest advocates throughout the process, and I could hear the pleasure it gave him to officially inform me that I had been recommended to the Bishop for Postulancy. I felt like I bird suddenly being released from the tight hold of a tether – I was flying high!

I tried not to fly too hard and too high until I actually had word from the Bishop, and when that finally came, I am sure that my shouts of "Yes," and my screams of joy were heard all the way back to Southern Virginia. Days later, I received a formal letter from the Bishop, and, suddenly, I was an official participant in the ordination process of the Diocese of Southern Virginia.

I BELONGED TO "THE PROCESS"

The "Process" is, on the one hand, very structured and real, with its levels, rules and requirements, and its scheduled interviews and evaluations. On the other hand, it is a rather nebulous entity that looms over your life like a watchful parent. It hangs around in your consciousness as an ever-present yardstick by which your progress is measured. Every grade, every paper, every sermon became grist for the mill that churned away in Virginia, while I slaved away in Tennessee.

I would get occasional reminders of the upcoming steps and dates for interviews, but my main contact was through an advisor appointed by the Commission. My advisor was a clergyman I knew quite well, and he was a great help to me over the next year. Unfortunately, he rotated off the Commission and was replaced by a woman who wasn't totally supportive of women's ordination. I couldn't help but question the wisdom of her appointment as my advisor, but I figured it was the Commission's way of way of testing me and allowing this woman the opportunity to get to know me better.

My other main point of contact was the Bishop. As part of the process, seminarians are required to write "Ember Day Letters" to the Bishop communicating any concerns or problems, but mainly to reflect on the seminary experience and its impact. Ember Day Letters, so called because they were due on the Ember Days (four sets of three days each), which were set aside in the church year for fasting and prayer throughout the history of the church. They have become preferred times for ordinations as well as the specified "touchpoint" between seminarians and their Bishops.

So, here I was, a second-year student – a Middler – in one of the Episcopal Church's premier seminaries and a Postulant for Holy Orders in one of the most conservative Dioceses on the issue of the ordination of women, and writing quarterly to a Bishop who was an opponent to the very thing which I sought. Many times in the next 12 months, I asked myself questions like, "Are you nuts?" and "What are you thinking?" and "What do I do when the money runs out?"

CHAPTER EIGHT

Candidate for Holy Orders

A MIRACLE

As I approached the next step in the process – candidacy – the answers to those questions became clearer for me. One, I decided I was nuts to think that I was suitable for the priesthood but that God seemed to want me anyway. Two, I found that what I had been thinking was not nearly as important as what I was doing and what was happening over the past year. What I mean is that my thoughts didn't really seem to have a lot of impact as everything I was doing seemed to be out of MY control and much more in the hands of God than I had ever dreamed possible.

The willingness of my Bishop to admit a woman to the ordination process for the first time, the transformation of my own yearnings, the strength I had found to be what many people called "a pioneer," and the sudden acceptance of BACAM and the Commission on Ministry to my "calling" were all nothing short of miraculous in my mind and in the minds of many members of our Diocese.

The fact that I was even allowed in the door was a major topic of conversation all over the Diocese and I began to hear from people I knew back home with their thoughts and reflections on what was taking place. The most amazing concept that came from some of these folks was their conviction that God was using me as a catalyst in the Bishop's journey through his own admitted "emotional turmoil" over the idea of laying his hands on a woman's head and saying the words of ordination.

Amazing may not be the best word to describe that idea – I think it's more like "Hunh?" And then, "I do not want to be used in the Bishop's life for anything," but what was becoming more and more clear to me was that ordination is much more about what God wants than what I want. Of course, there were also those who were just as convinced that I was the one doing the using. They saw me as a shameless "gold digger" who was taking advantage of our Bishop's gracious willingness to allow me to just pursue a theological education. Many of them believed that I had "hoodwinked" the Bishop by telling him that I wasn't interested in ordination and then changing horses in mid-stream. Thankfully, it was a long way from Southern Virginia to Sewanee and I didn't have to deal with them first-hand.

This next step was crucial, as a Candidate for Holy Orders was only one step away from ordination. It usually came sometime in the last semester of the Middler year, which is by far the most difficult year of the theological education program in most seminaries. At Sewanee, our Core Curriculum was crafted around the Middler year with its historical, theological, ethical, and liturgical romp through the years between the ascension of Jesus and the early 20th century. The course was based in Church History, taught by the Rev. Donald Armentrout, an avowed Lutheran pastor, who masterfully laid out the historical development of Christianity. As we traced this history, we also learned how the theology, ethics, and liturgics of the church grew and changed as the church and the world around it changed.

It was a fascinating approach to the immense amount of information we needed to absorb and I thrived under Professor Armentrout's succinct and entertaining lecturing style and his uncanny ability to present such an immense amount of historical facts in the exact order they occurred. At the same time, we were exploring with Professor Robert Hughes the theological beliefs of the growing church as they emerged and evolved throughout the history of the church.

There were deep theological discussions in our weekly seminars, as well as what he called "Locus Papers," which we each prepared for each doctrine according to our research into the teachings of one theologian. I had chosen William Porcher Duose, theologian and Professor of Theology at Sewanee and with each student distributing copies of their own theologian's contribution, we were constructing a comprehensive history of the theology of the church. The ethics Professor Jack Gessel traced the development of ethical thought and Marion Hatchet taught us how the church moved from secret house meetings to the worship structure of the modern church.

We also began Pastoral Theology courses and continued

our homiletics training, so the Middler year was just brutal. We
all looked forward to the end of the school year and a break from
books and papers. Scotty and I were more than ready to hit the
road, as we had plans to meet my mother for a relaxing week with
her cousin and family in a huge beach cottage at Pawley's Island,
South Carolina. For seven glorious days we ate fresh seafood, sat
in the sun, walked the beach, played cards, and did whatever we
wanted. To say it was heaven is a gross understatement. I gloried in
the absolute "nothingness" of the days – nothing to write, nothing to
read (except a good novel), and nothing to study.

SUMMER FIELD WORK
        You know the saying, though, about "all good things?"
Well, this one came to an end, as we turned north to southeastern
Virginia, where I was scheduled to spend eight weeks as a
Seminarian-in-Residence, training under the Rector of a large parish.
He had arranged lodging for us with a member of the Vestry – Jill,
a single woman with a teenage son in a nice townhouse near the
church. This was a perfect match, wouldn't you say? We moved in
on a hot June day, I went to the church and met with the Rector.
He informed me that he was leaving the next day for a 6-week
continuing education program at Virginia Seminary, I was to wear a
clergy collar with a tiny strip of black tape across it at the throat, and
"not to worry, the new Deacon will be here in 2 weeks and I'll be in
touch by phone."
        Well, I left his office thinking that if God was in charge of
THIS part of the process, he had a strange sense of humor – leaving
me "in charge" of a huge parish for two weeks to deal with supply
clergy on Sundays and then putting me in the position of working
with a brand new deacon, a woman straight out of seminary. The
Bishop had approved her call by this church, even though he still
wasn't making any announcements about his intentions regarding
her ordination. He was on Sabbatical for the rest of the year so the
whole Diocese was left wondering what was going to happen to
their new Deacon when it came time for her priesting.
        She asked me that question one day and I asked her what
the Bishop had told her when he interviewed her. She said that she
would have to be ordained a Deacon by her own Bishop, and when
the time came for her to be ordained to the priesthood, he'd let that
Bishop come into the Diocese and ordain her. She was worried that

he would really do that so I told her, "If Bishop Vaché said that he would do that, he will."

She didn't look convinced. "How do you know that?"

I didn't even have to stop and think about it. "Because I trust him. He has accepted me and my call and supported me through some really tough criticism and backlash in this Diocese and I'm still in the program. If he said he will allow you to be ordained, he will." She seemed to be assured, but I could well imagine her anxiety and feelings of being in limbo. Even with my outward confidence, I was still anxious, but I had things to keep me busy – enrolling Scotty in a sports camp the Bishop had offered to pay for, unpacking and getting settled in a small room after living in a good sized apartment, and getting to know our hosts. I was busy finding places for all the stuff I had brought with me when the phone rang and it was for me! Not too many people knew I was there, so I went to the phone in the hall with a sense of foreboding. Was I right, or what?

It was the parish secretary with the news that an elderly member of the parish had died and the new widow was waiting for me at her home. I was numb. I was supposed to be working with a priest, who would do all these things and I would tag along and "learn from the master," so to speak. But, he was off to Alexandria, Virginia and I was the only thing close to a clergy in sight!

So I donned my clergy shirt with its "black-striped" collar and drove to the woman's house. There was no ambulance, no hearse, no cars at all and I couldn't find the house number. I was standing in the muddy street, looking around, when I heard a woman call from behind me. "That's the house; they're waiting for you in the kitchen."

So, I went up on the porch, found the door unlocked and stepped into a formal entryway which, in turn, led into a pristine, white-carpeted, formal living-room on the left. I could see a swinging door on the other side of the living room, which was a common entryway into kitchens in the south, so I lifted my foot to go across the living room when I remembered the mud I just walked through in the yard. Not wanting to leave my footprints on this white carpet (surely she wouldn't appreciate having to clean her carpet before the funeral), I moved straight ahead where I could see a door leading into a pine-paneled den. I turned the corner and was confronted by a white-sheeted form on the floor, which I instinctively knew was the now-deceased elderly member of the church.

Needless to say, I chose the white carpet, tip-toeing to the kitchen door to leave as little mess as possible. When I pushed opened the door, I was greeted by a woman who said, "O thank God, you're here." She was a neighbor and the new widow was sitting at the kitchen table, hunched over a cup of coffee, wiping her eyes. She looked up at me, and I instantly felt like I was right where I was supposed to be. I introduced myself as I sat down, took her hand expressed my condolences, wondering what in the world to say next.

I was quite amazed to hear the next words coming out of my mouth: "Can you tell me what happened?" My chaplaincy training from the summer before had kicked in and I had automatically gone into the "pastoral" mode with Step #1: Get the person to talk. Telling what happened is the first step in the healing process.

She gulped a few times as she tried to control her tears and I waited while she gathered herself and the neighbor put a hot cup of coffee on the table in front of me. When the woman was calmer, she began, "I was in here washing the dishes and I heard him calling me. I answered him, but there was just silence. So, I figured he didn't hear me and I answered again. He still didn't say anything."

Her eyes started to fill with tears again and I squeezed her hand. She continued, "I went to find him and, when I opened that door," (she pointed to the other swinging door in the kitchen) "there he was – lying on the floor. I yelled, 'Honey, what's wrong? Did you fall?' But he didn't answer. He couldn't." She started to cry but managed to say, "He was gone! I called 911 and they came, but he was already gone."

I asked her the next question I had been taught to ask, still amazed at how natural it all felt to me, "So, how are you feeling now?"

She looked up and tears spilled down her cheeks and she said, "Lost. I'm lost."

I assured her that she would soon feel not quite so lost and that time would heal her pain, but in the meantime we were all going to be with her. "You aren't alone," I told her. "Your friends and neighbors are here and I'll be here anytime you need me – just call," and I wrote down my phone number for her. She looked so grateful and fragile that I could feel the tears springing up in my own eyes. I had not lost any close member of my family, except for my grandmother, so I didn't have any of my own experiences to draw on and I was deeply grateful at that moment for my CPE training.

The doorbell rang as I was thinking I should go and, when the neighbor ushered in the funeral director, I could hear the stretcher banging against the door frame and rolling into the room next to the kitchen. I figured that it was time for me to go so that she could deal with the details of what came next. I stood up and must have looked like I was leaving, because she looked at me with pleading, tear-filled eyes and said, "You're going to stay, aren't you?"

Well, of course I was staying! I assured her that I would stay as long as she needed me, and I settled back down in the chair as the funeral director sat down across the table from us.

I wondered if it was obvious to this man that this was my first experience at a funeral planning meeting, and was both relieved and amazed at the deference to my "collar." He didn't seem to notice the stripe either. I held the widow's hand as she made the hardest decisions of her life: picking out a casket and setting times for the visitation and funeral. Her hand shook as she signed the financial agreement with the funeral home and I was very glad I had stayed. She was too.

Before I left I did think to tell her that I would call the Rector to find out which supply priest he wanted me to call. Suddenly, I realized that we hadn't covered funeral planning in seminary yet, so I didn't have a clue what I was doing. Luckily I had decided to keep a prayer book and Bible in my car so I excused myself to retrieve them. I needed something firm and familiar to bluff my way through the next step in the planning but, as I headed out the door, I realized I was the only one who seemed to notice.

I returned, we began to talk about the service. and I reminded her that there would probably be a supply priest doing the service. I was shocked when she asked me to say a few words about her husband since the supply priest didn't know him! Can you imagine? She felt like I knew him from the story she told me and the things she shared with me about the man she had loved for more than 50 years. I was incredibly honored and touched and I remember thinking, "Wow, she didn't even bat an eye; she didn't seem to know or care that I was not your normal, every-day, run-of-the-mill clergy person. She accepted me because of the collar I wore and because she needed me."

Well, that bubble burst the following Sunday after church. The new Deacon had not arrived yet but, because I was a woman and wore a collar, many members of the parish assumed that I was the new Deacon. I was called "Deacon" more than once, and it took a lot of explaining to get folks to understand who I was, what I was doing at their church, and where was their new Deacon??

As I left the church for the coffee hour, I was stopped by a woman whom I had not met but who, obviously, knew me; at least, she thought she did, because she called me "Deacon Bowman" like most other people. Actually, this encounter was more a "roll-over" than a "stop." She accosted me angrily, without so much as a "nice to meet you," and proceeded to ask me what did I think I was doing. I must have looked puzzled because she went on – actually I don't think she ever planned to NOT go right on – "Why do you have to be ordained – why can't you just be a lay person like me? I do lots of stuff at this church and I don't need to be ordained."

Of all the things I learned in Field Work, this was the hardest to take – women can be our most vocal opponent AND our biggest obstacle as we break into traditionally male roles. This woman was a prime example, as her venomous comments were very shrill and were heard by a number of parishioners. It was unnerving and embarrassing, but I thought later, "Well at least she was up-front about her feelings." Not so with the woman who had so graciously opened her home to me and Scotty for the summer. Several days after we arrived at her home, we were having coffee and chatting over breakfast. I was interested in getting to know her and her son, but she was more interested in discussing "women's issues." She had her "pet peeves" and was very vocal about how she experienced and witnessed discrimination against women in the workplace.

At this point, I have to confess that "women's issues" were not (and still aren't) my favorite topic of conversation. It isn't that I don't think they are important; I have experienced much of the mistreatment that she wanted to rant and rave about in our discussions. I know that the "glass ceiling" is a reality – that women are often not paid the same as men for the same work, and that women are passed over for promotions past a certain level just because they are women.

It isn't that I am not sympathetic, and it isn't that I am not interested in these real issues. What they mean to me has nothing to do with their importance – it has to do with my priorities. When I meet a person, male or female, or when I'm having a conversation with someone, I do not enjoy what I will call "rantings and ravings." I find it non-productive and exhausting to hash and re-hash the evils of our society and the mistreatment of women, so I tend to hang back when the discussion takes a turn in this direction.

I guess part of this has to do with my upbringing and my father's tendency to run from confrontation. I was taught to never "argue" the issues because there was no "arguing" allowed in our home. When the conversation began to heat up, my Dad would either stop it or leave the room; my mother would pretty much agree with most anything, thus putting an end to such conversations. Since I never learned how to argue, I was not very adept at "political" discussions and heated conversations, so I tended to avoid them whenever possible.

Also, I find such conversations tedious, stressful, and basically a waste of time. Ranting and raving about an injustice doesn't get many favorable results – it just turns people off and ends up alienating them. I tend to be much more like my mother, who was an expert at letting people be where they were, and I learned from my father that avoidance can be much more pleasant than confrontation. With such a "double dose" I was an abject failure at the kind of conversations my summer host expected and craved.

As my "priestly formation" progressed, I was also learning that clergy who "rant and rave" about any issue are basically an anathema (a hated thing) to most Episcopalians. We just don't "rant and rave." It isn't considered seemly to raise one's voice in church and I discovered the hard way that clergy don't have to actually raise the decibel level of their voices to be considered to be ranting and raving. The slightest negative tone of voice can send Episcopalians into "shut-down" mode and lead to such comments as: "I wonder what's wrong with the Rector – she yelled at me."

Not to rant and rave, but I cannot remember hearing such comments about male clergy. If a man gets carried away and raises his voice in the pulpit – he "got a little excited"; if a woman does that, she is emotionally out of control. If a man raises his voice in a Vestry meeting, he is being assertive although a little out of line; if a woman does that, she is pushy and *over* the line. This phenomenon is not reserved for clergy; it happens in businesses all over the world – the double standard is in effect. It has been since the beginning of time and, I believe, will always be a fact of life. This is another reason that I don't tend to want to waste time ranting and raving about something – it doesn't do any good. It doesn't produce change, and it only alienates people.

The other topic she wanted to discuss was the Rector and his sexist leanings and how surprised she was that he agreed to have a woman as a Field Work student and that he had hired a woman to be his assistant. She continually brought this up and pointedly asked me what I thought of him. She seemed to think I was the perfect sounding board for all of her criticisms of the Rector and his policies, his sermons, etc. I was so uncomfortable with these questions because it was not my place either to listen to her complaints about her Rector or to discuss his shortcomings, his beliefs, or his behavior. I put the instant "kibosh" on any such conversations, gently but firmly changing the subject or explaining that I was uncomfortable with the things she was saying.

So, the summer was difficult, as I felt like I was walking on eggs "at home" and constantly on display and under a very critical and biased microscopic eye. There were members of the church who were very excited to have me there for the summer because it was a victory for women in the Diocese; but I still felt them watching me to see if I was a worthy representative of such an important step forward for women.

There were church members who were definitely not excited to have me there for the summer because of their own prejudices against women in ordained ministry; I felt *them* watching me and waiting for any opportunity to say – to themselves, to each other, and even to my face – "See I told you women shouldn't try to be priests."

There were also members who were huge supporters of me personally and of women in ordained ministry in general; though I cleaved to them for moral support, I also felt them watching me to be sure I lived up to their expectations as a "model" for women aspiring to the ministry, especially in our Diocese.

Then there were my favorite people – the ones who didn't have a clue that there was any difference between their Rector, their new Deacon, or me. We were all "clergy" to them and most of them just shook their heads at the others in amazement, I guess wondering why they wasted so much time on all the extraneous stuff instead of getting whatever ministry they needed from us. Unfortunately,

there were very few who accepted me as just an "almost priest" like
the many other Field Work students they had encountered through
the years in this parish, which was an official training ground for the
Diocese's ordination process.

The Rector seemed to be oblivious to all of this; the issues I
have mentioned never came up in our supervisory sessions, which
were very few since he was only there for the first few days and
the last two weeks of my stay in his parish. The one thing I guess
I learned from him was the ability to trust that others will do their
job. I liked him too, probably because he was a lot like me and didn't
tend to confront issues publicly or even get into any discussions
about them.

I left my summer field work site with an odd feeling of
having not learned a lot about parish duties, since I only preached
twice, had minimal roles in the worship services, and many people
were away for the summer or on Sundays. I had a difficult time
writing the paper that was due on our return to seminary as so many
things had just not been addressed.

There was one delightful and rather telling encounter with
the owner of a small hardware store where I bought the necessary
supplies to repair a broken kitchen cabinet door. I stopped by on the
way home from the church, so I had on my funny striped collar, and
when I went up to the counter, I noticed the man looking oddly at
me. I was used to that so I told him what I needed but he just stared
at me. Finally, he asked me, "Gee, did you hurt your neck?"

I was clueless. I said, "No."

He asked, "Then what's that thing around your neck?"
Now that was a first so it was all I could do to explain to him what
a clerical collar was without laughing. His next question nearly did
me in: "So, is the black stripe because you're a woman?" I barely
made it out of the store.

I did have a side ministry that I thoroughly enjoyed. The
Diocese has an outdoor chapel at a quiet, mostly private beach some
30 minutes away that was the summer home of Virginia residents
from all over the state, and many owners rented out their homes
when they were not in residence. The population swells in the
summer time when many families come to spend vacations, and
there are always a number of young people around.

My ministry there included a weekly prayer service with
lively music and a short program of some sort. I played the guitar

and led the singing. The purpose was to bring Christ's presence to
the summer residents and to promote the summer chapel. Weekly
services were conducted by vacationing priests who got to stay
in the apartment behind the chapel for free. I was able to take
advantage of this several times as an active priest in the Diocese, and
it is indeed a holy place for vacating!

There were never very many people at my Wednesday night
services but I met some very special young people who did find my
music and message to be a help to them and a break from the same
old/same old. One evening we were singing one of my favorite
songs "They Will Know We are Christians By Our Love" and a
young couple, who had been out for an evening stroll, ventured up
the walk from the road. They stood for a moment as we finished
the song and, before I could welcome them and invite them in, they
began to applaud! The others joined in and I suddenly found myself
the very embarrassed subject of a standing ovation! They turned
around and continued on their way. I never found out what made
them offer such an accolade but it was one of the high points of my
summer!

There were also several meaningful experiences including
my first funeral. One of the two sermons I preached had such an
effect on one young man that he went home and told his mother
that he "had to be a priest because Susan said so." (I didn't know
this until some years later after he had indeed become a priest and
neither of us know to this day what it was I said!)

I guess if nothing else, I have that to carry from this
experience.

SUMMER RETREAT

For some reason that eluded most of us Southern Virginia
seminarians, we had the distinct honor of attending a weekend
retreat with the Commission on Ministry, the Standing Committee,
and the Bishop before returning to our respective schools. As if we
Middlers hadn't been through the most difficult year in seminary,
we now had to suck it up once more for this command performance
that ended with the dreaded "Middler Exams."

It was a valiant attempt at bringing all of the students and
their spouses together with all of the evaluators to "get to know each
other better." We were told to "relax and enjoy" the experience, as if
anyone in such an intense evaluative process can ever relax around

those who have the power to end or significantly alter the best laid plans. This may sound somewhat paranoid, but I had not forgotten the conversation I had with my sponsor after I was admitted as a Postulant. Basically, he said to me that I now belonged to the Commission on Ministry, that I should think of the Commission as my parent, a loving and supportive parent, who would guide me through the process toward ordination. (Years later, I recalled that conversation with a bit of bitter irony as my "loving and supportive parent" acted more like a distant supervisor who cared more about the process than they did about me.)

So back to the "relaxing and enjoyable retreat" in the summer of 1982. The students met with advisors regarding whatever steps were coming up next and then each student met with a small "mini-committee" made up of members of both the Commission on Ministry and the Standing Committee. Problems or concerns were addressed, such as grades, family, money, etc. and we all knew that after we left, each student was thoroughly discussed – from the Faculty's evaluation and recommendation to the student's own self-evaluation. As you can see, this was far from a relaxing experience.

That being said, I found myself actually enjoying the informal time when we could just "get to know" all the other participants, including the students who attended other seminaries. Then, just when we were filled with warm feelings from the Eucharist, came the dreaded "Middler Exam." This was an oral test administered by several clergy in the Diocese who were particularly knowledgeable about Scripture, Theology, and other Seminary courses. They were appointed by the Bishop to a rather ominous sounding group, the Board of Examining Chaplains. I was fortunate to be in the group interviewed by the Chair of the Commission on Ministry, who was a huge supporter for me and was a very gentle and caring priest.

There were six of us in the Middler (2nd) year, two attending Virginia Seminary, two attending General Seminary, and two of us attending Sewanee. They divided us up into two groups, each comprised of one seminarian from each Seminary. We were questioned on everything from the Old Testament to Church policy. Most of it was basic and I was lucky that I could answer all my questions with confidence. I remember one question distinctly: What is redemption? The moderator turned to one of the other

seminarians in my group, who gave a long, rambling answer that I
had trouble following. The second one didn't do much better.
    Then the moderator turned to me and asked, "What do you
think, Susan?"
    I easily answered him, "it's the free gift of salvation that we
received when Jesus died for us on the cross."
    Looking impressed, he then asked, "and where do we find
that in the Bible?"
    I immediately responded, "Romans, Chapter 5."
    To this day, I don't know why he was so surprised; after
all, I had just completed Don Armentrout's Church History course,
during which this "flaming Lutheran" would regularly bang on the
podium and yell at us: "You Episcopalians, you think you can earn
salvation but you can't! Dontcha see? It's a gift! Romans 5 – Paul
said it and I believe it!"
    So, I passed the Middler Exam with flying colors; in fact, all
of the moderators agreed that the two seminarians from Sewanee
were the most well-prepared and seemed to have a much more
integrated knowledge of Theology, Scripture, and Church History.
I will always be grateful to Sewanee, its Middler program, and its
effectively arranged courses that taught us the doctrines of faith as
they arose in Church History, giving us a much more comprehensive
theological education.
    By the time it was over, I was exhausted and everyone was
getting packed and on the road as quickly as they could – except
me. The last thing on the agenda for the weekend was my interview
for candidacy. I think I was so tired that I didn't have the energy to
get stressed out over it, so what I felt as I sat down at the table was
a strange kind of anticipation that bordered on excitement. I knew
I had done well in the Middler Exam, which had been dutifully
reported to the group during their preparation for my interview. I
knew my grades were good and that the faculty had given me a very
positive recommendation, based on my performance at seminary.
I also knew that several key antagonists were absent from this
meeting and I was hopeful that our relaxing and enjoyable weekend
together would set the stage for a brief and positive interview.
    It was just that – to the point and no surprises. As I left
the conference center and drove to Lake Gaston to pick up Scotty,
I remember feeling such a sense of relief that, not only was the
marathon over, but I thought I had actually made a rather good

showing! Even though I didn't dare speculate over what the combined group had said about me after I left, I couldn't think of any negative experience or major concerns that could interfere with my candidacy. By the time I arrived at my parents' house, I had decided that, since there was nothing I could do about any of it, I was going to put it all out of my mind and get on with the one thing every seminarian dreams of – Senior Year!

The next day, Scotty and I were on our way back to Sewanee and I found myself enjoying the ride through the Smoky Mountains of North Carolina. We decided to stop in Chattanooga for a quick trip up Lookout Mountain. I was tired when we climbed the "Mountain" but I felt hopeful and very excited about being a Senior. Scotty was also excited about his new status as a Jr. High Student. He had barely survived the 6th grade with a teacher whose least favorite students were boys and seminarians' kids, in that order. He would have a long bus ride up and down the mountain every day but I could tell that he was really looking forward to a new experience. I was so excited about finally being a Senior that I actually was able to survive the next few weeks until I finally got the word from the Chairman of the Standing Committee.

When the call came, I had gotten so involved in my new courses that, for several days, I had not thought about what was happening in Southern Virginia. I was fixing dinner and I answered the phone with an almost impatient tone as I had my hands full of ground-beef-almost-meat-loaf. I was precariously balancing the phone between my shoulder and my ear to keep from getting the phone goopy. When I heard who it was, I was so shocked that I actually dropped the phone. I quickly wiped off my hands and rescued the phone with apologies but my caller didn't seem to notice. He began, "Susan, I'm calling to let you know that, following your interview, the Commission on Ministry voted to recommend you to the Bishop for Candidacy." I was holding my breath. "They voiced the same concerns about your weight and Scotty's welfare and it was a close vote."

I thought, "Gee, I don't think I needed to know **that**."

He went on, "The Standing Committee met the following week to consider all of the seminarians' status and we have recommended to the Bishop that you be admitted to Candidacy." At that, he stopped and I felt a little shiver of panic as I waited for the "But" to follow. "We all agreed that you should pursue some

counseling around your weight issues, and that you should find
someone to help Scotty with his issues over school." Still, I waited
for the "But" to come. It didn't. He continued with this stunning
statement that I know was still reverberating all over Southern
Virginia. "The Bishop has agreed and you are now a Candidate for
Holy Orders."

SENIOR YEAR
 I was absolutely blown away – it was actually happening – I
had finally gotten into the last steps of the process with only one
more hurdle before ordination. I could barely stand still even though
my meat-loaf-wannabe was crying to get into the oven. Scotty
was still at a friend's house, and my neighbors weren't home yet.
I had no one to tell!! I threw dinner into the oven and grabbed the
phone, dialing the first number that came into my mind. My mother
answered the phone and after I finished telling her my amazing
news, she asked, "What did you say?"
 I tried not to sound as deflated as I felt because I realized
that I was probably speaking "Greek" to her. I slowed down and
explained what had happened and, God bless her, she tried to grasp
what it meant. However, I knew that she was happy because I was
happy. No, happy doesn't even come close. I was ecstatic.
 I hung up and started calling my classmates, none of whom
were at home yet. This had been my early day, so I was probably one
of the few seminarians who were not in class. I really needed to tell
someone who really knew what this meant, but I had to be satisfied
with just dancing around the kitchen giving high fives to the wall
until I finally realized that there was one person I really should call.
Dean Booty had been such a huge support for me throughout the
entire year and I knew that he would appreciate the huge import
of this news. So, I picked up the phone and dialed his office even
though I figured he had probably left for the day.
 He answered so quickly, I almost missed his quiet "Dean
Booty here."
 My response was anything but quiet and I could picture him
holding the phone away from his ear while I yelled, "Dean Booty –
I'm in! I'm a Candidate. They called! The Bishop said yes."
 Somehow he managed to figure out what I was saying
and I was so gratified to hear him say, "Susan, that is fantastic!
Great news! I'll get the calling tree started spreading the word.

Congratulations!" We both ratcheted down enough to carry on a normal conversation for a few minutes and when I hung up, I felt a deep sense of rightness. If this holy man of the church was so convinced that I should be in this process, then it had to be God's will as well.

Unfortunately, my grand announcement was eclipsed by the news we received the next day that one of our classmates had lung cancer. It was a huge blow to us all as everyone loved Dave. We knew he was going to be the best priest ever and it was unthinkable that his love of Jesus and his considerable pastoral skills were not going to be shared with the church. We all gathered around him for the next few weeks as he underwent tests and was even examined by a well-known specialist flown in from Gainesville, Florida by Dave's best friend, the owner and CEO of Walmart Stores. We were all frantic as the news kept getting more and more ominous but Dave seemed to just get more and more serene. He was a man of rock-solid faith and he knew that he was in God's hands and that was OK with him.

It wasn't OK with me, though, and I spent as much time as possible with Dave as he waited for a final verdict. It finally came and he was scheduled for extensive surgery to try and remove the cancer. Dave and his family had been warned that the cancer was probably of the "oat cell" variety (because it looked as if someone had cast seeds everywhere, resulting in multiple growths in so many places that it was rarely removable).

There were three of us gathered in Dave's room on the afternoon before he was to be transferred to the hospital in Huntsville, Alabama for surgery. We sat with him and talked about our new classes and what he was and wasn't missing. All of us were ignoring the huge elephant in the middle of the room, named "inoperable cancer." Suddenly the door was flung open and a large figure appeared in the doorway. The three of us jumped up off the bed looking very guilty.

It was our Theology professor with his academic gown flowing out behind him, and in his booming voice, he demanded, "What's going on here?" We were all dumbstruck, including Dave, so we all just looked at him. Obviously enjoying himself, he reached Dave's bedside in two strides, looked at the three of us and demanded, again, "What's going on? Are you praying for Dave?" We just looked at him and I think one of us must have said something that sounded like "Yes," because he grabbed my hand, pulling me toward the bed and said, "Well, come on, you can't pray for healing without laying hands on him, and you can't reach him way over there!" He instructed us all to put one hand on the person next to us and to place the other hand somewhere on Dave's body. He placed his left hand on Dave's chest, looked around the circle until he had everybody's attention, and, in a quiet, but intense voice, he prayed, "Father God, watch over this your servant, David, and remove this cancer from this body. Amen."

We all stood silently and in that moment, I felt something course through me from my hand still in his hand to the other hand on Dave's arm. It was so strong that I made a sound and they all looked at me and it was all I could do to keep from running from the room. I had never participated in such a prayer in my life, and I had never had such a feeling before. I was thinking that maybe I should tell them, when the Professor said, "Now *that's* how you pray for healing," just as if we had been in a classroom. With that, he left the room and all of us were in shock, to say the least. I thought about saying something to Dave about what had happened but I was so blown away by it that when I tried, I found I couldn't speak.

Thankfully, the nurse appeared at that moment, and shooed us all out. It was time. We moved out of the room to make room for the stretcher, and the others stood watching from the hall. I knew that they would see him into the waiting ambulance with an appropriate sendoff, so I took off down the hall in the opposite direction. I couldn't get out of that hospital fast enough.

For two full days, we all waited for word from Huntsville. We knew it would take longer than usual for him to recover from the deep anesthesia that is required for lung surgery, so we were prepared for the long wait, but it was agony. There was hope, but it was a slim thread to hang onto, and we all knew it. I had this secret knowledge about what I thought had happened that day in his room, but I didn't dare tell anyone. What if Dave still died? I would sound like a hysterical fool, and I would feel like one too. I would just wait. Finally, the Dean got a call from one of our classmates who had stayed in Huntsville throughout the ordeal. He reported that Dave had made it through surgery but that it was oat cell cancer. The surgeon had removed as much as he could, including one lung and the lower portion of the other one.

We were crushed! Our prayers for a total healing had gone

unanswered. He may have a few months now, but that was all. The whole campus was in mourning, but they were still praying. Not me! I was angry! I had felt something that day and I knew that it was God taking the cancer out of Dave's body, just like Bob had prayed. I still hadn't told anybody, but I just knew God was healing him at that moment. When I heard the report, I was furious! I had been floating, waiting for the news that, when the surgeon opened his chest there was no cancer. I knew that God had taken it – I just knew it! I left the classroom and walked for hours, yelling at God for fooling me and at myself for being so gullible and believing that God healed through our intercessions.

I didn't go to class the next day. I did what I always do to sooth my savage beast. I went shopping. After a few hours of walking the stores and finding nothing I felt like buying, I still ended up with a load of bags and packages. I arrived home just before dinner to hear the phone ringing. I was out of breath from getting my packages in from the car, and from the tears that started when I caught sight of the cross on the mountain shining in the late afternoon sun. I could hardly hear the voice on the other end. Finally, I realized that it was one of my classmates trying to tell me something, and he was so excited that he could hardly talk.

Finally he calmed down enough to tell me what was being reported to all of Dave's classmates at that moment. He said, "Susan, you won't believe it. They didn't tell Dave everything when he first woke up the other day." Evidently, the anesthesiologist had decided to wait another 24 hours until Dave was fully conscious before telling him what had transpired in the operating room. He said that he had been practicing for many years, and that he had never seen anything like what he saw that day. When the surgeon opened up Dave's chest, the cancer was indeed oat cell cancer and it was everywhere. There was a collective moan as they all knew what it meant.

The surgeon said, "Well, he asked me for as much time as I could give him, so I'll take what I can."

When he began to remove the cancer, the Anesthesiologist said, "it was all stuck together, and when he lifted up a part of it, it all came off in one piece. It was like peeling a sticker off a window. It was a very large mass and didn't leave much of the lung, so the surgeon removed the entire lung and the lower lobe of the other lung which had also been covered with cancer." My friend was in

tears by then, as I was, but he managed to tell me, "When he was
done, Dave's chest cavity was clean – there was no more cancer to be
seen. He will have a long recovery; he will have to be very careful
with only two-thirds of a lung, but he will be fine."

The next morning in chapel we all cheered and clapped
and sang, and the Dean gave copious thanks to God for Dave's
miraculous healing. It's all we talked about for days and everyone
was sure that all of our prayers had been answered. I still hadn't
told a soul about what happened that day in Dave's hospital room,
and I certainly wasn't going to say anything now – it might seem as
if I was taking credit. But I knew.

I spent a long time with God asking for forgiveness for my
lack of faith and trust, and I came away knowing that God did,
indeed, remove the cancer from Dave's body – he just chose to use
the surgeon to do it. I decided that God must have agreed with
us when we said what a wonderful priest Dave would be. I also
concluded that God had a lesson to teach some of us, especially me.
For years, I didn't share this story, but now it needs to be told. I was
able to share it with Dave before his eventual death, and together we
gave thanks to God for his wildly successful 10 years of ministry in a
small town in Alabama.

Oh yeah, I learned one more thing from this brave and
faithful servant of God. Some years after we graduated, I got word
that one of his sons had been killed in an automobile accident after
falling asleep at the wheel of his car on the way home from work in
the wee hours of the morning. Dave was summoned by an usher
just as he climbed into the pulpit on Father's Day. A State Trooper
was waiting to tell him the news. The boy had died instantly when
his car hit the water; needless to say, Dave was overcome with grief.

When I spoke with him, it had been several months since the
accident, and he was able to share with me this very moving account
of the service at the grave. His Bishop had performed the funeral,
and so was with him at the cemetery. When everyone had left,
the two of them stood beside the grave in silence. Suddenly, Dave
screamed a list of obscenities at God that would make a sailor cringe.
He told me that there was another silence of about two beats, and
then the Bishop screamed at God, repeating the exact same words,
thus joining Dave in his grief at the deepest level he could.

I was in tears by this time and then he said something I will
never forget, something I have passed on to many grieving parents,

widows, children, anyone who has lost a loved one. He said, "Susan,
I was standing in the deepest pit, at the very bottom, as low as I
could possibly be, and I knew with every fiber of my being that what
I was standing on was the rock and the rock was Jesus. I wanted to
just let go and sink but he wouldn't let me."

A few months after surgery, Dave returned to classes and he
was just like he used to be – kind, loving, generous, witty, and one
of the best friends I ever had. This "near-tragedy-turned-lesson-in-
faith" had consumed us for the first month until Dave had recovered
from surgery but soon we were back in the "swing" of school. It was
time for the annual election of student leaders and I decided that I
would like to be the Student Body President. In talking with other
classmates, I discovered that one of the other women in my class was
also considering running, and I was soon embroiled in a huge debate
among the women students over who should run.

Some of the women thought that one of us should withdraw,
as two women running would split the "female vote." I listened
politely, and then, more politely said that all that sounded like a lot
of politics, and I wasn't interested in playing the game they were
suggesting. I made it clear that I wanted the position because I had
distinct ideas about the position and how it should be used to effect
some needed changes. I was convinced that if God wanted me to
be the Student Body President, it wouldn't matter if 50 women were
running. So I ran and she ran, and a male student ran and I won,
hands down. I had my mandate.

I was an effective President, working closely with our
Dean to organize and promote a weekly "folk mass" with more
contemporary music, a band of guitarists, and a more casual
atmosphere to encourage the attendance of children. Over the
objections of the Liturgy Professor, we started a Friday night service,
which allowed working spouses, and children of the seminarians
and faculty to attend a weekly worship service with some of their
seminary family. The "regular" weekly worship service was held on
Wednesday at noon, followed by lunch at The Sewanee Inn. Since
many students were in their field parishes on Sunday morning, this
had long ago become our "Sunday service," and it was a cherished
tradition.

None of the seminary students wanted to give that up
because it was a nice break in the middle of the week. In addition to
a community celebration of the Eucharist, we got a nice free lunch

with good, hot food and real napkins. We felt pampered, and we wanted that to continue. Since it was necessary to have a service each week that was planned and executed by a team of students (this is called "liturgical training"), most of the students felt like the Wednesday service was "work," and many of them enjoyed the more relaxed atmosphere of the Friday service and the opportunity to worship as a family with their families.

My efforts were greatly appreciated by the students, but not by some of the faculty, which showed on my 1st-semester evaluation. It began with the glowing parts of the evaluation in which they mentioned my good grades, my faithful participation in classes and worship, and a steady growth in my spiritual life and my sense of calling to the priesthood. There were "concerns about getting involved in the less traditional worship movement pervading the church," a remark that could only have been written by our very conservative Liturgy Professor who had adamantly opposed my proposal in the Liturgy Committee meetings. He refused to take any part in the Friday night services, which were instituted over his loud objections.

I was taken aback by this comment for several reasons. One was that I was appalled by the negative attitude towards the "less traditional worship" movement that had begun to gather momentum in the church in the past few years. There was an unspoken, but very clear, "rule" against raising one's arms in praise during worship, and one of the new Junior students had actually received a warning from the faculty that "such ecstatic showing off was not tolerated in the traditional Episcopal worship of the School of Theology." My efforts at promoting an alternative worship experience began shortly after that confrontation, and many saw this new service as a way to circumvent the seminary's official disapproval of such innovative and inappropriate public expressions of faith.

I was also convinced that this negative part of my recommendation was meant to scare me off. The power of a seminary faculty's recommendation, whether positive or negative, was well known throughout the theological education community, and every student lived in fear that something would trigger a negative report to the Diocese and the Bishop. I spoke with the Dean about it, and he assured me that it was added as a concession to those who opposed the new worship service and didn't really pose any danger to me as far as a final recommendation for ordination would be concerned. I relaxed some but every Friday night I still couldn't help but hope that God would suddenly turn some professorial hearts and they would join us in worship. That didn't happen, but the negative vibes did decrease enough that we all were able to enjoy our "less traditional worship."

PARISH FIELD WORK
        During the Senior year, all seminarians are required to do Parish Field Work, (in addition to the summer field work) at a location in their own Dioceses. There are numerous sites in Sewanee but, due to the number of students, there are a number of sites which are an hour distant or more. I was fortunate to draw a local parish about four miles from campus – St. James. This was a sweet little church with about 50 members and about 25 attending each Sunday. It was one of the few spots in the Church where I felt totally accepted. I didn't have any authority, of course, and they were accustomed to seminarians of all types – male, female, foreign. So, as far as I can tell, no one batted an eye when I showed up on a Sunday in the fall of 1983 with Edna Evans, my Homiletics Professor, who was a long-time member of St. James.
        Yes, there ARE drawbacks to everything – I had drawn a plum parish but I was also going to be watched every minute by the same person who evaluated my sermons in class. This felt a lot like "Double jeopardy" at first, as I thought about Edna's strict evaluations of our sermons. I figured that everything I did on Sunday mornings would be scrutinized with the same critical eye. I was as nervous as a cat on my first Sunday, as I was introduced to the congregation by the Warden. I spoke for a few moments telling them about myself, and I kept looking over at Edna expecting her to be taking notes, but she was reading the bulletin! "How rude," I thought, before I realized that she had heard it all before and then I thought that maybe she was trying not to crowd me and make me feel just like I was feeling.
        I relaxed a little but I only had to read the prayers and serve the chalice, so I didn't worry about any negative feedback. The following Sunday though, I was scheduled to preach, and I spent more time agonizing over how Edna would like it than I did writing it. Even though I had become accustomed to preaching in class and receiving her feedback (I had even become somewhat comfortable preaching in Chapel), somehow, it felt like I was a brand new

student again. Now I was preaching for people – not academics or visiting bishops – just regular people in the pew, and I realized that I wasn't exactly sure how to write a sermon for them.

Finally, on Saturday night, I calmed down enough to remember the things Edna had taught me about preaching, and I laid out my draft and reviewed it as I knew she would – looking for my one sentence, and making sure that everything I said was pertinent. I tightened up the rhetoric and illustrations, so that it was what she would call, "a work of art." It took most of the night, as I kept going off on tangents in an effort to speak to the ordinary folks who would be listening to me. I'd read it again, and had to keep coming back to my one sentence and cutting what was not necessary. Finally, at some ungodly hour of the morning, I stopped. I didn't really finish, but I stopped. I had reached the wall where there was nowhere to go but to bed. I had done all I could. I liked it but then I was biased. I thought I had followed all of Edna's rules, but then I was the student who didn't always obey all of the rules.

I dragged myself up several hours after I had finally fallen asleep, got dressed, and took off with Scotty for our new church home. I was warmly greeted, and spent the first hour discussing with the adult Sunday School class what they would like to study for the year. They had expressed a desire to learn about the "new" Prayer Book (even though it had been adopted in 1979, it was still considered "new" four years later), and I had put together a lesson plan to trace the development of the Prayer Book from its beginnings to the present. They loved the plan and we got started that morning. It was a topic that had been drilled into us in Liturgics and I had all my class notes so I was comfortable with teaching the class. I was also grateful that Edna had a policy of not attending Sunday School because the members of the church had a tendency to rely on her for all the answers, which diluted the seminarian's authority (little as it was) and distracted everyone from the topic at hand.

That should have been a tip-off to me about how professional Edna would be in this field work site, but my paranoia and fear were much stronger than my common sense at that point. Consequently, I was surprised that she didn't even arrive at church until the Sunday School class was almost over. I wondered how she would evaluate me, but, when I asked her, she just smiled and said, "I have my ways." It was later that I realized that she got feedback from the members of the class, and they formed the basis for her evaluation of that part of my field work. Clever and effective.

There was still the dreaded sermon, though, and I was in a sweat by the time I rose to the podium to deliver the message. I took my time arranging my manuscript, trying to give my heart time to stop pounding so hard I was sure they could hear it in the back pew. I had a momentary feeling of panic as I looked down at the short prayer I had typed above my opening sentence. It was what was said before every sermon I had ever heard, until I came to seminary. I had always wanted to say the words, "May the words of my mouth and the meditation of our hearts, be always acceptable to you, O Lord my strength and my redeemer," and I almost did, but just in time, Edna's voice said in my ear, "Never start your sermon with a prayer. You can say your prayers during the hymn. Just get up there and preach." I was so undone that I had forgotten her instructions and had almost messed up my first sermon in my field parish, that my voice came out in a thin, whiny tone. I stopped and faked a little coughing bout so I could get my bearings.

When I got my breath, I felt somewhat steady so I started again. This time my voice came out clear and strong and I thought, "Gee, I actually **sound** like a preacher." I finished the opening, which was a story about a preacher giving his first Christmas sermon in a new church. He was so nervous that he called his mentor and asked him what he could do to relax, and he suggested that he stash a small glass of vodka under the pulpit, and to just take a few sips before he started. The new preacher thought that would work so he got a small glass and filled it with vodka before the service and went into the church to put it under the pulpit where he could get to it. He was really nervous, so he thought, "I'll just take a little sip now; maybe it'll help." He took a sip, then another, and figured if a small sip would make him feel better, a swallow would do an even better job.

He looked around and saw no one, so he took a big swallow and put the now half-empty glass on the shelf and went back to prepare for the entrance hymn and the beginning of the service. After he got in place, he thought about the vodka and thought, "I'm parched and really nervous; I think I'll take another sip." He did and then he figured he'd better drink it while he had the chance, so he turned it up and placed the now-empty glass on the floor next to his feet. The moment finally arrived and he stepped into the pulpit, feeling very relaxed and ready to preach. When he looked down at his sermon, he thought, "Gee, I don't really need this – I know this story," so he started telling the familiar story of the birth of Jesus, went on about what Christmas really means and how all good Christians should remember that "Jesus is the reason for the season."

He finished with a flair, wishing everyone a "Merry Christmas." When the service was over, he noticed that most people went out of the church by the side aisles so he only got to speak to a few of the members. One of his Deacons was the last one out of the church and the new preacher asked him, "So, what did you think of my first sermon?" The Deacon paused a moment and then said, "Well, Pastor, I think it was pretty good until you got to the part where the shepherds were out in the fields playing craps with their flocks by night. That wasn't too bad, but I think you lost them when you talked about the "low-down" angels and the wise guys. I think that everybody could have overlooked all that until you sang Happy Birthday to Jesus ending it with 'You look like a monkey and are one too.'"

Everyone was laughing and I knew I had their attention, so with perfect timing, I moved into my sermon on Jesus reading from the Torah in the Synagogue and how he got everyone's attention by claiming to have fulfilled the words of Isaiah in their presence. As I continued, my confidence gained momentum until I reached the final point of my message. I can still recall the thrill that shot through me as I asked, "How did God get your attention this week?" I knew in that instant just how good the sermon really was. All my work had paid off. I was on a roll. I finished with a hearty "Amen" and sat down, still shaking, partly from the remnants of the original fear, partly from the abject relief that it was over, and partly from the power of the message I had just delivered.

It was Edna's practice to offer feedback on the sermon directly following the service after everyone had gone home. She wanted it to be fresh in both minds so I sternly threatened Scotty within an inch of his life if he didn't quietly entertain himself and sat down in the pew to await the verdict. She started with her usual praise as she believed that students listened to negative feedback much better if they have something positive under their belt. She said that the sermon was well-written and pertinent to the congregation even though she thought that the first illustration was a tad weak. The congregation seemed to enjoy it but she thought I could have used something more powerful. I had loved that first story so I wasn't liking this so far.

Then she said, "Now, for the serious feedback." My heart
fell – she hated it! "I looked up to see her smiling, and she said,
this was one of the best constructed sermons I have ever heard. In
all my years teaching homiletics, no student has ever followed my
structural plan for a sermon so perfectly, and the effect was just
what I tell my students it will be – awesome!" I was stunned but
she went on, "Almost every person told me what a good sermon it
was before they left and I was in such agreement, that it took a lot to
come up with that criticism about the first illustration. It was actually
everybody's favorite, but I had to find something of teaching value!"
She laughed and handed me my manuscript, on which she had
written in large red letters, "A+" and said, "I told you that you were
going to be a great preacher."

I felt like I had wings as I walked out of the building, but I
was slightly irritated at myself for doubting Edna's professionalism. I
should have known that she would be just as straight and fair as she
was in class, and I was suddenly happy that I would now have so
many additional opportunities to preach for her and learn as much as
she had to teach me about preaching. I became a voracious student of
everything there was to learn in that tiny little parish with its devoted
members and the one person who made me into a devoted student
and a powerful preacher.

"THE VISIT"

As I look back on my Senior year, I am reminded of the
movie "Jaws" and all of the sequels that spawned the saying, "just
when you thought it was safe to go back in the water...." By the
time the Christmas vacation arrived, I was firmly ensconced in the
ordination process. I was getting good grades, receiving excellent
reviews from the faculty, and enjoying my relationship with the
Dean and the Liturgy Committee. Then came "The Visit."

Just after Christmas vacation, I received a call from the Rev.
Douglas Burgoyne, President of the Standing Committee, who said
that he and my sponsor, the Rev. Bob Morrison, were going to be
coming to Sewanee to discuss with me a letter that the Bishop had
received from the woman I had stayed with the summer before.
Remember Jill? She's the one who wanted to discuss everything
from discrimination of women to her less-than-perfect Rector.

Anyone reading this can just imagine my abject terror – two
of the most respected clergy in the diocese were taking three days and

spending a lot of money to come to Sewanee to discuss a letter. This letter, needless to say, took on gargantuan proportions immediately. I couldn't imagine what horrendous things she must have said to cause this expense of time and money when a simple phone call could have sufficed. My imagination was running around like a wild bull in the streets of Pamplona, and, one minute my emotions were running wildly trying to outrun my thoughts and the next minute I was trying to chase them down and make some sense out of them.

I thought my visitors would never arrive, and I dreaded the moment when they would drive into my yard. Of course, they did arrive and we exchanged hugs and heartfelt pleasantries, since both of these men were my close friends. But, "the letter" loomed large between us.

We went to dinner at a local restaurant and I enjoyed it as best I could, but I was dying to know what could be so bad that they had flown to Sewanee to discuss it with me. And why did it take not just one person but two of them! The more I thought about that, the more nervous I became, and dinner was fast becoming an ordeal as I found that the food I usually enjoyed was like cardboard, and my mouth was so dry that I could barely swallow.

Finally, Doug said, "OK, let's get to it. Here's why we came – the Bishop received this letter, and we'd like you to read it, and then we'll talk about it." I took it – it felt like a lead weight – what on earth could be in this letter? As I was opening it, Doug said, "It's from Jill (not her real name)." I just wanted to throw it down on the table and run screaming from the restaurant. Instead, I opened it and began to read. After all these years, I can still remember the opening words:
"Dear Charles:

As you know, I graciously opened my home, at your request, to Susan Bowman and her son for the eight weeks she spent at our church as an intern. You also know that I am not in favor of women's ordination but I agreed anyway."

It was all I could do to remain upright in the chair, I was so shocked. After eight weeks under the same roof with this woman, I was just discovering this important fact. After all the conversations we had, she had never even hinted that she felt this way and I was flabbergasted.

The letter went on for several pages, detailing all the reasons why she did not think that I should be a priest. Of course, the details have dimmed over the years, but I remember the gist of her complaints, as follows:

- I was a poor houseguest. I had broken a cabinet door in the kitchen and had not fixed it. I had spilled the dirt from a house plant in my room and had not cleaned it up. My room was messy with the bed often unmade. Scotty had put his foot through the floor of the attic and I had not mentioned it or had it fixed.
- I was a poor conversationalist. Regardless of the number of times she tried to start conversations with me about serious topics, I would not engage in any meaningful dialogue with her.
- I was a poor mother. I "used the TV as a babysitter" and allowed my son to sit around the house watching TV even though she had suggested that he could earn some money by mowing lawns in the neighborhood. She had even offered him the use of her lawnmower.
- I was a lazy intern. I had only preached two sermons in the eight weeks that I was there and I only held one bible study during that time.

By the time I got to the end of the letter I was overwhelmed by a raging tumult of feelings that threatened to wreck my composure and send me into a fit of angry tears. I was furious and I was completely dumbfounded at her lies and misinterpretations. I was hurt and humiliated by her insinuations. Mostly, I was scared that this one person might be given the power to derail my candidacy for ordination and completely ruin my life.

Everything inside of me was screaming to defend myself, to deny everything, and to discredit the author. I have always had a tendency to be defensive. During this process, I had worked very hard to control that part of myself, because I had learned how such an attitude affects those around me. I had begun to acquire the ability to accept criticism gracefully and admit to my mistakes and shortcomings with a more honest and accepting demeanor. In early interviews in the process, it had been a real issue and I had made a concentrated effort to control my urge to do the "YeahBut" dance. That's when you listen politely to a complaint and then say something like, "Yeah, but here's why" or "Yeah, but here's what really happened."

It took everything I could summon up to put the letter down on the table and calmly tell my friends, "Well, there's certainly some truth in this." I will always remember and be eternally grateful to those two kind and gentle priests for their next words. Almost in unison, they assured me that they didn't put a lot of credence in her complaints due to her admitted bias against women being ordained. Then, they told me that the Bishop wanted me to answer each complaint with my own "side of the story."

They had just given me permission to rightfully defend myself, and I felt a surge of hope, because I knew that most of what she had said was untrue or skewed. I felt sure that, once I had set the record straight, her power over me would be dissipated. So, I began with the first complaint and went through them point by point.

- I did indeed break an already loose cabinet door (I forget now exactly how I did that). At my earliest opportunity, I went to the local hardware store and bought a new hinge. (Remember the "because you're a woman" collar story?) When I started to fix it, Jill took it and insisted on doing the job herself. I had turned a plant over on my way out of the room one morning and, since I was late for Bible Study, I waited until I got home to clean it up, leaving a note that I would take care of it then. Finally, Scotty adamantly informed me that it was her son who stepped through the attic floor. Scotty didn't tell anybody because the boy told him that he'd "better not tell." He said he would fix it and we moved out that day.

- I was very uncomfortable discussing "women's issues" with her as I am with anybody because it's not an "issue" for me. While I'm cognizant of the plight of women, especially those of us in traditionally male roles, I don't dwell on it, I don't waste time and energy in pointless conversations or angst sessions, and I certainly don't get into finger-pointing sessions when the object of the pointing is my Bishop. I also refused to continue any conversation she began with "You know what bugs me about the Rector..." and she wanted to talk about him a lot. I found that a very uncomfortable situation and, while I may not have handled it expertly, I thought I made it clear without being rude that I would not discuss the Rector, the Vestry, the Associate Rector, or any parish politics with her.

- When I expressed to the Rector my concerns over having an 11-going-on-12-year-old son with me all summer, I was assured that there would be lots for him to do. He said that members would invite him over and many of them

had pools or went to the beach often. This never happened
during the entire eight weeks. The Bishop did pay for
Scotty to attend a two-week Sports Camp nearby, but the
rest of the time, he was pretty much on his own. I was very
uncomfortable with him roaming a strange neighborhood
in a metropolitan area. He didn't even know how to get to
the apartment for the first three weeks or so. He had never
handled a lawnmower in his life because we had never had
a lawn to mow. Consequently, I wasn't about to let him take
someone else's lawnmower and use it without supervision.
There wasn't much for him to do but watch TV. Finally, I
sent him to his grandparents for a week but the other five
weeks were miserable for him.

- I was only invited to preach twice, even though the Rector
was gone for six weeks on his continuing education leave. I
was without supervision for much of the internship because
of his absence. Their Deacon was brand new and getting
settled and wasn't expected to supervise me. I was given one
two-hour slot during the week for a Bible Study (the "Beach"
doesn't lend itself well to summer activities that don't include
sand and sun and surf). I also led a youth program at a local
private beach where the Diocese has a summer chapel. I was
out there at least once and sometimes several times a week,
a fact which she overlooked. I also performed daily visiting
and hospital ministry; I was gone from 9:00 in the morning
until sometimes 6:00 or 7:00 almost every day so I was a little
put off by her charge that I was "lazy."

I finished "my side," and our dinner ended on a friendly
note as both Doug and Bob assured me that my explanations were
more than satisfactory. They said that the Bishop would be pleased
with how I handled the whole situation. They praised me over and
over for my honesty and my willingness to meet such difficult words
head-on. As they were winging their way northward, I made a
conscious effort to put "the letter" out of my mind and concentrate
on finishing my papers and graduating from seminary.

As that date loomed closer and closer, I was beginning to
nourish a real hope that The Process was becoming friendlier and
that I might not only survive it, but complete it successfully. You
gotta love an optimist.

CHAPTER NINE

"The Bomb"

The rest of the year was without serious incident, except when Scotty almost cut his thumb off making Pizza while I was studying in the library and when he got smacked in the mouth with a baseball while I was in class. Our neighborhood in Sewanee was a parent's dream. There were several spouses who didn't work outside the home "watching out" for our kids when they came home from school. It was the ideal situation for single parents like me. I was also fortunate to live in a duplex apartment, so there was another family "attached to us," as Scotty described it. The couple who lived there were at home, so they were right there when he came over dripping blood on their floor. He had slipped while slicing pepperoni and the end of his finger was still attached, but just barely.

One of them took him to the emergency room and the other came to find me in the library and took me to the ER. He was very brave but he had a very sore finger for a month. I bought pre-sliced pepperoni from that day and I don't think Scotty used sharp knives for another several years.

THE DREADED INTERVIEW

We survived that incident and before I knew it, I was finishing up final papers and preparing for a trip to Virginia and my interview with the Commission on Ministry and the Standing Committee. This was the final step before ordination. Finally, the school year was complete and, with Scotty safely ensconced with another family for the time I would be gone, I flew out of Chattanooga on a beautiful Spring day in May, not prepared or ready for what was to come.

My interview was scheduled for 10 in the morning. I arrived and was greeted warmly by my sponsor, who assured me that "the letter" was history and everything was fine. Armed with a cup of coffee, I was ushered into "the interview from hell." The first two

questions went like this:
- I understand that you are a poor housekeeper (sort of a statement that sounded like a question – "Is that true?").
- Who's going to take care of your son when you're working, especially when the phone rings in the middle of the night, and you have to go to the hospital to attend a dying member?

When I heard the first one, I was dumbfounded; I had been told – twice – that "the letter" was a dead issue. So why was this question even asked? Later, when I was re-living the interview with friends in Sewanee, one of the men said disgustedly that they would have never asked **him** that question. In fact, all of the men agreed that the questions were sexist, and that none of **them** had ever had to discuss who was going to take care of **their** children.

The interview went downhill from there as they probed and prodded into why I refused to lose weight, why I had stopped the counseling sessions (they weren't convinced that the counselor had moved out of town), why I couldn't control my son, and what kind of "less than traditional worship" was I advocating. I managed to answer every one of their questions honestly and openly. I was not defensive from the very beginning, when I said calmly "I never have been great at housekeeping. I just always seem to have more pressing things to do." I acknowledged that I continue to struggle with my weight, and I even shared with them some of what I had discussed with the counselor before she left Sewanee. It wasn't earth-shattering stuff since she had said that mostly I just needed to change my eating habits and stop munching when I get stressed. However, they had dwelt on the issue and what they saw as my obvious inability to deal with the emotional issues that kept me overweight. They questioned the reasons for my divorce, why I had chosen to raise my child as a single parent, and why I had stayed single so long (it had been 10 years by then – at this writing it has been 37 years!).

Just when I thought it couldn't get any worse, they informed me that they had received negative feedback from, not one, but both people that I stayed with during the past two summers. The priest, who had offered his and his wife's hospitality while I was in Richmond doing CPE, had just joined the Commission. Upon hearing the issues in "the supposedly dead letter," he decided that he was duty-bound to share some of the problems they had experienced with Scotty and me that summer.

Again, they had to do with Scotty's inactivity, and again, I had been told that members of the parish would be inviting him over regularly for pool parties, etc. That never happened once. Bored stiff, Scotty had evidently explored the house when they were out, curiously checking out the contents of drawers and closets. He didn't do any damage or take anything – he was just bored. I did finally send him to stay with my parents, but not until he had left the freezer door ajar one night while they were on vacation. He was getting something for our dinner out of their larder of frozen vegetables from their garden.

He had pulled out a drawer, and when he shoved it back in, the drawer didn't go all the way in, and he didn't notice it. The drawer kept the door from closing tightly, and, when they arrived home the next day, they blasted Scotty. When I arrived from the hospital, he was in tears and threatening to run away if we didn't go somewhere else to stay.

I called my parents and took him to their home on Lake Gaston the next day where he stayed until the end of my CPE course. I tried to talk to the couple about what had happened, but they were too angry and I left Richmond with nothing resolved between us. Even though I had apologized numerous times and tried to discuss it with them, they had refused. I even wrote them a letter after returning to Sewanee, but I was still the "non-communicator." Since it was all just too much like the next summer, they concluded that I didn't take these issues seriously and didn't seem to be willing to deal with them.

I was shaking by the time they had finished grilling me on every negative aspect of my life they could find. I kept waiting for them to comment on my whopping 3.75 GPA, and the faculty evaluation, which I had been given a copy of and had almost memorized. The entire faculty, even the two professors who traditionally refused to vote on female candidates, unanimously endorsed me for ordination. They described me as a "bright student who had grown tremendously in three years, a well-liked and highly respected leader who had made great contributions to the community, and a well-trained professional who was ready and able to be ordained a priest in the church."

One member of the Commission made a brief reference to

the evaluation, commenting that it was nice. The unspoken "but" left me with the distinct impression that they felt that I had the whole faculty fooled, including the dean. He was a highly respected Anglican scholar of many years, who had written numerous books, held many successful positions in the Church, and was Chair of the National Church's Board of Examining Chaplains. In other words, he was no "lightweight" and he certainly wasn't some upstart faculty member eager to please. He was serious and intuitive; since we had spent many hours discussing school issues, he knew me well and he said what he thought – that I would make a great priest.

THE AFTERMATH

After returning home to Sewanee, I spent many hours going over and over the disastrous interview with my classmates and several of my professors. I even talked with Scotty's counselor several times because I was so disturbed and angry about some of the things they had said. It was only a few days later that I received a phone call from the Chair of the Standing Committee who informed me that the Commission on Ministry had recommended me for ordination with the following conditions:

- That I pursue professional counseling to deal with my weight problem;
- That I address Scotty's problems from the two summer experiences and seek professional advice about being a single parent with a highly stressful position; and
- That I be re-evaluated by the faculty after they were told of the problems I had encountered in the summer placements.

BACK TO "THE END"

I was thinking, "Fine, I'll jump through their hoops – a little counseling can't hurt," when he dropped "The Bomb." "Susan, after much prayer and discussion, the Standing Committee has decided **not** to recommend you for ordination. There is no appeal process, but we may be willing to grant you another interview in a year." As far as I know, I didn't speak. I just dropped the phone and my next remembrance was my neighbor rushing in to find me sitting on the side of my bed staring at the wall. Scotty had tried to get me to talk and when I didn't respond, he ran next door and told them that he thought someone had died.

Well, that's pretty much what happened – I died. After

so much preparation, so much agonizing over what God wanted me to do, and so much hard work, I was dead in the water. The Bishop's comment in the upstairs room at Christ and Grace Church in Petersburg three years earlier was proving to be prophetic – "My concern is what you will do if you are not ordained after seminary." But, I thought of nothing at that moment, as I sat staring at the wall, and, when I finally began to come back to the world, the only words that ran through my completely fried brain was "How could they??"

It was, without a doubt, the most devastating moment in my life. I had lived through marital discord ending in divorce, but that was nothing compared to the loss and the pain I was feeling now. I really thought I'd never come out of this hellish place – it was a black hole in my soul that felt permanent and endless. I sat for a long time on the bed, crying helplessly, while Bob tried in vain to comfort me. There was no comfort for me – I had nothing now. No ordination, no job, no future. I couldn't see beyond the emptiness that engulfed me every time I heard those words in my mind, "The Standing Committee has decided not to recommend you for ordination." As hard as I tried, I could not make myself stop crying. Whenever I felt like I could get a breath and speak, the words that were repeating themselves over and over in my brain would grab me and reduce me to wrenching sobs again. After a few of these vain attempts to recover my composure, I began to feel a rising panic that I couldn't control. I vaguely wondered if this was what a panic attack felt like, as I became acutely aware of my heart beating so hard it felt like it would jump out of my chest. My thoughts were in a panic as well, as the words became louder and more insistent – we're not recommending you – no appeal – another interview – maybe in a year.

Suddenly those last few words sunk in to my consciousness, and my panic was full-blown. I heard myself crying, "What do I do now? Where are we going to go? How can they just dump me with nowhere to go?"I felt like I was coming apart inside, and that was making me even more panicky. I had never lost control like this, and I just couldn't find a way to get it back. My mother's instinct was barely operating but it did kick in enough to make me wonder where Scotty was. I looked around but couldn't see him. I began to panic again, this time with a new target, my son, and I remember thinking, "They were right. I am a bad mother. I haven't even spoken to him...." And then, Bob was there with a glass of water and a pill

that he held out to me. "We called your doctor and he prescribed
this to help you get some rest." My brain screamed, "Rest! How
can I possibly rest?!" but my body screamed louder, "I need to get
out of this black hole!" I took the pill gratefully, while I wondered
somewhere deep in my despair how many pills the doctor had sent.
Then I literally fell over sideways on the bed. I have no remembrance
of how my feet got onto the bed and where the blanket came from
because the blessed gift of a drug-induced sleep had swept over me
before my head hit the pillow.

  I awoke sometime later, and realized that it was dark
outside. I wondered why I was still dressed and what time it was. I
looked at the clock and saw that it was after 9:00. I wondered why
Scotty was still up watching TV as I could hear voices from the living
room and could see the light on in his room. I started to get up, but
I was immediately aware of the dizziness and the fog that seemed
to fill my brain and keep me from actually moving. I laid there
wondering what was wrong with me when I saw a small figure in
the doorway. I couldn't see his face because of the light behind him
but I knew who it was. I lifted my hand to him and he came over
to the bed hesitantly. His quiet "Are you OK, Mom?" threatened to
bring up the tears again but I was still in the clutches of what I had
figured must be Valium, so I was able to nod and reach for his hand.
He sank down on the bed and hugged me and we cried some until
the drugs took me back to La-La Land.

  When I came to again, his room was dark and the door
was almost closed, but I could still hear voices in the living room.
I tried to get up again, determined now to find out who was in my
apartment at this hour of the night when I recognized a voice that
was saying, "I hope she'll sleep through the night, but if she doesn't,
give her this. The doctor said that it will take a few heavy doses
to get her on an even keel, and then she can take these to help her
get through the crisis." My brain took in the words but all I could
do with them was wonder: "what pill?"; "what doctor?"; "why
do I need a pill?"; and "What crisis?" My eyes popped open at the
word "crisis," just as the voice from the door said, "Susan, are you
awake?" The swirling thoughts subsided and I tried to focus on the
figure in the doorway.

  I said, "Yes. But I think I wish I wasn't." I could feel the tears
starting again and I said, "I just don't think I can ever stop crying."

  My friend came over and handed me a glass of water and

put another pill in my hand, saying gently, "You just need to rest and let this stuff work. Your doctor sent it over and it's helping." I was in no condition to resist so I took the pill, laid back down and fell asleep again with my friend sitting beside me and holding my hand.

Gradually over the next few days, with the help of friends and neighbors, I began to come back from the brink. The lower doses of Valium were keeping the hysteria at bay while allowing me to begin to function and carry on lucid conversations with those who came and went with food and moral support. I had become slowly aware of the insistent and frequent ringing of my phone and as my mind cleared I realized that my friends had been fielding calls from fellow seminarians, friends and family from home and even the Dean had called. I became increasingly aware of the reality that I was going to have to climb up out of the pit I had been thrown into and begin to deal with this turn of events.

Scotty was very protective of me and didn't want to let anyone upset me again but I could tell that this had taken a toll on him. I knew that he had heard my hysterical recounting of the phone call and I was sure that someone must have explained to him what had happened but he was mostly silent, which was completely out of character for him – and sometimes I could see that he was trying to hide the tears. I wasn't surprised, after all, he was still a kid and he had been forced to watch his usually strong mother come completely apart right in front of his eyes.

Scotty and I had been on our own since he was two years old and his father and I had parted ways in divorce. I was the only parent he knew and, while he was a typical boy, he and I had a strong bond – we were a team and I didn't keep things from him. He was totally aware of what this journey meant to me and it was not just my journey; he was also part of it. Everything I did affected him and his life. So it wasn't just my life that got turned upside down when I entered seminary 600 miles from home. He had also been uprooted from his home, family, and friends; he had grown up faster than most kids as I became a full-time student and he had to take on way too many responsibilities for his age; he had lived through two summers of exile in the homes of strangers while I struggled through some of the most difficult experiences of my life. He was also looking forward to my graduation and our triumphant return to Southern Virginia. This was not only affecting me – it was his disaster too.

I knew that he was scared – I could see it on his face as the reality of the situation began to dawn on us both. Over the next few days, as we talked and as he watched and listened to the irate seminarians discussing the gross injustice that was being perpetrated on me, I watched his fear become anger – not only for all he had given up and what this meant for him – but it was a righteous, protective anger. He asked the same incredulous questions I had asked – how could they do this? What would we do now? Where would we go and how would we live if I didn't have a job? As a mother I was helpless – nothing I could say would bring back his security at this moment. I was scared but now I was getting angry! What did they think I would do now? How did they think I was going to provide for my child? What about him?

If all of this was too much for me – I could only imagine how Scotty was feeling as his secure, comfortable world was now virtually ended. The future felt as empty as this apartment was when we arrived three years earlier. It would soon be empty again as we had to move. We had been planning to move; but now, we had nowhere to move *to* and we shared this dreadful uncertainty. What would we do? Where would we go? How would we live? I could do nothing to relieve his anxious feelings or mine and so we both watched with a mixture of anger, uncertainty, and fear as neighbors and friends came and went, offering sympathy and support.

THE WAKE

The days following "the Bomb" really did look a lot like someone had died. There were people with us continually, answering the phone, intercepting visitors, finding room for the food in the refrigerator, comforting and reassuring Scotty that I would be fine, and trying to restore some semblance of normalcy in his life. They helped him get to school, went to pick him up when he couldn't handle it, and spent hours watching TV with him. The phone calls that had been coming from Virginia warmed my heart. Some were from friends and family but there were many calls from clergy and other people I knew from around the Diocese who had made my answer to God's call into their issue with the Diocese and its outdated stand on the ordination of women. It was common knowledge all over the Diocese that more than half of the Standing Committee members were anti-women's-ordination and that they probably would have taken the same action if I had been the perfect seminarian with no issues and no disgruntled letters to the Bishop. Those were the ones who called with their own righteous anger on my behalf.

Shortly after "the bomb" dropped, the Bishop called. He was sympathetic and even somewhat surprised but as I listened in horror, struggling to control my tears, he made it clear that he was unwilling to go against the Standing Committee's recommendation. This was something Bishops did only in the direst of circumstances and then it is done with fear and trembling. Every Bishop of the Episcopal Church will attest to the one unbreakable commandment – "Thou shalt not ignore the recommendations of the Standing Committee." He also believed strongly in "the process" and "letting it work"; therefore, I knew that, while he was highly supportive of my continuing in the process, he was not willing to circumvent this roadblock for me.

Well, you could hear the outrage all over the mountain! My fellow students were incensed that my academic success had been completely discounted and ignored. The faculty members who heard about it were stunned that their well-thought-out, serious evaluation had been questioned and discounted as uninformed. The Dean was livid! He dragged the phone number out of me and placed an immediate call to the Bishop and the Chair of the Standing Committee. This accomplished nothing except to increase the Dean's ire but, as I later discovered, he had "only just begun."

He wrote a scathing letter to the Standing Committee and the Bishop making it clear that he and the faculty were indignant and appalled at their apparent disregard for the opinion of the faculty and Dean of a major Episcopal seminary. He reminded them that seminary faculties take their responsibility to the greater church very seriously, and that their evaluations were carefully crafted to accurately portray the success or failure of each student in the process of priestly formation. He demanded that they re-consider their actions; he even sent a copy of the letter to the Presiding Bishop, making it abundantly clear that they did not appreciate being ignored by people who didn't know me nearly as well as they did.

Clergy friends called, one after the other, offering support, pledging to weigh in with the Bishop and the Standing Committee members. They made those calls, only to report that they had done all they could; the Committee was immovable. I love them all for

what they did and with every attempt I got my hopes up, only to
have them dashed again and again. It finally became clear to me that
my ordination just wasn't going to happen and, with that thought,
came the realization that I did not have a job. The chances of an un-
ordained seminary graduate getting a parish position was two-fold
– slim and none. Every prospective employer, whether a Church
Vestry or Rector, would not even need to know the reasons for my
rejection; just the fact that I was not being ordained was enough to
scare them away.

I was suddenly terrified. School was over, graduation
was in a few weeks, I had to vacate my apartment within 30 days,
and I had nowhere to go, nowhere to live, no money, and no job. I
thought I couldn't sink any lower but now I knew what the real
bottom looked like. For several days, I vacillated between anger at
these people for waiting until the last possible moment to ruin my
life and anger at myself for thinking that I could break through the
stone wall of discrimination against women in the priesthood that
was still obviously impenetrable.

It took about two weeks for the furor to die down on the
mountain as life had to go on, especially for the Senior Class, who
only days away from final exams and graduation. It suddenly dawned
on me that I was one of those. Nothing they did or said in Virginia
could take away the Masters of Divinity Degree I had earned and
would be awarded in a few short days. Thankfully, none of my classes
required written examinations, and I was exempted from one oral exam
by a sympathetic professor who said that anyone who had maintained
an A average throughout his course, deserved an A, period.

The debris left by the storm was palpable in the community.
Another of my classmates had encountered delays within his
Diocese because of a negative recommendation by the faculty.
The community had rallied around him and sweated it out, but he
had survived and was on the ordination track. I was the only one
who wasn't making plans for an ordination service, and that fact
was threatening to derail all the joy and excitement of upcoming
graduation celebrations. As miserable as I was, I wanted desperately
for all of us to put my disaster aside and really rejoice at the end of
our seminary ordeal. Until I communicated this to my classmates,
my personal ordeal had threatened to put a huge damper on the
one event that all Seniors look forward to with great anticipation for
three years – the "Crossing."

THE "CROSSING"

At the School of Theology, there is a delightful and ancient tradition called "The Crossing." It took place in St. Luke's Chapel several days before the academic graduation ceremony in the University Chapel of All Saints. It is, by far, one of the most moving experiences of my life. It was eventually eclipsed by my ordination but at that moment in time, it was the single most powerful milestone of my life. It's called "The Crossing" for two reasons:

1. Graduating seniors are recognized for successfully completing the process of "priestly formation," and for "crossing over" the fine line between seminary student and "almost-ordained" cleric. Most of the graduating students were continuing in the ordination process although there were a few who were not aspiring to the ordained ministry, but were receiving Masters in Sacred Theology degrees. So the "crossing over" was really a moment when we all traversed from the realm of student to the somewhat nebulous status of "educated theologian."

2. In a very moving and spiritual ceremony, each Senior is endowed with a "St. Luke's Cross" by the Dean of the seminary. It is a Celtic cross (with a circle around the top of the cross) which has been designed especially for the seminary; (called "St. Luke's Seminary" because it was housed in St. Luke's Hall on the University campus.) "The Crossing" refers to the ceremonial draping of the beloved cross around the neck of each future graduate making him or her an eternal member of the family of St. Luke's Seminary.

"The Crossing" was a monumental event for me as I was completing a chapter in my life that had seemed impossible but had become my destiny. As I accepted the cross from my dear friend, the Very Rev. John Booty, our Dean, I felt a huge sense of rightness, even in the face of my recent rejection. I knew that I had taken St. Luke's by storm; I had grabbed hold of everything I could, from a new way to learn to a new way to read the Bible; from "manual acts" to one-sentence sermons; from being a church member to being a church leader. I had excelled at every phase of St. Luke's program of "priestly formation" and, even if the "powers-to-be" in Virginia weren't ready for me, I was ready to meet the church as the Rev. Susan Bowman.

> "A woman is like a tea bag, you cannot tell how strong she is until you put her in hot water."
> *(Nancy Reagan quoting Eleanor Roosevelt)*

BUT NOT YET

There is no doubt that I was in "hot water" by the time I received my Masters of Divinity degree and prepared to leave "the Mountain" to return to Virginia. The days following graduation continued to be just as hot; now my predicament grew even hotter. The day approached that I would have to vacate my seminary apartment, but I still did not have a job. I was quickly running out of money, as I had done a masterful job of budgeting my grants and student loans to last until Graduation and no longer. I was forced to take out an additional loan of $1,000 to be able to pay June's rent and to feed us until I figured out what we were going to do.

It was scary and degrading beyond belief. Here I was with a Master's Degree from a prestigious University, on top of a Bachelor's Degree from the College of William and Mary. However, I had no job, no prospects, and a handful of rejections from the "Process" that had partially supported me for three years only to cut me off with nothing at the last moment. All of my classmates were preparing for ordinations, and almost all of them had positions in churches throughout the Southeast. Even students who had struggled with their Bishops over placement issues, were packing up with "Ministry Agreements" in their pockets.

I was the only one in my class without "plans." For three weeks, I thought I was in hell – the one reserved for candidates for ordination who dared to be different. Scotty knew what was happening, and I could read the terror in his 11-year-old eyes and hear the uncertainty in his voice. Still, he was a rock during those days, not adding to my difficulties, but actually providing me with support and even a little humor along the way.

Just when I had decided there was no hope, the Chairman of the Commission on Ministry, who had promised that he would work on finding me a position, was true to his word. Finally, I heard from him with the news that a Diocesan-supported home for emotionally disturbed girls was looking for a Chaplain and would consider hiring a layperson. I was invited to come for an interview, the

Bishop bought me a ticket, Scotty stayed with friends up the street, and I took off from the Chattanooga airport with some hope in my heart for the first time in weeks.

A TIME FOR PRAYER
    I need to pause here for a "sideline." As I have said, I was raised in the Episcopal Church of the 1950's and 1960's in an area of the country where any outward ecstatic expression of one's faith was highly suspect. Good Episcopalians did not talk about Jesus; the only one who mentioned him by name was the minister, and he always ducked his head when he said "Jesus" in a worship service. I can't remember anyone in my family talking about Jesus and, while we always said the grace before dinner, no one prayed any words out loud except:

> "Pardon our sins, O Lord,
> and bless this food to our use
> and us to thy loving and faithful service.
> Amen."

    Sometimes we would add "and make us ever mindful of the needs of others," but we didn't "say prayers" before bed, and there were no "family prayers." I cannot ever remember seeing my parents pray anywhere but in church, and then they were either listening to the minister pray, repeating the prayers from the book in unison with everyone else, or praying silently (like after communion or when first entering the pew before church when we went to the 8:00 service). I did not, therefore, learn to "pray." In fact, I didn't pray, except as my parents had, until I began working with the youth group in my church and watching and listening to them pray – out loud!
    Imagine my shock – and discomfort – the first time I heard a teen-ager praying out loud without a book. This kid was actually making it up as he went along. I had never heard anyone in the Episcopal Church do that, much less a teen-ager! I was amazed, and as I listened to him I felt good – it was an uplifting experience – until I suddenly realized that, if they asked him to say such a prayer, they might ask me next!!
    It was one of the defining moments in my spiritual journey, when I realized that I was almost 30 years old, and a teen-ager was

light-years ahead of me when it came to communicating with God.
In fact, I began to realize just how much I did not know about God.
This was when I began to feel the tug to seminary. I loved these
kids and I desperately wanted to be able to help them with their
own struggles about life and their faith. I wanted to be to them what
my friend was to me – their spiritual leader, mentor, and priest. I
wanted to minister to them on every level, including the sacramental
level; but even more than that, I wanted to know what they knew –
and more!

By the time I arrived at seminary, I was light-years ahead of
where I was, but I was still light-years from where I needed to be. I
was struggling with how to pray – the words to use. After all, I had
always had the words given to me; all I had to do was read them,
and after so many years, all I had to do now was say them. I knew
them all by heart, and they were in my heart, deeply engrained
in my spirit. Now they came out of my mouth naturally, without
thinking. Impromptu, off-the-cuff praying was something else,
however, and I was having a difficult time getting words to come out
of my heart, into my brain, and out of my mouth.

Of course, words came, but I needed the "right" words. It
was a long time before I learned the lesson that I have subsequently
taught to so many Episcopalians: God doesn't care what words you
use, just use them. God doesn't care how you say it, just say it. God
doesn't care how well it flows, just let it flow!

All through this entire ordeal, I was praying. I spent hours
contemplating what the priesthood meant, whether God was calling
me to it or whether I was calling to God, saying, "I want to be a
priest." I had developed the habit of turning off the radio in the
car and engaging in "windshield prayer." All over Sewanee and
southeastern Tennessee, whenever I was alone in the car, I began to
pray out loud. I talked to God with just the words in my heart, not
trying to force them through my brain first. I found it freeing; that
is how I learned to "say a prayer" when asked, even when I didn't
have my trusty Book of Common Prayer.

So, it's difficult for me to pray sometimes. I even find that it's
awkward to just talk about praying. I used to be ashamed of this and
I tried to hide it for years. But, through years of spiritual direction,
I have concluded that, because of my upbringing, talking about
praying just isn't something I do naturally. Actually, praying was
not something I did naturally either. It has taken more than 20 years

for me to realize that and to admit that I may never be one of those preachers who just take off in prayer at the drop of a hat and rattle off the perfect prayer without even thinking about it. I still struggle for the right words and I still feel more comfortable praying from my prayer book and so sometimes I still find myself **not** praying when I need to be praying.

In that plane from Chattanooga to Norfolk, I desperately needed to be praying. I was at a terrifying crossroads in my life and in my career. I had no job, no place to move to, and a deadline for moving out of our seminary apartment. I didn't have much of that $1,000 loan left and I would have to start paying it back to the tune of $57 a month on top of my major student loan as soon as I was employed. I knew that this was my only chance for a job in southern Virginia that was anywhere close to what I had been trained and educated to do or what I wanted to do. It was the only way that I was going to be able to stay close enough to the official process to be considered someday for ordination.

The Chapel
Jackson-Feild Home

INTERVIEW AT JACKSON-FEILD HOME

Yes, Jackson-Feild is spelled right. It was a Virginia family name that was given to this home for young girls in southeastern Virginia. Having lived in the Diocese most of my life, I was familiar with Jackson-Feild, since it had been a Diocesan institution for years. Many of the churches in the Diocese provided an annual offering towards the home's expenses. I wasn't very familiar with what they did at JFH, but I knew that it used to be an orphanage. At any rate, I knew in my heart, that if I didn't get this job, I would have to look for secular employment and that my dream of being a priest would be dead or at least seriously wounded.

I needed to be praying about this, and I was. I remember sitting in the plane as we took off, praying to God to "GET ME THIS JOB!" We were somewhere over Baltimore I think when I realized that God didn't take too kindly to demands, so I began to alter my prayer. It now went something like: "PLEASE GET ME THIS JOB!" By the time we landed in Norfolk, I had progressed to "Please God, help me get this job," and by the time I arrived at Jackson-Feild Home in the tobacco fields of Jarratt, Virginia, my prayer had become a simple, "Please God, help me!"

During the interview, I found myself praying before I answered each question, and it had now become just one word: "Please!" I repeated that word over and over all the way home to Sewanee, and for the next two days as I awaited word from the Director of the Home. Finally, he called and I vividly remember sinking to the floor of the kitchen in utter disbelief and relief when he said, "Susan, we'd like you to be our chaplain."

THE MOVE

I was still in a fog, when the Bishop called several hours later to congratulate me and offer to pay my moving expenses back to Virginia. That was when I cried. I knew that my parents would reverse their trip of three years earlier to help me get moved, but I had three times as much "stuff," and they were three years older. I had dreaded confronting this issue and was so grateful to the Bishop for sparing me any further agony. He gave me the phone number of a van line he used for his clergy, and we started packing!

The move was classic "God is in charge" stuff. I couldn't afford another trip home, so I arranged for the mover to come on a Friday morning so they wouldn't make it to Virginia until Monday. Scotty and I took off as soon as the van was full, and were in my parents' living room before midnight. On Saturday morning, we met a man with an apartment near my brother's house in Lawrenceville at 9:00 am, and by noon, I had the key and a year's lease in my hand. I called the mover's dispatcher and gave them the address. We had a home at last.

It was the perfect location, within blocks of family, close enough to my parents that Scotty could ride a bus from school to their house if I had to be late getting home or was away overnight.

My son was now almost 13 years old, was as tall as I was, and was now insisting on being called "Scott." He was excited about being home, proud of his mother, and anxious about being the "new kid" at the local public school. He didn't totally understand what had happened, but he knew that I had been hurt, and he was keeping his feelings about all that close to his teen-age heart; but I knew he was hurt and angry. He didn't talk about that because he didn't think it was OK to be angry at the church or at God, and I'm pretty sure he was angry at both!

Of course, all that got shoved aside as we settled into our new home – the top floor of an old Colonial home on Main Street in Lawrenceville, Virginia. We had four huge rooms, an old-timey bathtub, and a tiny kitchen. The washer and dryer were on the first floor, in the front hall, and there was a nice woman in the apartment on the first floor who had a dachshund that had such long toe nails, we could hear him walking all the way upstairs. Imagine how loud the barking was!

Scott got settled in school and I began my new job as a Chaplain for about 30 teen-aged girls, all of whom had been abused in life, mostly by parents or other family members. Most were alcoholics or drug addicts, and had been assigned by the court for treatment in our facility. It was a residential facility, where the girls lived in "cottages" with "housemothers" and attended the local schools.

THE GIRLS

They were all "tough" from so much abuse, angry at just about everyone in their lives, but they were mostly hurting. They came from all walks of life and all parts of the state. There were black girls and white girls but mostly, they were just girls. There was little distinction between them in their minds, except for the occasional racist comment that was a natural part of the teen-age existence in the South at that time. They all knew that they were in the same boat and their issues with each other tended to be more centered around their needs and their pain than around the color of their skin.

The treatment used was called Positive Peer Culture, a popular method in the 1980's, which consisted of group meetings, where the girls were encouraged and often forced by their peers to reveal their feelings about their lives and how they got to Jackson-

Feild. This resulted in many screaming matches, thrown furniture,
fights, and often a quick escape to the chapel, and my office where
they felt safe. Of course, I was not allowed to "harbor" them, and
I had to escort them back to the group; but this always gave me the
opportunity to let them know that I cared, that I was going to be
praying for them, and that we could set up an appointment for later
that day or the next day.

I hated sending them back but I loved being their "escape."
I was the route they took in a crisis, because it had to do with God.
My relationship with the staff grew, as they began to trust that I
would "work the program" and not allow the girls to avoid doing
the hard stuff. It was a terribly difficult position to be in, and I
agonized over each girl who came through my office.

I was also concerned about the issue of confidentiality. Since
I was not an ordained minister, the law protecting clergy from being
forced to reveal confidential information when shared during a
confession didn't apply to me; but, I *felt* like a priest and I knew that,
if I ever shared what those girls confided in me, my effectiveness as
their chaplain was toast. After sharing this with the staff at a cottage
meeting one night, I got called in to the Director's office the next
morning.

This was a serious issue, because of the new "mandated
reporting" laws. These laws required that anyone in an official
capacity who received reports of an abused child through
counseling, teaching, or any means, must report the abuse to the
authorities. This put the Home right on the top of that list, and all
staff were considered mandated reporters as well. The Director
informed me that any information on abuse that was shared with
me by a resident of the home must be reported to him immediately.
I said, "Steve, if a child came to me and begged not to be sent home
for a visit because her father was getting in the shower with her
every night, and if she made me promise not to tell, I could not and
would not share that information with you or any member of the
staff."

He almost rose from his chair as his face began to turn red
from anger and frustration, but I asked him to hear me out. I said
that my position as their chaplain bound me to keep confidences
confidential but, I continued, "you can bet your bottom dollar that
if I got that kind of news from a girl who was desperate not to go
home, I would find a way to let the staff know, if it meant camping

out on her bed, that they should not allow her to leave the campus. He looked at me as if I had grown a horn in my forehead and I said, "So, if I ever do that or anything that desperate, you can be assured that something is going on at home or somewhere that frightens her. Then you can find out what it is on your own. But I cannot tell you."

He was somewhat mollified but still concerned about the legalities and liabilities the Home would face in a situation like this. I agreed to speak with the Bishop about it, and I went back to my office and made the call. It was a few days before I could connect with the Bishop but, when I did, I posed the question to him. "What if a girl confided in me that she was being abused when she went for home visits, should I tell the staff what she told me?"

"Absolutely not!" he said.

"And what if a judge says I have to or be held in contempt?" I asked.

He didn't miss a beat. "I'll come visit you in jail." I not only had my answer, but I also realized that he was treating me as a priest. It was a hopeful sign and I grabbed it and held on to it.

CHAPTER TEN

"Meanwhile"

STILL A CANDIDATE

Meanwhile – the time between what is over and is no longer, and before what is next but is not yet. This was how Bishop Jones, our Interim Dean when I started seminary, defined the years that he and his wife were spending in Sewanee following his retirement. I learned from him that this can be a special kind of time. After graduation, I realized that I was in just such a place. It didn't seem "special" at first; it was just where I had to be between graduation and ordination, since I had been put on hold by the system. As I pondered my situation I decided that I was the "Meanwhile Chaplain," between my seminary training that was over and was no longer, and before ordination, which was next but not yet. It was an odd place to be, sometimes uncomfortable, as people didn't quite know how to treat me, what to call me, etc. I hated it at first, because I was still angry. I couldn't stop thinking about all my classmates who were getting ordained, starting their ministries wearing the coveted "clerical collar," and writing the "The Rev." before, and a + after their names.

COMING HOME

Actually, from the time I landed in southeastern Virginia again, I felt like a returning hero who had been stripped of my awards. I had survived three years of seminary, ending up with a 3.75 average and the dubious distinction of being the first woman to be President of the Student Body. I was the first woman to ever attend Sewanee from the Diocese of Southern Virginia, but in the world of the ordained clergy, I was nobody. I was in limbo, "no man's land" (now there's an unfortunate use of the wrong words for the right feeling), and I really struggled with my "not yet" status.

The Bishop was extremely supportive of me in this unexpected spot in which I had landed, and I will be eternally grateful to him for allowing me to join the Deacon's program even though I was not ordained. I knew the other participants and the instructors well, and I was pretty much treated like the others, except that I wasn't asked to read the Gospel at the closing Eucharist of our monthly meetings. The Deacons in the program were sympathetic to my situation and they basically thought I had been dealt a crummy hand but all they could do was commiserate, comfort, and act as if nothing was wrong.

I knew that something was wrong though, and, from the 2nd or 3rd session, was beginning to feel sorry for myself. When December rolled around and the Deacons in the program began to schedule their ordination services, order priestly vestments, and send out invitations, I could only write down their dates on my calendar, knowing that I couldn't possibly attend any of them. I felt like a schmuck, but I knew I'd cry through every word of the ritual that I wasn't going to be allowed to participate in either as clergy or as an ordinand.

As part of the Deacon training program, we were each required to have a mentor – an experienced priest to help us with the "newness" and the whole process of becoming "clergy." My mentor was the Rev. Richard Draper, the Rector of my parents' church in Lawrenceville and a member of the Board of Directors of the Home. We talked about how bad I felt when I was with my friends who had already been ordained and, while he was sympathetic, he was equally adamant that I had to "get over myself." I tried! I struggled and struggled with my harsh feelings towards the Standing Committee, which had sidelined my career and dashed my hopes, and my anger at the Bishop for not over-riding them. I thought I was okay about that, but as time passed and the reality of my non-ordained state began to impinge on my life, my anger became a serious threat to my spiritual wellness.

"Ordination is God's business," Rick said at least 10 times in every session. "When the time is right, it'll happen." I nodded obediently, agreed wisely, and then went home and cried myself to sleep. I had become convinced that God didn't have a thing to do with MY ordination, that he had totally abandoned me, and that I was doomed to roam the church as an "almost priest." I had met with the Standing Committee in October, and they were "pleased with my progress," but thought I needed more time. As Christmas loomed, I was facing another special celebration when I would have to be an observer, not a celebrant. Rick kept encouraging me to relax and let God "do his thing," but I just wasn't in a "whatever-you-say-God" mood.

THE HOOPS

I had obediently found a therapist to explore my past and, while it was somewhat helpful to re-visit some of my experiences, I didn't discover anything new about why I had trouble controlling my weight and keeping a neat home. It was the time I spent with a spiritual advisor that opened my eyes and heart to experiences that I had long ago labeled as "my own thoughts" or "my vivid imagination." By telling another person about them, something I had never done, I discovered a whole new realm of my being – my spirit. It was here that God spoke to me. It was here that I could actually have a personal relationship with God. Gradually, I began to find that there were some things I did need to explore further.

As I said earlier, I had been raised as an Episcopalian in Southern Virginia in the 1950's and 1960's when things like "a personal relationship with Jesus" and "God said to me" were expressions that caused raised eyebrows, to say the least. That kind of talk evoked looks of horror by some, and responses from most like "we don't talk like that – we're Episcopalians, not Baptists!" So I had stashed away in my mind all of the "Baptist-like" things I had experienced and labeled them as "not real" and unacceptable.

As I began to explore these ideas with a priest, who believed strongly in the personal presence of God and Jesus in daily life, I began to think that maybe I had been hearing God's voice all along. The blowing curtains in the retreat house, the feelings of being drawn to Sewanee, and the sense that God was calling me all took on an even deeper meaning. I realized that these things were real. They weren't figments of my imagination or "just me" thinking about what I wanted to do. They were real experiences which happened and were very real "in my spirit."

Now, you would think that, after three years of seminary including courses on Spiritual Theology, I would have figured that out. However, what I was now figuring out was that, when the spirit is "squashed" or "underdeveloped" (mine was both – squashed by a non-spiritual upbringing and completely unused), it takes a lot of work to catch up.

A DREAM?

As I began to explore my spiritual life in some detail, I was amazed at the depth of my own spiritual yearnings. During all those years that I spent in total "spiritual ignorance," I was also in denial of my own spirit's connection with God through the Holy Spirit. In fact, I distinctly remember thinking that the "Holy Ghost," as the church called it for centuries, couldn't be real because there is no such thing as "ghosts." Everybody knew that, except for the unenlightened and superstitious folks who believed in things like throwing salt over your shoulder if you spilled it or broke a mirror. They would look you right in the eye and say, with all seriousness, "Of course, there are ghosts – I've seen them in my attic."

I had not seen ghosts and didn't believe in them, so I had dismissed the "Holy Ghost" and with it, any chance of having a spiritual connection with God. I guess that's mostly why Christmas, my very favorite church holiday, came and went, and yet I was pretty cranky and didn't really enjoy the holidays. I went up to my old parish, St. Michael's in Colonial Heights, on the Sunday after Christmas, trying to get away from everything and get some "strokes" from some old friends. One of them convinced me that I should come back for the New Year's Eve party she was hosting. The couple I was staying with invited me back to spend the night, and since Scott was with his father for the week after Christmas and would be returning on New Year's Day, I agreed to come back up for the party. I could then more easily pick Scott up on the day after the party. It was fun; I was really glad I went, and by 2:00 am my friends and I were enjoying a final New Year's egg-nog. I was ready for bed by 2:30 and I fell asleep easily, thanks to the lateness of the hour and just the right amount of booze to make me sleepy.

At exactly 8:05 am, I woke up. Actually, my eyes popped open, and the first thing I did was feel the covers and pajamas to see if they were wet. I **knew** I was. I had had a dream that was so real that I just **knew** that the water that poured down on me in my dream had gotten me wet. My first thought was that my friend was going to be mad because I had gotten her bed wet!

It was so bizarre. The dream that was so utterly real, that I thought it had really happened. I was in some kind of building that resembled a prison, but I was not in the area that had cells. I was in the stairwell, where I couldn't seem to get to the door at the top of the steps, where I knew there were people who needed my help.

There were people in the stairwell who just would not let me get to the top of the stairs; it was as if they were trying to prevent me from helping these people (just like the Standing Committee who had blocked my ordination). I struggled and struggled to no avail.

Suddenly I found myself in a bathroom, fully clothed, next to the tub where the shower was running and the curtain was open. I was talking to God, who for some reason I was calling "Grundy." (My only clue about this is that, not far from Sewanee is a town called Grundy. Grundy, Tennessee was well known as the Stolen Car Capital of the South, and every seminary spouse looking for a teaching position, prayed mightily that God would provide one anywhere in southeastern Tennessee, besides Grundy.)

Anyway, God was instructing me to get into the shower, but I was steadfastly refusing. Several times, I heard the "invitation" to get in, and each time I refused, finally saying, "I'm not getting in the shower; I have my clothes on. As long as I'm out here, you can't get me wet." Immediately, the showerhead turned right on me and I was instantly drenched from head to foot. Not being a total fool, I gave in and stepped into the shower and at that moment, I woke up. This dream was so real that I knew in a nano-second that God had spoken to me.

I was still feeling the covers and the front of my pajamas, convinced that I and the bed had to be soaked, when my host called through the closed door that it was time to get moving. I answered her in a daze; but my brain finally cleared, and suddenly, I couldn't wait to tell somebody! I jumped out of bed, dressed, had breakfast with my friends, went to pick up Scott from his father and took off for home. I couldn't wait to tell Rick about this dream. Imagine my chagrin when I found him unavailable until the next day. "The nerve," I thought; "just when I need him the most, he's enjoying a Sunday afternoon with his family!"

I finally got to tell him about my dream, and he smiled and asked me, as every good mentor would, "so what do you think it means?" I was sincerely hoping that he was going to offer me more than the opportunity to figure it out for myself. I had been thinking about it for 24 hours, and I really wanted him to tell me what it meant. We talked about the possibilities for awhile and then he looked at me and said, "I think God just baptized you with the Holy Spirit."

Being the good conservative, traditional Episcopalian that I was, my first reaction was, "No way! We don't do that stuff in our church!" But, I knew better. I had learned that what I had thought

"baptized in the Holy Spirit" meant was very different from what
it really is. Over the past months, I had actually been praying that
God would touch me as he had touched many of my classmates and
good friends. They were all good Episcopalians and I still like them
all! They had not become ranting, raving "super-Christians" with all
the answers, and they had not tried to push their experiences down
anybody's throat, including mine.

A NEW ME – A NEW JOURNEY
        So, after those first few moments of panic, I thought to myself,
"Yes! Finally!" Rick and I talked for hours that day about what this
meant for me, and how to let God continue to speak to me and mold
me into his priest. For at least the next two weeks, everyone I met
remarked on the change in my demeanor and my disposition. Most
people asked, "What happened to you? You're so . . . different." At
first I was slightly miffed. I thought that I was a pretty nice person,
and all their questions made me feel like I had suddenly become a
nice person. This meant that I mustn't have been nice before. Then
I thought about what they were saying – that I was **different** – not
better, but different. I started to think about how different I felt, and I
began to see what they meant. Here's what I saw:

- I smiled a lot more.
- I was "mellow" (I didn't get uptight about stuff)
- My voice had dropped about an octave and was now as
  mellow as the rest of me
- I listened more
- My face was brighter and my countenance was lighter

        I remember thinking once, when I saw my face in a mirror,
that I didn't look so "weighed down" anymore. I felt different too:

- Happy – I actually wanted to smile and it felt so good that I
  did it constantly.
- Perfectly at ease with myself and my situation.
- Quieter and more centered.
- Connected to people as I began to hear what was being said
  around me.
- Free from the burdens that had me shackled.
- Totally connected to God

Well, there you have it! I was connected through the Holy Spirit to God, so I could feel this power and calmness all at the same time. I felt centered for the first time in my life, centered in God and not in my own needs and concerns. I found myself praying a lot more. It was easier and more focused. My "baptism" by "Grundy" in the "spiritual shower" was definitely more than just a dream – it was an intervention.

CHAPTER ELEVEN

Deacon

A NEW INTERVIEW

    After New Years, I received a call from the President of the Standing Committee informing me of the meeting date for our new interview. They had told me in October that would interview me again in January and they were true to their word. The President had changed and was now the Chaplain of the Episcopal college right in the town where I lived and he had scheduled the meeting for his convenience there at the school. I showed up at the appointed time feeling confident and at home – for two reasons:

1. I **was** at home – or at least half a mile away.
2. I was a different person and I knew they would see the changes.

    We met for less than 15 minutes and when they asked me to step outside in the hall while they conferred I knew in my heart that the answer would be "Yes." I could feel their approval – it was palpable. The atmosphere was so different from my last interview that I felt like I had landed on another planet – I'm sure they did too.

    In three minutes flat, the door opened and a smiling President invited me back into the room. Actually, he took my hand and led me into the room where every person was smiling and he said, "Susan, we have seen exactly what we wanted to see. Whatever you have done is what we were looking for and we're happy to inform you that we will be recommending you to the Bishop for ordination to the Diaconate." I felt weak in the knees – I was really glad I had sat down because I'm certain I would have fallen right on my face especially when they all rose to their feet as one and applauded.

    After almost five years, I was finally there! I had finally gotten through "the process." I was finally going to be ordained. The next day, the Bishop called and we joyfully set a date for the much-awaited ordination day. My Bishop had a rather unique sense of humor, as I've described, so I could hear the chuckle in his voice as he suggested that I be ordained on the feast day of Polycarp of Smyrna. I didn't dare tell him that I didn't have a clue who Polycarp was or where Smyrna was – I just let him have his fun and grabbed the date – February 23, 1985.

ORDINATION DAY

My incredible mother was ecstatic and she began all of the chores she had been planning for months. She made me a killer red stole out of the most gorgeous material that stubbornly refused to accept a needle, which made her task of cross-stitching a cross with silver thread on each end of the stole a more than daunting one. It took her days and I thought it possible she might decide that this "God thing" wasn't really worth it after all. But she persevered and we all lived through "the stole" without too much angst. It was finished in the early hours before dawn of February 23rd so it was a true labor of love.

The day that dawned was an atypical February day, even for Southern Virginia. By 1:00 when we all began gathering for the one-hour trip to Colonial Heights where the ordination was to take place, it was 65 degrees, the sun was shining brightly, and the convoy of vehicles from places like Georgia, South Carolina, and Florida following our Virginia cars took off amid much hilarity and confusion. We made it without too many stops for the little ones (after all, it was only an hour's trip) and by 2:30 we were anxiously awaiting the arrival of the Bishop, who was the key player, besides me.

He was a stickler for punctuality and arrived right at 3:00 and immediately convened a brief rehearsal during which I moved in and out of consciousness as I began to realize what a huge thing was about to happen to me **and** to my Bishop. He had recently ordained the first woman to ever be ordained in our Diocese and certainly the first he had ordained **ever** so it wasn't a totally new thing. But, I was the true "first" as I had been through the process as the first female he ever accepted for Holy Orders. I knew, and he knew, that this was a special day, not only for both of us, but for the whole Diocese.

There were some members of my home parish, St. Michael's, who opted out of this historic event – I knew who they were and I understood their angst over the situation. They loved me – I had been a faithful member of St. Michael's for almost 10 years – but they just couldn't accept a woman as an ordained person. Many of them wrote to me and some called me to apologize but I told them all there was no need for apologies. I appreciated the dilemma they were in and completely understood why they had chosen not to attend. I concentrated on all who **did** attend and the joy we shared that day but mostly, I was just on such a spiritual high that nothing could tear me down.

As I started down the aisle in front of the Bishop, I realized that my face hurt from smiling so hard. I felt like a new bride in a way. I was starting a new life with a new title, and a new companion. I could feel God's presence all around me and I have never felt so "right" in my life. I was in the right place, it was the right time, and we were doing the right thing. As I stopped at the front pew and acknowledged the Altar with a bow, I felt a tiny tap on my back, as the Bishop touched me with his staff. I was almost overcome with love and respect for this man who had put his integrity on the line and had so faithfully worked through his objections to women's ordination. As he reached the Bishop's chair at the top of the chancel steps and turned around, I could see the telltale twinkle in his eyes that said, "Let's do it."

Bishop Vaché was the consummate liturgist; every move he made and every word he said was rich with tradition and perfectly executed. He graciously welcomed Don Armentrout, my Church History Professor, who preached a stellar ordination sermon. As a Lutheran, he didn't really buy into the Anglican orders of ministry which required that a Bishop perform all ordinations, but he knew what it meant to his students and he knew very well what it meant to me. As he got to the end of his sermon, he looked at me and invited me to stand for the traditional "charge to the newly ordained." I could barely keep from swaying as I stood before him and he said, "Susan, I charge you to serve God and his church faithfully as a Deacon under the direction of your Bishop and I charge you to use every piece of knowledge, training, and confidence that we worked so hard to stuff into you in three years." (There was a chuckle from the Bishop and a few others.) Don ended with "Go with God into the world making disciples for him and for his church and may God bless you in your ministry."

I swallowed the lump in my throat and picked up my program. The Bishop was standing and indicating that I was to join him at center stage. This was the moment I had dreaded. The Prayer

Book requires the ordinand to kneel in front of the Bishop during the entire ordination ritual and my knees weren't so great. It was also very warm as the temperature outside had soared to 73 degrees, so I was appreciative when the Bishop paused to request that someone open the windows or turn on the air conditioner. Finally, it was time, and I knelt before him as he began to read the long introduction to the actual ordination.

Kneeling upright on a wooden floor for any length of time is a trial for healthy knees. With knees that are anything but healthy, this was not my idea of a fun time. "Arthur"itis and I were long-time acquaintances and I was almost used to the pain. However, it was most difficult to keep my balance when I closed my eyes, as I was always taught to do during a prayer. I tried several times and could feel myself swaying precariously so I kept my eyes open. The Bishop was a tall man so when I did open my eyes, I had a direct view of the bottom of his stole which had a multi-colored trim along the edges that had the appearance of a comb with alternating teeth of red and silver metallic threads.

The Bishop had begun to intone the traditional "Veni Creator Spiritus" ("Come, Holy Spirit"), which has serious "lulling" properties so I had to concentrate on something or I was going to topple over. All I could see in front of me were the ends of the Bishop's stole so I began to count. Yes, that's right, I started counting the little sections – there were 15 red and 14 silver on the left end of the stole and 14 red and 15 silver on the right side. I remember thinking how symmetrical that was and then I felt the Bishop's hands land on my head.

It felt like someone had set a heavy warm pillow on my head but it didn't just lie there. He had warned me that "I push hard because I want you to know that God means what he's doing" and he wasn't kidding. As he pushed on my head, I braced myself so I would stay upright and I focused on the words he was saying, "Therefore, Father, through Jesus Christ your Son,…" As he got to "give your Holy Spirit to Susan, fill her with grace and power…," I suddenly felt like someone had lit a fire inside of me. I was burning up! I knew it was warm in the church but this was way past warm. It lasted only a moment – as soon as he finished the prayer with "and make her a deacon in your Church" and lifted his hands from my head, the heat subsided.

Suddenly I was standing beside him while he introduced

me as the newest Deacon in the Church to a standing ovation (of course, the people were already standing but it was still neat) that lasted until he finally had to almost yell the words of "The Peace" – I only knew he had because of the resounding "AND ALSO WITH YOU" that came from the congregation. As we "passed the peace" I whispered to Rick Draper, who had sung the prayers of the people, "Was my face red during the ordination prayer?" He laughed and said, "No you were as cool as a cucumber!" No way!! I had been burning up but now I knew why – the Spirit had filled me and set me on fire. It was an internal fire – one that no one had seen – but one I knew was there and would take a lot to extinguish.

Finally, the Bishop began to talk over the din and people sat down to listen as he talked about the reception and other things. I could tell he was so proud of me and so pleased that we had finally come to this place in the journey. Of course, I knew it wasn't over yet. There was still the Deacon Training Program to finish (the Bishop had graciously allowed me to be part of the program when I started at JFH – just another glimpse into his faithfulness in God's calling) and then the "mother of all interviews" – the final step in the process in which everything comes full circle.

That was the future and this was now. I had been charged, ordained, sent forth, and I had work to do so, on that bright day in February of 1985, that final step to priesthood was far from my mind. I had a bunch of incredible girls to shepherd and I couldn't wait to get to "work" the next day with my first Deacon's Mass, planned with the Bishop's permission, and reserved sacrament from the ordination service. The Director had felt it best that they not attend the service so this was the best way I could include them in the biggest moment of my life.

"MS. REV'REND BOWMAN"

I'm not sure how many of them truly understood what had

happened to me the day before but they were very excited to see me
in a clerical collar for the first time. They had cleaned the Chapel
from stem to stern and were waiting in the driveway when I arrived
on Sunday afternoon. I climbed out of my car to excited cries of "Ms.
Rev'rend Bowman," "Hey Rev'rend Bowman," "Let me see your
collar," and "When are you gonna do church?" They grabbed my
bag and proudly led me into the chapel to show me the fruit of their
labors. The pews glistened with Scott's Gold, the floors were clean as
a whistle, even with the unseasonable weather turning the property
into a slush/mud/snow lake.

Amid their excited questions and nervous laughter, we all
got vested and, as I played my guitar, we all processed solemnly
down the short aisle to the Altar where we gathered to sing
everybody's favorite, "They Will Know we are Christians by Our
Love." When we sang, "We will walk with each other, we will walk
hand in hand," a girl on each side of me reached out to grab my
hand and then realized that they were otherwise engaged with the
guitar. So, one laid a hand on my back and the other crooked her
hand in my elbow and before we had finished half of the verse,
every hand in the church was in the hand of another. At the end
of the verse, I could feel the excitement building as we got to their
really favorite part. The Acolyte with the cross looked at me with a
questioning eye, and I nodded, just in time for them to finish that
verse, at the top of their lungs, "and together we'll spread the news
that GOD IS IN OUR LAND."

After the lessons were read perfectly by the girls, except
for the Gospel which was my duty as a Deacon, I said, "Today's
sermon is going to be a very special one because I want to tell you
about my ordination and what it means, my new duties as a Deacon,
and the Deacon's Mass we are celebrating." They were listening
to everything with great anticipation and they got more and more
excited as I said, "I climbed the steps to where the Bishop stood and
they had put a pillow there for me to kneel on, but it still hurt as I
knelt down in front of him."

I heard one girl groan, "Oh, I know that hurt."

I was accustomed to their sermon "abridgements," and I
acknowledged her, "You bet it did."

"The Bishop was great, though; he helped me kneel down
and held on to my arm while I got as comfortable as I could be on
these knees." They all chuckled appreciatively. "Then he started that

long prayer I showed you last week," I continued, "and suddenly I thought I was going to fall right over in a heap."

"Woo-eee! That Bishop would have been so shocked, I bet he'd have fallen over, wouldn't he?" came from a girl in the back.

They laughed at the picture that made in their minds and then I told them, "Listen – here's how I kept from falling over." I picked up the end of my stole and showed it to them, "he had on a stole like this but it had these little silver and red squares along the bottom of each end and that was all I could see – the ends of his stole were right in front of my eyes. So I counted them."

My free spirit in the back yelled, "You what?"

I repeated, "I counted them. I had to have something to do to keep from falling over." Everybody was laughing by now, so I let it die down and I looked around dramatically. They got really quiet and I asked, "Anybody want to guess how many squares there were?"

Our sermons always went on like this as I encouraged the girls to be inquisitive about what I was preaching and they always seemed to feed me with the best straight lines. My sermons may not have been exactly what Edna Evans would have approved, but they were effective. Those girls remembered more of my sermons than any congregation ever. After they zeroed in on the correct number of squares in the Bishop's stole, I said, "So, here I was, really into this stole, when all of a sudden, his hands crashed down on my head and I almost went down again."

There was another appreciative groan from the back pew. "But I was expecting that because the Bishop had told me he wanted to be sure that I knew he was serious and that God was serious. I just stiffened my legs and hung on until I heard him say, 'make her a Deacon in your church.'" Before they could respond, I said, "And you know what?"

"What?"

"I felt like he had lit a fire right inside my heart." There was silence in the church.

From the back pew came a suspicious, "Whatchoo mean – a fire?"

I told them, "I felt like somebody had turned up a heater right inside of me to about 200 degrees...."

"That woulda burned you slap up!" came from the back and we all laughed.

But I brought them back, "I felt like it would but, you know,
I've learned that God doesn't burn us up. God heats us up with his
power and his love, but he doesn't destroy us."

Right on cue, my faithful questioner asked, "So why'd he
make you so hot?"

I hadn't expected that one, so I had to think quickly, but God
was right there with the answer, "because he knew I'd need to be hot
to get through to you!"

The laughter exploded like a firecracker and when it died
down, I heard, "Well it worked."

I walked back to the pew where she sat and hugged her and
said, "Thank you for making my day just perfect."

The girls were hushed as I gathered them around the Altar
and explained the "Deacon's Mass." I took the bread in my hand
and said, "The Bishop took the whole plate of bread, including this
bread, and he put his hands over it and asked God to make it the
Body of Christ." They all nodded sagely as I had been teaching them
about communion for the last several weeks. "Then the Bishop took
the cup of wine (of course, we had to use grape juice) and asked
God to make it the Blood of Jesus." There was a holy silence as they
watched me imitate the Bishop's movements. "Then he did this right
over top of them" (I made the sign of the cross like the Bishop did),
and asked God to make them holy and us holy and everyone who
would eat the bread and drink the wine holy together."

I stopped and looked around, "So God did it and now we
can have the Body and Blood of Jesus just like we all did yesterday
in St. Michael's." I felt the tears pricking my eyes and I said, "I really
wish you all had been there with me," and they were all tearing up
and even my tough girl from the back pew was sniffling. It was a
powerful moment, one I would carry with me for a long time as the
most perfect communion moment I had ever experienced.

These girls were so hungry for something of God in their
lives; they loved "acolyting" (carrying the cross and candles and
serving at the Altar), they learned every song I knew and loved
to sing them over and over. While some of them started coming
to Chapel to get out of the stress of the cottages, most of them
wanted what I was offering. Our Bible Studies were lively and they
sometimes would almost get into a fight over who was going to
carry the cross.

We "did the dishes" as they called the ablutions, two of the girls solemnly carried the chalice and plate back to the little kitchen that served as a Sacristy, and put them carefully on the counter like I had taught them. We raised the Chapel roof with a rousing rendition of "Pass it on" and in every verse, they sang/shouted "That's how it is with God's love, PRAISE GOD! once you've experienced it, you'll want to pass it on."

After securing the Chapel, we adjourned to the dining hall for a raucous post-ordination party and it wasn't long before there was a lively discussion about what to call me. "Susan" was out as staff could not be addressed by first names. "Reverend" isn't really correct, but my explanations about that fell on deaf or non-comprehending ears and then all that was left was to decide which was right – Rev'rend Ms. Bowman or Ms. Rev'rend Bowman. Each girl had a definite opinion and, the debate soon ended as one of the girls who had successfully completed the program, said diplomatically, "Anything that's OK with the Chaplain is just fine." And that was the end of it. I didn't care what they called me, as long as they called me.

ON THE ROAD AGAIN

One of my duties as the Chaplain was to "take JFH to the Diocese," the perfect job for a Deacon, who is ordained to bring the world to the Church and the Church to the world. Deacons offer the Prayers of the People in the liturgy as God's servant who brings the needs of the world to the attention and prayer life of the church. Deacons are also charged with bringing the Church to the world as those who are "Permanent Deacons" traditionally hold down jobs and careers which involve some kind of ministry – to the homeless, to youth, etc.

My temporary role as a Deacon fit right in with this concept of the Diaconate and I loved it! Week after week I took the girls – whole groups at a time – to churches around the Diocese, where we would worship with the church members, I would be "the Deacon at the Mass," and usually preach the sermon. I was a good preacher, thanks to my training in Sewanee, and I used my skills and my love of the girls to bring their plight and the needs of the home to the attention of the church and its members. JFH was a Diocesan-supported institution, which received subsidies from the courts and social services agencies which place the girls, but there were many things, such as the Chaplain's program and the chapel, that could not be funded by those sources. So the home relied on donations from Diocesan churches as well as from the Diocese itself.

Our weekly jaunts were a high point in my ministry, even to this day, as I watched these girls who were hurting from a life of abuse and neglect, get up in front of a church full of strangers and tell about their lives before JFH, their new lives at JFH, how the program helped them deal with their pain and problems, and usually how much they loved "Ms. Rev'rend Bowman."

We made some good friends all around the Diocese and we always were delighted to receive a delivery of some much-needed items from one of "our parishes." In the midst of all the traveling, I completed the Deacon's Training Program, I baptized my first new Christian, with the Bishop's permission – one of the girls at the home – and my ministry there continued to be full and exciting.

Christmas was truly an experience of Christian love as all of those parishes and many others would heap gifts on these girls who had nothing but themselves to hold on to and most had nothing to go home to when they left. Many of these girls found solace in the loving care they received from the generous churches of the Diocese of Southern Virginia. We had a huge party after the Deacon's Mass on the Sunday night before Christmas, complete with Santa Claus and it was an especially joyful celebration that year because just 5 days before I had faced the final interview of "The Process."

CHAPTER TWELVE

Priest

THE "MOTHER OF ALL INTERVIEWS"
My final interview with the Commission on Ministry for ordination to the priesthood took place at the conference center where I first attended BACAM five years before. I was very clear about my calling to ordained ministry in answer to their first question, "Why do you feel a need to be ordained?" Through the many steps of this process, I had honed it down to this crisp and clear statement: "I want to help people (especially young people) to know about God, Jesus, and the Holy Spirit, and I want to be able to minister to them sacramentally through the Eucharist, Confession, Absolution, and other priestly ministrations."

The thing I remember most is how I felt. I wasn't nervous; I was confident and calm. I wasn't anxious; I was serene, and I could tell that it showed in my face, my demeanor, my voice, and my words. Rick was present beside me, despite his physical condition; he had undergone oral surgery to remove his wisdom teeth, and he was in awful pain. During the interview, with his wife literally holding him up, he spoke eloquently about our work over the past year and a half. He reported how God had touched me, filled me, and was already using me as a priest in the lives of "my girls." In addition, many people around the Diocese had been touched by my preaching and presentations at various churches.

He praised me and gave them his unqualified recommendation that I be ordained a priest. With one last burst of his flagging energy, he pointed out to the Bishop, the Standing Committee, and the Commission on Ministry that the fact that he had made it there (three hours round-trip) and sat through the interview (more than an hour) in his condition, spoke louder than anything he could say through his clenched teeth. He made it abundantly clear that his actions spoke louder than his words, and that he would not have even gotten up from his bed that day, if he didn't believe in his heart that God was calling me to the priesthood, and that I was ready to be ordained.

There was a profound silence and then someone started applauding. In less than five minutes, he and his wife were out the back door, in their car, and on the road back to Lawrenceville. Before they had time to clear the city limits, the Chairman of the Commission on Ministry called me back into the room and delivered the good news that the Commission had unanimously recommended me for ordination. The Standing Committee had also voted to recommend to the Bishop that I be ordained, and the Bishop was ready to set a date for my "priesting." With his characteristic wry humor, the Bishop pulled out his "brains" (as he called his calendar), flipped a few pages, and announced that he thought the Feast Day of the Conversion of Saint Paul would be a "highly appropriate" occasion for the ordination of a woman to the priesthood. There was laughter, more applause, and I felt like God had swooped right into that room, and gathered us up into one great moment of joy, that can best be described with these familiar words: "God's in heaven and all's right with the world."

ORDINATION DAY (#2)

The day dawned gray and cloudy; it was January 25, 1986, my parents' 45th wedding anniversary and my ordination day. By 10:00, it was sleeting, and by 2:00, it was worse. Thankfully, the Bishop was like the United States Post Office, "Neither snow, nor ....." He arrived as promised at 3:00, and, in spite of the weather, the church began to fill up by 3:30 for the 4:00 service. The Bishop was in grand spirits, joking around with the other clergy who had braved the elements, particularly about the irony of ordaining a woman on the Feast of St Paul, the reputed male chauvinist of the New Testament. Of course, we all know that he has gotten a bad rap all these years, but it made for a little levity on an otherwise gloomy day.

The freezing rain let up just in time for us all to trek from the parish hall to the front door of the church for the processional. There were a goodly number of clergy present, so we made quite a scene in our finery coming down the hill from the parish hall to the church. The Bishop led the way in his red and white robes with his gold and white miter on his head, while the wind whipped our vestments around our legs. The processional began on time, and the church was almost full, a testament to the support that I had in the small community where my family lived and worshiped. People who weren't quite sure they supported women's ordination as a concept, accepted me as a reality and came out to be part of history and to support me and my family.

Ordinations are typically what I will call graciously ostentatious. Every member of the clergy wore their finest red or white stoles, depending on the day or season. The church was in its glory as well, with flowers on every flat surface and the attendees decked out in their Sunday best. It was, in a word, grand! Our Bishop was a striking figure, who carried out the functions of the Celebrant with grace and dignity. From the first words of the liturgy, all the levity was put aside, and Charles, as the clergy called him in private, was gone – he was the Bishop (God's vehicle) and I was the Ordinand (God's chosen). When it was time for the ordination, I knew he had been there many times before, and once before there had been a woman before him. I knew in my heart, that he knew in his heart, that this was right.

There was a long introductory prayer, during which the Bishop was required to offer the traditional opportunity for "anyone who can show any reason why this ordination should not take place to speak now." There had been instances around the country of people rising from the congregation to object to the ordination of a woman, so we all held our collected breath, while the Bishop glanced quickly around the church. He had a definite look on his face that said, "don't even think about it." The next line was "So, is it your will that Susan be ordained a priest?" and the people answered, "It is."

St. Andrew's is a small church, but those two words echoed through the building like a thunderclap. The Bishop smiled, and then placed his heavy hands on my head. There was a slight pause, while the clergy gathered around and each added a hand to signify that ordination is for the whole church. He had warned me ahead of time that, at that moment in the service, it feels like the whole weight of the church is on your head, and that it's hard to actually stay upright. Wow! He was exactly right! I felt the weight of his hands first and then they started to pile on. The circle was big, as there were about 15 to 20 clergy present. The ones on the periphery actually had their hands on the backs and arms of those in front of them, which added to the pressure. By the time they were all in place, and the Bishop continued with the prayer, I was struggling to keep from toppling over on the rug. With my weak knees, I was barely able to kneel anyway, and the pressure of all those hands (all men but one) actually caused me to sway. I know that I was only staying upright through the support of those hands that were, at the same time, turning me into a "bobble-head." I was grateful that the rest of the prayer, while the most important, was also blessedly brief. It ended with the simple prayer that God will "make her a priest in your church."

When the prayer was over, and the Bishop signaled the priests with a flick of his finger to remove their hands, I almost fell over from the sudden lack of pressure. The Bishop knew well what it felt like, and he left his hands in place just long enough to allow me to re-orient myself. When the prayer was over and the loud AMEN was echoing throughout the church, he leaned down, took my hand, and said quietly, "Welcome." It was finally done – my journey had brought me to my goal and it was complete. It had taken many years, many heartaches, much pain and agony, and a lot of joy and laughter to arrive at this moment. I felt them all rush through me, as my mother and family members draped me in the vestments of the priest. My brand new chasuble and stole were made by my loving mother, who was still wiping her eyes up in the choir. Then the bishop helped me to my feet and presented me with a Bible that had been purchased for the occasion by my spiritual director, the Rev. Norm Baty. He then put his arm around my shoulders, turned me around, and proudly presented me as "the newest priest in the Church of God."

I almost fainted! The applause was deafening; there were even a few cheers and "whoops." My mother was still crying, the Bishop was still grinning, and I was numb with relief and shock. After the applause died down, I invited the congregation to pass the peace with the traditional words that I said for the first time in my life, "The peace of the Lord be always with you." The standard Episcopal response, "And also with you," bounced off the walls of the church and filled me with the most incredible sense of God's peace that I had ever experienced. The Bishop hugged me, wished me God's peace, and we moved off to greet the other worshipers. This went on for some time, until the Bishop called us back to some semblance of order and made his traditional explanation about the Bishop's chair. Here's how it went: "Since the Diocese of Southern

Virginia does not have a cathedral, which is traditionally the seat of the Bishop, each congregation has a chair that symbolically makes that church the Cathedral for the day." He could never resist adding, "So, I guess you could say that the Bishop carries his seat with him." It always got a laugh, and this day was no different.

While one of our perpetual Deacons prepared the communion elements, the Bishop and I sat and listened to the choir, which had prepared the loveliest music for the occasion. My parents could hardly sing a note; in fact, they were there trying not to cry. Things only got better, as I concelebrated the Eucharist with the Bishop and served the communion bread for the first time. I had been so busy, I hadn't had time to think about the really big moment to come – the Blessing. Now, as I sat next to the Bishop while the Deacon did the ablutions (that's church-speak for washing the dishes), I began to feel panicky. I had memorized the blessing that I had heard countless times from countless priests, and I had practiced and practiced until it felt almost automatic. I was still worried that my mind would go blank, or that I'd leave out something really important.

Finally, it was time. The Bishop faced the congregation and said, "I will now ask our new priest to pronounce God's blessing." He turned to me, bowed ever so slightly and stepped aside to give me center stage. I stepped up, took a deep breath to ward off the panic, and began: "The peace of God which passes all understanding, keep your hearts and mind in the knowledge and love of Jesus Christ our Lord." Just as I had seen priests and bishops do for my whole life, I raised my hand and began to make the sign of the cross over the congregation as I went on, "And the blessing of God Almighty, the Father, the Son, and the Holy Spirit be with you this day and forever more. Amen." I could hardly breathe. The power of those words had always brought me comfort and a sense of divine protection, but today they packed a huge punch. I had actually spoken those words to this congregation as God's agent of blessing. I was very thankful that there was a Deacon present to give the Dismissal, because I couldn't even think straight at that moment. I opened my hymnal to the final hymn and tried to sing, but it was the third verse before any noise would actually come out of my mouth.

I preceded the Bishop down the aisle, and, when the hymn was over, the Deacon stepped forward and, in a loud, clear voice,

brought my ordination service to a close, "Alleluia! Alleluia! Go in
peace to love and serve the Lord." The congregation responded,
"Thanks be to God. Alleluia! Alleluia!" It nearly blew the roof off the
church; we could scarcely hear the strains of the organ playing the
postlude over the excited voices of my friends and family as they
began to move toward the doors to follow us to the Parish Hall for
the reception.

We didn't waste any time getting there, as the temperature
had dropped, and the rain had become mixed with tiny pellets of ice.
I fully expected that many people would head straight for their cars
to go home before it got any worse, but every person headed up the
walk to the Parish Hall. It quickly filled up with stomping feet, as
they dried their shoes to keep from tracking the mud onto the floor.
We were disrobing in the basement, and it sounded like a herd of
elephants above us, but no one really cared much about anything
except the incredible thing that God had just done. As the Bishop
packed up his vestments, I was flooded with such a deep respect for
him that I felt my throat closing with the huge lump that always told
me that I was becoming overwhelmed with my emotions. I got busy
packing up my own vestments before I made an utter fool of myself
by bursting in to tears, and we all quickly made our way upstairs to
the reception.

It was a delightful party, with delicious looking food
spread out on several tables, but I had no time for any of it, as I
was constantly surrounded by well-wishers with their hugs, hand-
shakes, and flashing cameras. The crowd finally began to clear
out, and my father began to look anxious as we still had a good
half-hour to drive in the freezing rain. We were on our way to the
Kennon House, our favorite restaurant on Lake Gaston, where my
parents had reserved the back room for a grand buffet dinner and
celebration. Some folks headed for home because they were afraid of
the weather getting worse. It was still raining, but, fortunately, the
temperature had risen, so that it was just rain, and we were able to
make the drive without incident. It was a raucous crowd that finally
gathered in the warm and cozy dining room for some of the finest
food in Southside Virginia.

We waited and waited for the Bishop, who was rarely
late, so we were a little worried about him. Finally, one of the local
clergy said the blessing and we started serving ourselves dinner.
The Bishop arrived before we had finished going through the

line, just in time to jump in and get dinner. He and his driver had misunderstood the directions and ended up in North Carolina. They back-tracked quickly and arrived a little sheepishly, amid much teasing and joking about the "errant Bishop."

Dinner was grand, as usual, at the Kennon House, with crispy fried chicken, homemade mashed potatoes, fresh green beans (in January?), their killer dinner rolls, and sumptuous desserts. Then, there were the remarks and testimonials. The Bishop started off by welcoming and paying tribute to his "punniest Priest" by re-telling one of the many "punny" stories we had shared over the years. Everyone groaned obediently and laughed at the stories told at my expense by family members, long-time friends, and now-colleagues. We took time to pay tribute to my dear parents on their 45th anniversary, without whose love and support I would not have made it through the long journey. It was one of the most wonderful "parties" that had ever been thrown for me, and I reveled in it – every minute and every word.

THE NEW PRIEST IN ACTION

The next morning, I was scheduled to be the Celebrant at the Sunday Eucharist at the Episcopal church in Alberta, Virginia, one of the three churches in the Lawrenceville charge. When I got up, it was snowing, and I was afraid it would get called off; but, the snow let up as we started out for Alberta. By 8:00 am, I was standing in the back of the church waiting to process in for the first time at the **back** of the line – the place reserved for the priest who was celebrating the Eucharist. It was a heady moment, but nothing will ever compare with the first time I said the words of consecration and institution, made the sign of the cross over the elements, touched them and asked God to make them the Body and Blood of Christ for us. I felt something like an electric charge running through my hands, and I had another of those moments of utter clarity, when I knew that I was doing exactly what God wanted me to do.

We left almost immediately after the service in order to arrive back in Lawrenceville for the 9:30 service, where I was to be the Celebrant once again. It gave me such a thrill to celebrate the Eucharist in that holy place, where I had become a priest less than 24 hours before, that I had to struggle past that lump that was spending more and more time in my throat. The people, who had watched me struggle with the process and who had supported me through it all, were now before me in the church that had become my second home for the past three years. They were almost all there on that snowy morning, and we blew the roof off again with our lusty singing and enthusiastic responses; then we tramped off to the Parish Hall in the snow, for yet another reception, for me and my new role in the church.

That afternoon, there was a meeting of all the churches in our Convocation preparing for the upcoming Diocesan Convention in February. Rick and I struggled up there in the snow; at this point, I wasn't missing anything that would be my "first" experience as a priest. I was warmly welcomed by most of the clergy and laypeople present, but the shock of the day was when the Rector of St. Paul's in Petersburg, Virginia, where I was born and raised, invited me to be the Celebrant at the main service on Easter Sunday. I was astounded. Rarely do clergy give up "their altars" on such a vitally important feast as Easter, and I was touched and moved by his gracious invitation.

I accepted readily, but when I tried to thank him, I choked up at his generous gift. There were so many people congratulating me, and then there was a business meeting, so it wasn't until Rick and I were on the way to JFH for Sunday services, and yet another "first time" celebration of the Eucharist, that the reality really hit me. I would be standing behind the Altar of the church where I had sat wishing I could grow up to be a minister. I would be in the chancel, inside the communion rail, where I had never been allowed to enter, because only the minister and the Altar Guild were allowed in there

Rick and I arrived at JFH, where the staff and girls waited with a huge celebration. We had a moving and exhilarating worship experience; all the girls I had trained to read and acolyte behaved and performed perfectly. The chapel was full, even as the snow fell outside. Even some parents who had been part of their daughters' successful treatment returned with the girls to celebrate my "big day." As I, once again, uttered the sacred words of institution over the bread and wine, served the Eucharistic bread, and pronounced God's blessing, I was filled with wonder and awe at what an amazing thing God had done with my life. I was a priest, and it felt so right.

After the service, there was a scrumptious dinner in the dining hall with cake and balloons and lots of laughter and tears. It was not what we had all wanted, as most Deacons are ordained to the priesthood in the parish where they are serving, but the chapel just wasn't big enough; so, we had moved it to St. Andrew's in Lawrenceville. The girls and staff had attended the ordination, so they weren't feeling too left out.

We were exhausted by then, but there was one more stop, a tiny little church in the country near JFH where I truly learned how to be a pastor. Emmanuel Church in Callaville, Virginia is the 3rd part of the Lawrenceville cure, a sweet little church that doesn't hold much more than 25 people, but it was always more than half full with some very faithful Episcopalians who loved God, each other, and their church. They came to love me, and I grew to love them over the year of my Diaconate, when I developed the habit of "dropping by" to assist Rick with the services on my way home from JFH on Sunday evenings. This night, the church was overflowing. Even with the snow flying, every member of this little congregation had come out to celebrate with me, and I have a permanent picture in my mind of these people in their pews hanging on my every word and rejoicing with me in my new role.

It was an absolutely unbelievable and L-O-N-G day. We started out for Alberta at 7:30 am, and it was well past 9:00 pm when I finally pulled up in front of my apartment. I felt like I had been wrung out like a sponge, but it was the best feeling I ever had at the end of such a long and draining experience. Somehow, God managed to squeeze everything out of me, yet he left me with the most amazing sense of accomplishment, humility, and completeness.

As I crawled into bed at last, I found myself wondering where I would have been at that moment, if I had spent the past year and a half as an ordained parish assistant somewhere. What if I hadn't endured the agony of rejection and the long, winding journey that I had just completed? I started my prayers with a question that I had asked God many times: "Why did I have to go through all of this? Why couldn't I just have gotten to this point the same way as everybody else I knew?" As usual, I heard no booming voice, and I saw no flashing lights. In fact, for some time, there was such profound silence that I thought God had finally finished with me and gone to bed!

I decided that God must be like any of us, waiting for some kind of appreciation from me for all the blessings of the day. I said, "Sorry, I should have started with this: Thank you, thank you, thank you! You made this the most glorious day of my life, and I am so grateful to you for bringing me to this day and making me your priest." I still didn't hear anything, but the silence wasn't quite so deafening, so I continued with some specific thank-you's: for the Bishop and his courage, for Rick and his faithful support, for my parents for their steadfast love, for Scott and his love and faith in me, and for all those who had helped me survive the ordeal and come out of it whole. My eyes were beginning to droop and burn, so I knew sleep was imminent. I ended my prayers with the usual, "Keep me safe, keep me humble, and keep me in your love."

I had finally learned to pray, but what had I not mastered until that early morning "shower" was the art of "Letting go and letting God." I had been a "worrywart" all of my life, and, all through this long and painful process, I heard the words of those around me telling me to trust God. While my new spiritual awareness had allowed me to put most of the process in God's hands, I had not been able to stop worrying completely. I wish that I had found these words of Henry Ford during that long and difficult process, as they are exactly what I needed then:

> *I believe God is managing affairs and that He doesn't need any advice from me. With God in charge, I believe everything will work out for the best in the end. So what is there to worry about?*   **-- Henry Ford**

On some level, I think I had always known that everything would turn out for the best, but I could have saved myself many agonizing hours, if I had been able to live that out on a daily basis. I was totally aware that, as my father's daughter, I would never be able to let go completely, as Henry could, but now that I had finally reached my goal, I was faced with the truth, that it was only because "Ordination is God's business."

PART THREE

THE MINISTRY

MINISTRY IS . . .

    My father was a very traditional Episcopalian; in fact, he was a traditional everything! He lived by the book and, as a churchman, that book was one that was written by the low church of the Diocese of Southern Virginia. This was where he became an Episcopalian, had a long and active life as choir member and Church Treasurer in two churches, and died an Episcopalian who still called his "minister" by his first name and who refused to cross himself at the end of the creed or any other time.

    I remember visiting at the lake one weekend when he handed me a sheaf of papers and said, "Rick handed this out at Vestry and I can't make hide nor hair out of it. Maybe you know what it means." I took it and recognized it immediately as a newly mandated program by the Diocese about the "Ministry of the Laypeople." I flipped through it and immediately saw what had him so agitated – the term "Lay Minister." I could see in his face that this was not going to be an easy go, so I took a deep breath and started to explain as gently as I could.

    "Dad, this is just an explanation of the ministry of the church by laypeople."

    He frowned, "Laypeople?"

    I smiled, "That's you, Dad. And Mom – you're lay people." He still looked confused so I pointed at myself and said, "I'm ordained." I pointed to him and said, "You're lay."

    The light dawned but he said, "What a dumb word for that."

    I knew things were going to get worse but he still wanted to know what this thing was all about, so I pressed on. "This is talking about the ministry of the lay people of the church..."

    He interrupted, "Is that what 'lay minister' means?"

    I gritted my teeth and said, "Yes, you're a lay minister."

    He jumped out of the chair, his face turning red and he

yelled at me, "Not me! I'm not a minister! You're a minister! Rick's
a minister! I'm not a minister and they better stop calling me that or
I'm quitting!" I knew this was not going to set well with him but I
didn't quite expect such an angry outburst and I figured I'd better
tread very lightly. Of course, his "non-confrontational-there-will-be-
no-arguments-in-this-house" policy took over and I could see that he
was starting out of the room.

I laid down the papers and said, "Dad, it's just a word. If
you don't want to call yourself a minister, you don't have to. If you
want to call Rick a minister instead of a priest, you can. The only
thing they're trying to do is to help lay people understand that they
have a purpose in the church beyond showing up every Sunday and
putting their offering envelopes in the plate so you'll have something
to count every Sunday afternoon."

He stopped in his tracks. "You mean I don't have to be a
minister if I don't want to?"

I so wanted to tell him that it didn't matter what he called
himself, he was still a minister; but I knew better, so I answered him
with just what he wanted to hear, "No, you don't."

He picked up the papers and tossed them into the trash
can and said, "Good. Now I can just go on being a member of the
church."

"Whew," I thought, "I dodged that bullet!"

This scenario was playing itself out all over the Diocese,
indeed all over the Episcopal Church, as the new emphasis on lay
ministry was falling on many deaf ears as well as many outraged
ears like my father's. Ministry had long been the purview of the
ordained and it was a hard sell to get the un-ordained to claim their
part of the ministry of the church. For centuries, the ministry of the
church was seen as three-fold: Bishops, Priests, and Deacons but the
church had begun to stress what has been in the back of the Prayer
Book for many years. That is that the ministry of the church is four-
fold: The Laity, Bishops, Priests, and Deacons – and in that order.

In other words, the lay people of the church are seen as the
primary ministers of the church with the ordained ministers set aside
for specific ministries within that body. Many people like my father
had never been taught that and now didn't much want to hear it.
They liked church the way it was with the "minister" in charge and
the lay people following along and doing what they were allowed
to do. Most of them didn't want to do "clergy things" like serve the

chalice, read the lessons, visit the sick, or even say the prayers in church. Of course, there were also lay people who welcomed the new idea of being a "lay minister" and people like me jumped at the chance to minister in other ways like reading the lessons and serving communion.

To say the least, it was a time of great turmoil among the laity as well as the clergy, many of whom did not want to give up their historic roles to lay people. They liked them in their place – in the pew. There were more clergy who welcomed this re-ordering of the ministries of the church to be more in line with the intentions of the framers of our Prayer Book, but it was a slow and painful evolution.

MY MINISTRY

I had, of course been involved in ministry in the church since the beginning. Our youth program was called Youth Ministry and there were many more lay people than clergy involved in it. I had been a Lay Reader and then a Lay Eucharistic Minister as soon as the Bishop would allow women to fill those traditionally male roles, and I had performed pastoral ministry as a CPE student, a summer intern, and as a Lay Chaplain. My work at JFH was a ministry for me as a lay person, just as it was after I was ordained. All through my long journey, I had been a lay minister and now, I was an ordained minister. I could now do those few things that were reserved for the ordained – the Sacraments.

Part Three chronicles my ministry as a priest of the church.

CHAPTER THIRTEEN

Southern Virginia

COMING HOME

The weeks flew by after my ordination and suddenly it was Holy Week. Easter Sunday was coming up and I began to mentally prepare myself against all of the voices which were crying, "You can't go in there" and "Only the minister is allowed behind the Altar." I had been behind an Altar every Sunday since January 25th and was even becoming accustomed to that position but none of them were the forbidden Altar of my youth where only men and Altar Guild ladies in white gloves were allowed.

When I arrived at St. Paul's on a beautiful Easter morning, I was sweating before I even got in the building. I was so nervous that my voice shook when I greeted the priest who had so graciously invited me and who now hailed me across the front yard of the church as I made my way toward the beloved church of my childhood. I struggled to stay in the present as I had images of the undercroft filled with people waiting for the minister to say the blessing so we could fill our plates with southern fried chicken and biscuits from the traditional Lenten covered dish supper spread.

I fought off the images of the choir room where I vested every Sunday for the processional to my place in the choir stalls. I tried not to think about the force field that I had breached just a year ago when I laboriously climbed into the same pulpit I had dreamed of standing in some 33 years before. I pushed aside my fears and tried mightily to appear cool and collected as I followed the Rector into his office where we began to vest for the service. "I'm supposed to be downstairs practicing with the choir," my brain screamed as I pulled on my alb instead of a choir member's cassock and surplice. "What are you doing?" I heard as I kissed the back of my stole and draped it over my head, "You don't belong here!"

By the time we reached the back of the church I was exhausted but I had managed to shut out the voices and regain my composure. As I slipped on the chasuble, I told myself, "You are a priest and you do belong here so shut up and get to work!" I started down the aisle **behind** the Rector in the position reserved for the Celebrant, feeling a lot like a returning student who had made it big and was coming back to show everyone that it's possible to achieve your dreams.

Of course, that's not what I was and I sternly reminded myself of that as we took our places at the front of the church for the Liturgy of the Word. The Rector preached a stellar Easter sermon, which made me think of the many deaths and resurrections I had survived to be in this place at this moment. Finally, it was time for the Liturgy of the Table and I moved toward the Altar wondering how I was going to get into the chancel. I could already feel the resistance of that force field that had always kept me on the outer side of the rail. I closed my eyes as we approached the gate, said a quick prayer, "God let me in, please," and miraculously stepped into the chancel like I belonged there!

The Altar that used to sit flat against the wall, forcing the priest to celebrate with his back facing the congregation had been moved out so that the Celebrant could now face the people. I moved into that space with the Rector so that the acolyte could perform the ritual hand-washing. I felt like I was moving through quicksand, so slowly it felt like slow-motion but I was there! It was such a victory that I was able to quickly bring myself out of the mire and into the reality that I was exactly where I belonged.

I turned to the congregation, raised my arms and said, "The Lord be with you," and was greeted with the loud and enthusiastic response, "And also with you." Many of those voices came from those who had known me all of my life. I know that there were some who didn't think women should be ordained but their love for me and my family had overshadowed their doubts and resistance and brought them to worship with me in this very special service of resurrection. It was a moment I knew that I would never forget.

"LADY FATHER" IS BORN
        As a Priest in the Church, I felt a new respect from many people, not just those at St. Paul's. The "collar" carries with it an authority that is unspoken and sacred for many people in the Episcopal Church. It isn't as strong in some areas as in others, certainly not as strong as it is in the Roman Catholic Church. But

I felt the difference. There were several "old-school" priests in our Diocese who didn't want to be called "Father" and many times you'd see them in their "civilian" clothes – a shirt and tie. They tended to prefer the vestments of the more protestant era of the Episcopal Church – the cassock and surplice. That's what my "minister" wore – he didn't ever call himself a priest and he was known by most as Mr. Swann. My parents called him "Syd"; I'm sure I never heard anyone call him "Father Swann."

There were, however, several priests who were definitely called "Father." Father Bill Hoffman's wife even called him Father Bill and, while I enjoyed a relationship with Father Norm, my spiritual director, that allowed first names, he was still "Father Norm Baty." He was my biggest support in my first days as a priest, and I had sought out his advice several times after returning from seminary and liked his quiet authority, his gentleness, and the way he listened to everything I said before he spoke. He was the essence of what a spiritual director is, so I latched onto him. For four years he helped me find my way inside myself to where I could meet the Lord in prayer and in meditation.

As I continued in my role as the Chaplain at JFH, I continued my spiritual awakening by getting re-involved in the Cursillo and Happening programs in the Diocese and, as a Deacon, served as a Spiritual Director on a Happening weekend with several of "my girls." It was an amazing experience; the staff loved having me serve in this new role after serving as the "Mom" at eleven weekends before going to seminary. It was somewhat strange at first but I quickly warmed to my new image as "Reverend Susan" or "The Deacon." It didn't take long before the girls from JFH had everyone calling me Ms. Reverend Bowman and I loved it! The girls blossomed in this new environment and they took back such a positive experience that one of them decided to become baptized. After their enthusiastic reports, more girls attended the next Happening. The idea had been a hard sell for both our staff and the Happening staff but, everyone agreed that it was an unqualified success as our girls found a new way of relating to God, and the others found a new appreciation for the blessings in their lives. There were some tight bonds formed that weekend that resulted in a continuing relationship between them.

As a priest, I was invited to serve as a Spiritual Director on a Cursillo weekend with my spiritual director, "Father Norm," and his almost twin, "Father Bill." (I swear, when you saw them together from the back of their identical bald heads, you could not tell them apart!) I played a little guitar back then and so I got to help out with the music. However, I was primarily a Spiritual Director, celebrating the Eucharist, hearing confessions, and spending many hours listening, talking, laughing, and crying with the participants and staff. At the end of the weekend, when Father Bill did the Spiritual Director's traditional recap, he shocked me and everybody in the room with this proclamation:

"I wasn't too happy with the Bishop when he said we had to have a woman on the Spiritual Director's team – I really was not too keen on ordaining women. But, I have spent this weekend with the Rev. Susan Bowman, and I'm here to tell you that the 'Lady Father' is OK!"

I wept, along with most of the others in the room who knew him and how he felt about this traditional title of the priest. "Father" meant priest to him and the fact that he gave me, a woman, that title was mind-blowing to say the least. The room erupted in applause and I was on top of the world!

Of course, one problem with riding that high is that it's easy for people to knock you down, and one woman tried. She was newly-ordained, one of those who had waited in the wings while the Bishop worked through his angst, and she looked great in her sparkling new clerical collar. She wasn't smiling and I briefly wondered why, when she said, "Didn't you just die when he called you a 'Lady Father'?"

She said the last two words with a little bit of a sneer and I was taken aback and couldn't believe that anyone was going to rain on my parade! I looked her right in the eye and said, "No I wasn't. In fact, I'm profoundly honored that Father Bill would give me that title!"

She went away shaking her head. To this day, I don't know exactly what was so offensive to her about that title but I knew that many women cringed when they heard it as did many people for whom the term "father" brings to mind things like abuse and neglect. But I don't tend to associate words with something else when they mean something special to me. "Father" is a priest – period. In my mind, "Father" does not indicate a male priest, even though it definitely conjures up a male figure and, it has been used for centuries to mean a priest, all of whom were male for so long. I know it does in the minds of others and I guess that's where she was coming from but I have come across many

more people who just "whoop" when they hear someone call me "Lady Father."

When I left the conference center that night, Father Bill said to me, "I want to see 'Lady Father' on your license plate!"

I said, "OK!" never thinking about how much it could cost to have a vanity plate. It was a few years later that I discovered that sad fact and I had just given up the idea. Then I attended a retreat in St. Helena's Convent in Vails Gate, New York and the "Priest of the Week" was a fantastic priest who was also just slightly crazy. I quickly related to her and I could see how much she loved life and everything about it. I was a little down and before we had been talking 10 minutes, I felt my spirits lifting. So when she asked me about the Diocese of Southern Virginia, I found myself telling her about my ordination journey.

I ended by telling her the story of Father Bill and the "Lady Father" and she screamed with joy. She jumped out of her chair and said, "I want to see it – where's your car?"

I was almost ashamed to tell her that I didn't have it on my license plate and when I did, she demanded to know why. I said, "Well, I just can't afford the vanity plate charge."

With that, she whipped out her Discretionary Fund checkbook, saying, "This Diocese desperately needs to see 'Lady Father' on your car." She wrote out a check for $50 and gave to me, making me promise that I would put "Lady Father" on my license plate. I went straight to the DMV, ordered a new license plate proclaiming "Lady Father," and it remains on my car today, 20 years later! Thanks to a dear priest in Virginia and another in New York, "Lady Father" was born and will live on as long as I do.

THE JOURNEY CONTINUES

Father Norm and I met every week during my first years as a priest as he struggled to help me learn to pray and meditate. I had never been much good at either, even though I had tried mightily. I remember one seminary professor telling us that if we did it (meditation) right, we would feel it. As he said that, he scratched his head lightly with both hands indicating that it would be like a little electric charge running around our heads. I never felt that and none of the other members of my class did either; we just figured he did somehow and wrote it off as not necessary. Years later I found that there is no "right" way to meditate. You connect to God whenever and however you can; each person is different – each person connects with God in his or her own way.

MY JOURNEY TO THE ATTIC

The way I found was an inner journey that Norm taught me when we first started working together. It was the first time I had ever experienced a "guided meditation" and I remember being nervous and feeling a little silly. As we went through it, I began to really get into it, until, by the time we had repeated the journey many times over several years, I had discovered a personal relationship with Jesus I never knew I could have. I began by thinking of my "self" as a house, one that I had always dreamed of living in, with a wide wrap-around porch, a large entryway with a sweeping stairway up to the 2nd floor. By exploring that house through many guided imagery sessions, I "discovered" my inner self in the attic of my "house." There **was** a place in the attic of my real house where I played as a child. Years after the house was built, Daddy had installed floor in an unused corner of the attic to accommodate the overflow of stashed belongings that seemed to grow inordinately.

I distinctly recalled that place where I could only get by crawling out a narrow walkway and climbing over one of the air-conditioning ducts. At the time, it was empty, except for one lone ladder-back chair where I used to sit (not in it but beside it on the floor) and play with my dolls. Sometimes I would just sit and read, when there was enough light. It was a special place and, in our meditations, Norm brought me there again and again, until I began to realize that I wasn't there alone. The reason that I sat on the floor was that Jesus was sitting in the chair and had always been there!

He had been in my life all along but I had somehow locked that out of my consciousness, probably because it wasn't "seemly" for an Episcopalian to have "talks with Jesus" in the attic. We didn't talk **about** Jesus, much less **to** Jesus. I vividly remember my parents and their friends talking about those "ranting and raving" Christians on TV who claimed to have a personal relationship with Jesus and how we could have one too if we just sent in enough money to line their pockets. These "televangelists" gave a bad name to all Christians who spoke personally about Jesus and so I grew up thinking that anybody who claimed to have such a relationship was not only crazy, but highly suspect!

This "awakening" was a long time coming and it was painful because I had to face years and years of denying God access to my spiritual life and I had to reconstruct that spiritual relationship that I didn't even know I had until Norm helped me find my way back to the attic where I must have known the Lord with my child-like faith. I was a new person! I didn't become one of those "I found Jesus" people who run around talking about Jesus and pushing "my way" of Christianity on everybody. I just became the real me – the one who did know Jesus and did have a personal relationship with Jesus – and I became an even better version.

THE "FIRST"

My other ministry in the Diocese of Southern Virginia centered around the churches of the Diocese. Many Sundays when the girls and I did a presentation at a parish in the Diocese, the local priest was away – it seems the clergy were happy to have someone do their services when they were away and not have to pay a traditional supply priest. The girls got to come and teach people about the ministry of JFH and how they could support that effort, so it was a win-win situation for everyone.

As a born-and-bred Episcopalian, I loved the pomp and ceremony, the procession, and the choir and, while I loved worshiping with my girls, I missed all of that. So on these Sundays, I was "in my glory." I loved being a priest, I loved doing what a priest does, while seeing my friends from all over the Diocese at the same time. The Bishop figured out quickly what was going on and said that it wasn't fair to me. As a fully ordained priest, I was entitled to the supply stipend like any other priest, so I was quickly placed on the Diocesan supply list. I was pleased that while the invitations continued to flood into our office, I also began to get requests from clergy to supply for them without any presentation, and these were a real blessing to me.

BLESSINGS AND "NOT-BLESSINGS"

I quickly discovered that, while I was feeling blessed, they

were not a blessing for everyone. As I began to visit parishes out
of the mainstream of the Diocese, in the far reaches of the Diocese,
I found rather strong pockets of resistance to women clergy. In
fact, several times, I encountered people who left the church in a
huff when they saw me at the back of the church in the priest's
garments. Consequently, I made it a practice to ask those who called
to schedule a supply priest if they were sure that their congregations
knew that a woman was going to celebrate the Eucharist. I expected
that some people would not be happy about that but what really
took me by surprise was this scenario:

> I would arrive at the church to be met by very
> helpful lay people, usually the Warden or
> whoever was scheduled to serve at the Altar. As
> I was vesting, invariably, someone would say
> something like, "I wonder if Joe will be in church
> today," and then, to me, "He's kind of against
> women's ordination."
> After the service, I would many times be met by
> "Joe" who would usually say something like:
> "You know, I knew you were going to be here
> today, and I started to stay home, but I decided
> that no one was going to keep me from my church.
> So I came and you know what? I don't know
> about this whole women's ordination thing, but
> YOU are OK!" Or, "I like **you**!" Or "**You** can come
> back here any Sunday!"

These encounters confirmed for me the truth that
the only real way to change hearts is with one-on-one
contact between human beings.

One of the most uplifting and touching scenes was at the
Church of the Apostles in Virginia Beach, a combined Episcopal/
Roman Catholic Parish which operated with the blessing of both our
Bishop and the Roman Catholic Bishop. Unfortunately, the Pope
wasn't too enamored with the setup and, on a regular basis, they
would have to upset their regular routine to obey their Bishop's
directive to "lay low for awhile." I was asked to supply for the
Episcopal part of the team one Sunday, which was enough of a shock
for me. I couldn't believe that a Roman Catholic Church and priest
would be willing to have a woman celebrating the sacraments in
their midst. The real shock came when I arrived, was shown their

setup and given very brief instructions as to the logistics of the
service, without any apparent concern as to my gender.

The room was set up in a diamond shape, with two dividers
placed lengthwise in the middle. When the worshipers arrived, they
never knew which side would be which, so they sat anywhere they
wanted for the Liturgy of the Word. The clergy sat in two chairs
placed between the dividers, where the pulpit was located. It was
the first time I had ever preached to people on both sides of me and
nothing but a plyboard divider and an empty chair in front of me
(the priest kindly moved to a side chair so as not to be a distraction).
At the offertory, they sang what they called the "Traveling Hymn,"
and everyone would "migrate" to the appropriate side of the
worship space, Romans on one side, Episcopalians on the other

At the Eucharist, the RC priest and I took up our places
behind our respective Altars, and we began the prayer in unison,
reading out of separate books, which had both been modified to
contain the same words. It was almost surreal, hearing his voice
coming from someplace I couldn't see and blending with mine. In
fact, we were so "in sync" that we actually flubbed the same word
at one point. It was the most amazing ecumenical experience I had
ever had, and I had a strong sense that Jesus was totally pleased
with this church and their efforts to "be one, as he and the Father are
one."

The entire experience is engrained in my heart and mind
but the most memorable moment came at the end of the service.
Most people were out of the church at the time when suddenly, a
5-year-old girl ran in from the hall, threw herself around my legs,
and hugged me so tightly I almost fell over. She turned and yelled to
her horrified mother, "Mommy, she IS a woman – I told you so!" She
looked at me, pointed again, and seemed to be screaming at anyone
who would listen: "She's a woman!"

The girl's mother was in tears when she arrived in front
of me, looking a little sheepish, but I was grinning from ear to ear.
When she looked at me and said, "Thank you SO much for being
here today – it's probably the only time my daughter will ever see
a woman being a priest." I joined her in her tears and we hugged. I
left for home a bit more humble and grateful that God had chosen to
use me in such a meaningful way in that little girl's life.

THE VICAR

I also had a new respect for myself as a Christian and felt

better equipped to do what God had called me to do as a priest. There was no doubt that God had been in "The Process" all along, making sure that I was becoming the best possible Priest I could be. I still felt God's presence as I struggled to bring that presence to the hurting girls at JFH. I loved them and knew that my ministry was making a difference for many of them but, at that point, I was aching to become part of a Christian community. I felt that I was ready for the ministry I had sworn I would never do – parish ministry. God has a way of doing that – putting you in places you swore you'd never go. In fact, it happened so many times in my life that I have sworn off the "n-word" – I never say "never!"

In my life I had said that I would
- never go back to school for another degree
- never be a priest
- never live in Lawrenceville, Virginia and
- never be a parish priest.

Here I was in 1987 and I had
- gone back to school and earned a Masters degree
- become a priest
- lived in Lawrenceville, Virginia and
- was now considering entering the parish priesthood.

Isn't God just a hoot? (That's what we Southerners call one who does stuff that makes you say, "Hoo-eee! I never thought I would do that!") Here I was poised on the edge of making the big step towards becoming a parish priest. I was burned out as a chaplain for the abused; I needed a change of venue as well as a change in purpose and practice in my ministry. There was a small parish about 20 miles west of Lawrenceville, that was looking for a priest and the Bishop suggested that I look into it. He also suggested my name to their Vestry/Search Committee and, before I knew what was happening, I was on my way to South Hill for an interview.

It was a match. They said they wanted the skills that I had, and their parish profile looked like a place where I could be happy. So in May of 1987, I tearfully but joyfully left JFH with my few books, my vestments, a Christmas Cactus that had somehow survived for three years in my window, and a new enthusiasm for ministry. I was thrust into a group of people who seemed to want all the things I did best and who greeted me warmly – at least most of them did.

I hadn't been there long before it became obvious that there was at least one member who was not "excited about the new lady preacher." Mary hadn't been to church and the Vestry thought it would be a good idea if I visited her, so off I went. We had a lovely "chat." I told her all about myself and how I became a priest, what I believed about the church and my part in her parish. She seemed to be accepting of me but still expressed reservations about women being priests. We parted graciously and she tried several times to enjoy the worship until the organist, her close friend who was also struggling with my gender, resigned saying that she was "retiring" and neither of them came to the church again.

The church had been on the brink of being able to shed the Diocese's "Sustained" status and become self-supporting, but the exit of too many pledging units pushed us firmly back into the group of parishes that had to accept a Diocesan grant each year to meet expenses. We struggled on for four years with the normal ups and downs of parish life. There were many outstanding people who worked with me to make the church viable, but there were others who seemed to be resistant. In reality, they were tired and seemed to be disinterested in most of the gifts I had to offer. They seemed to enjoy the worship, but didn't avail themselves of the other activities and opportunities for ministry.

There was a wonderful group of young people and I enjoyed them. In my first few days as their new Vicar, I was summoned to the home of a young teacher named Leigh, who had just given birth to her second child, a boy. I arrived for a visit and, before I left, she asked about baptizing the baby.

I started to explain about baptism, "There are certain days set aside by the church as most appropriate for baptisms...."

Before I could go on, she interrupted me. "The baptism has to be on his 4-month birthday."

This was a new one. "Why that particular day? I asked.

"Because," she said, "every child in our family has been baptized at four months old." I had watched her as she spoke of her family's tradition and I instinctively knew that the church's "appropriate days for baptism" were not going to cut it for this woman.

So I asked, "When would that be?" The date she gave me was quickly set as the day of the baby's baptism. I had learned the art of "pastoral back-pedaling." That's when you put yourself out there with what you think is a solidly based argument or statement only to find out that the pastoral needs in front of you are diametrically opposed to what you just said. You back up gracefully and throw the "appropriate" stuff out the window.

As much as I loved the kids and the fantastic organ, as well as so many of the people of this congregation, it became evident that I was spinning my ministerial wheels. I finally confronted the Vestry about the many programs I had tried with very little response, even though they were what they had said they wanted. Finally, one woman was finally honest enough to say, "We lied." At that point, I knew that I had to start looking for another church. I had to use the gifts that God had given me, and they wanted the type of ministry I was unable and unwilling to provide. They wanted and needed a priest who would be happy performing basic services and minimum programming. I needed more and I knew I would not be happy. So, in February 1991, after undergoing a hernia operation, I used my recuperation period to start the search process.

TIME TO MOVE ON

I updated my profile in the National Church search database and, before long, started receiving packets from churches looking for clergy who matched my profile. There weren't any openings in Southern Virginia, so I began to look at the information from churches from all up and down the East coast. One caught my attention with its vital youth program, Eucharistically-centered worship, and openness to women. In fact, they had approached their Bishop, who would not ordain women, and asked if they could interview a woman. Much to their shock, he had agreed. They didn't want to be in the position of wanting to call a woman and having the Bishop refuse to allow them to hire her. So, with his blessings, they invited me for an interview.

The parish was a medium-sized one with a large percentage of active parishioners, and I was enthralled with their physical plant – the church and rectory had been built in the 1950's when the church was founded; it was well-maintained by a faithful cadre of talented and dedicated experts, who were good at everything from plumbing repairs to building a portico over the side porch. For years, the focal point of this parish was the design, creating, and installing their home-made stained glass windows. We hit it off and in July of 1991, I packed up and left South Hill to become the first woman to be a Rector (a full-time priest in charge of a self-sufficient parish) in the

Diocese of Albany.

It was exciting and most of the people around me were excited for me, although there was some angst over their loss. We parted on good terms, though, and I have enjoyed returning to this sweet little church for a visit whenever I was nearby at my parents' home on Lake Gaston. I have continued to be in touch with several families, including my first "pastoral success." In fact, one of my favorite priest stories comes from the little boy I baptized during my first months. Leigh told me, "The first Sunday after our new priest arrived, we came out of Sunday School just as he was vesting for the service.

"Suddenly Drew was pulling on my blouse and yelling, 'Mommy, who is that man?' He was so panicky sounding that I looked quickly to be sure there wasn't a stranger in the building who shouldn't be there but I only saw our new priest adjusting his stole and looking a little puzzled at the commotion.

"I leaned down and whispered to him, 'Shh, he's our new priest.'

"With that, Drew threw up his arms in disgust and shock, yelling at the top of his voice, 'He can't be a priest Mommy! He's not a woman!'" You gotta love that.

It was sad to leave those folks and I was leaving the relative security of a Diocese where the Bishop had "come around," where I was accepted as a priest by him and most of the clergy, and was heading off to a Diocese where, as my Bishop put it, "that Bishop doesn't ordain women."

Sounding way more confident than I felt, I assured the Bishop, "Well, that's OK, I'm already ordained." With some tears and sadness over leaving family and good friends, I still went happily off to my new parish in upstate New York.

CHAPTER FOURTEEN

Diocese of Albany

THE RECTOR

I was on my way! Scott was going to be starting his second year at Clinch Valley College in southwestern Virginia. He had decided to stay resident in Virginia so he could continue to receive in-state financial aid as well as grants from the Diocese. By the time I was ready to move, my Bishop had announced his retirement and we had elected a new Bishop. He assured me that Scott would continue to receive funds from the Diocesan foundation as long as he remained a member of the church in that Diocese.

By the end of the semester, it became clear that this promise was not going to be honored and the school was no longer considering Scott an in-state student. Without the Diocese's assistance, I could no longer afford his increased tuition. So, in December I left for Virginia in a borrowed van (one of my new parishioners graciously offered her larger vehicle) to pick up Scott and his kitten, who threw up all over this woman's car during the trip. We had to stop and buy cleaning supplies to get the smell out of the car but other than that, we had an uneventful trip to New York and Scott moved into the Rectory with me. He transferred to the State University at Albany the year after they began to charge tuition to in-state students (yes, timing IS everything), and we settled in to life in the great Northeast.

Being the "first" is not all it's cracked up to be sometimes and, while I was accepted by many of the local clergy, others did not welcome me in that Diocese. I experienced this at a local clergy function. I was talking with one of my friends when a clergyman whom I had not met walked by and said to my friend, "Good morning." He didn't look at me at all and when my friend said, "Have you met Susan Bowman," he walked away quickly without even answering him. I must have looked appalled because my friend looked at me and said, "Don't worry about him."

The program was beginning, so we moved to our seats but I couldn't stop worrying about him. I had been completely snubbed by someone who didn't even know me. I can barely handle it when someone who does know me doesn't like me or ignores me, but to have someone who has never even met me treat me like a spot on the wall wasn't something I could just "not worry about." I was stunned but I quickly realized that I was just as angry as I was hurt. I wanted to get up and go over to this man and get right in his face and say, "I'm Susan Bowman. It's nice to meet you too." I also wanted to walk over to him and say, "Who do you think you are? I was ordained with the same words as you by the same church as you and you have no right to treat me this way."

Of course, I didn't do any of those things. I stayed in my seat and stewed over the unmitigated gall of this man and over the fact that many of the clergy in the room seemed to like and respect him. When the lunch break arrived, I wanted to leave but my friend said to me, "Susan I warned you about him and there are others who will do the same thing."

I interrupted him, "But why?"

He said, "They do not accept your ordination as valid so they do not even acknowledge your existence."

This was the most blatant discrimination I had encountered yet and I didn't quite know how to deal with it. He went on, "You really have to **not** worry about them because they don't count with the Bishop and they don't count with me or most of the rest of the clergy. We see them as what they are – dinosaurs who are out of the mainstream of the church. They can't hurt you and you're wasting your time by letting them get to you." I didn't want to but I listened to him and I stayed. When it was all over and I was going to my car, I was stopped by another clergyman whom I had just met that day.

"Can I speak to you a moment," he asked politely.

I stopped and turned, "Of course."

He went on quickly, "I saw what he did to you in there and I want you to know that I don't agree with him and that I respect the way you handled the situation. You had every right to confront him for his rudeness and I'm very impressed that you didn't rise to his bait. Welcome to the Diocese. I hope we can be friends." I almost wept. Here was a man I hardly knew who took the time to let me know that he was impressed with my maturity and control and I was grateful. We did become great friends over the years and I remain grateful for his support and the support of many others like him.

There were other occasions when this man and others completely and totally ignored me and the other women clergy in our Diocese, but I had much more on my plate to be concerned with and they were not worth wasting my energy or my time. With that decision and with the help and support of my new clergy friends and the most amazing Bishop, I was able to put those people aside and go on with my ministry.

ANOTHER HERO

Let me tell you about this "amazing Bishop." The Rt. Rev. David S. Ball had been elected Bishop of the Diocese of Albany as a strong opponent to women's ordination, which was considered an abomination by many members of the Diocese. They wanted to be assured that there would be no women "acting" as priests in the Diocese and they were confident that Bishop Ball would maintain that hard line.

They were not happy when he allowed a parish in Troy to hire a woman as an assistant, even though she would not be a full canonical member of the Diocese (the Diocesan canons restricted canonical residency to Rectors). They were not happy when he licensed a woman whose husband had been called to a small parish in the western part of the Diocese. Then when the Bishop crashed the canonical residency barrier by approving my appointment, he really found himself in "hot water" with those who had elected him. He told me not to worry about those folks and that he would deal with them. (Haven't I heard this somewhere before?)

Shortly after my arrival in the Diocese, the Bishop decided to institute a new program of ministry to his clergy. His plan was to schedule each priest to meet with him in his office once a year (along with his or her spouse), celebrate the noon Eucharist at the Cathedral across the street, and then join him for lunch. It was a great plan and the clergy loved it. However, when the Bishop broached the plan with the Dean of the Cathedral, pointing out that this would mean having women celebrating the Euchrarist in the Cathedral, he was greeted with this statement, "Over my dead body."

This wonderful Bishop calmly suggested that the Dean might be happier in another Diocese and he started the program immediately. He did wait and schedule the women for after the Dean had departed, not to placate the Dean but to save the women

from a potentially difficult experience. He made it crystal clear at
that moment that he was the Bishop and that he would not tolerate
such blatant discrimination. Interestingly, he still would not admit
a woman to the ordination process but he and I had become quite
close as he was always available for support and had become quite
fond of quoting me around the Diocese. At our first meeting as part
of his new program, we talked about the parish and some of our
programs. I told him about my family and gave him a brief synopsis
of my journey through the ordination process in Southern Virginia.

After our meeting we went off to the Cathedral where I
became the first woman to celebrate the Eucharist at any of the five
Altars. I was as shocked as everyone else when the Bishop got up to
serve me at the Altar, setting the table and washing my hands. At
that point I saw a woman leaving by the side aisle and I wondered
briefly if she was ill or if she just went to the rest room. I continued
and it was a moving spiritual experience for me and, I was later told,
for many others in the congregation, which had swollen from its
normal 10-12 attendees to 35! We had to relocate to a larger Chapel
one in order to accommodate those who wanted to support me, or at
least, be part of history.

After the service, the Bishop hugged me. The interim Dean
of the Cathedral (another wonderful Bishop – Vince Petit, retired
Bishop of New Jersey) also hugged me and then said to me, "Don't
worry about that woman who left. I'll go and see her. It's not your
problem, it's hers." He later told me that what set the woman off
was the sight of her Bishop, who she had never dreamed would
accept women as priests, actually serving a woman at the Altar.
She just couldn't handle the enormity of that, so she left the service.
She hastened to assure the Dean that it had nothing to do with me
– that she actually liked me and thought I'd be a good priest – and
implored the Dean to let me know that.

Bishop Ball and I went on to lunch at the University Club
where we were treated like royalty, had a lovely meal, and shared
stories. As we were walking back down the street to the Diocesan
Office, I said to him, "Bishop Ball, I want you to be absolutely sure
about me. I want you to know that you will never see me on the
steps of the Capitol with placards in my hand and you'll never
hear of me preaching anything from the pulpit but Christ and him
crucified. I am not fighting a cause. I never have been. I just want
to be God's priest and the best one I can be. That's all." He hugged

me again and went back to his office beaming from ear to ear.

THE PARISH
The parish was growing slowly as some people "dropped in" to see the "Woman Priest" and stayed. I started a weekly Bible Study, with about eight regular parishioners participating, which became a regular part of the life of the parish. We met at 10:30 for an informal Eucharist service right in the Parish Hall where we studied, and then worked our way

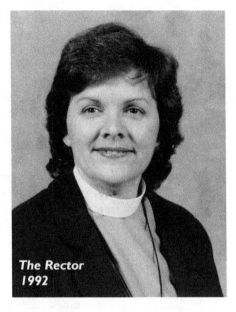

The Rector
1992

through many books of the Bible over the course of the coming years. It was my main source of Bible Study and my main source of support in that parish as we all came to know each other quite well.

The youth group was continuing, although it was a miniscule group compared to the huge youth groups that had been a signature feature of this parish since its inception. The former Rector had built the parish from local families. Hundreds of young people came to "youth group" with their friends – many times from other parishes and denominations – and stayed on as young adults to raise their families there. They wanted to assure that their children would have the same incredible church experiences that they had.

Of course, this wasn't possible as I pointed out to them during the interview process and for months after my arrival. I was *not* the former Rector and could not ever *be* him. I couldn't even be *like* him; I could only be me and do my own "brand" of youth ministry. I worked hard at learning the games that they had been playing for years and encouraged those who had grown up there to continue leading the recreational part of the program. They loved it, they knew the games, and they were good at it.

I listened to these folks as they described the program part of their youth group – mainly consisting of old film strips and now videotapes of short programs centered around Christian values. They used animals, cartoons, and other child-friendly methods of conveying the message of the parables and other Bible stories but I noticed that their past curriculum was curiously silent about Jesus. It reminded me of the old "Protestant" days in Southern Virginia.

We had also discussed the issue of women's ordination, including the atmosphere in the Diocese. We all agreed that it was exciting being a pioneer. One Warden said, "We have been pioneers for so long, this is nothing new for us." There seemed to be very few people in the parish who were opposed to hiring a woman as their priest and, soon after my arrival, I dutifully went off to visit them. One family was cordial and finally did come back to worship but one woman steadfastly refused to even let me in her home. When she answered the door, I said, "Hello, I'm Susan Bowman from the church. How are you today?" She looked at me, quickly taking in my collar and my introduction, and turned on her heel and walked off, leaving me standing on the porch.

I wasn't quite sure what to do but then her husband, who had been to church a few times, came to the door, followed by their granddaughter. He said, "I'm sorry about that. She can't help how she feels."

Everything in me was screaming "Unfair! She hasn't even given me a chance!" but I said to them calmly, "I understand. It's difficult for a lot of people to accept, so maybe with time...."

He interrupted me gently, "Oh, I don't think time will do it. I liked your sermon last Sunday and I'd like to come to church but... well, you know...." His voice trailed off and he looked around at his granddaughter.

She said, "I like you and I'd like to come too, but we just can't."

She turned away from the door and her grandfather said, "Thanks for coming and I'm sorry again."He closed the door and I just stood there, feeling like a total failure.

I had experienced rejection as a priest before; I had even been totally ignored but there was something about having the door closed in my face and being left standing on the porch alone that hurt on a level I didn't know I had. I was crushed! I was not only hurt and embarrassed by this rejection, but I felt so hopeless. There was nothing to do and I knew that there was no hope of ever seeing them in our church. I left as graciously as possible and went home wishing I didn't have to ever tell anyone what had happened. I felt like a total failure. I should have been able to win her over and now I had to report back to the Vestry that I had failed.

Most of them didn't seem too surprised and they suggested that I just let her be and maybe she would come around on her own. I didn't believe that would happen, but, several years later when her husband died, I reached out to her again. She answered the door when I rang her doorbell and when she saw me, she just shut the door in my face. Obviously she had not changed her mind. By then, I had grown a little tougher exterior so that such treatment didn't affect me as strongly. I had learned that people who had a problem with women being priests usually didn't have a problem with me personally. It was always their problem and not mine and I learned to let go of those folks as soon as possible. I was still sad as I walked down the steps and got in the car. I didn't like losing.

As the first few years passed, I felt like the parish members and the Vestry seemed to be satisfied with me and my leadership but I felt an uncertainty on some level that I was unable to identify at the time. I knew that I was not as skilled in the administrative part of my role as the Rector, and I felt disapproval and disappointment on occasion from some Vestry members and Wardens. I had learned in seminary that the best leaders are those who surround themselves with people who have the skills that they lack themselves. I had done a good job at that as many of the lay leaders of the parish were competent and successful in their own careers. I worked very hard trying to increase my administrative skills but, somehow, I felt like I never measured up to their expectations.

One of the major issues for me was the cloud of secrecy that surrounded any instance of dissatisfaction with my performance or any criticism of me by any member of the parish. I knew that there had to be times when people didn't like something I did or said, but they would never tell me; they would only tell one of the Wardens, who steadfastly refused to let me know who had complained to them. I consistently encouraged everyone to feel free to let me know if I offended them or did something they didn't like. Still, when there were times that people were offended by an assertive remark, which had been interpreted as pushy and even rude, they would not speak to me about it. Once, I asked one of the Wardens, "Why won't people talk to me about things like this? I've never raised my voice at anyone and I constantly let them know that I am open to their comments." I don't know how I sounded at the moment, but I know how I felt. I was hurt and frustrated at the lack of trust I felt from almost every person in the parish. The only answer I got was, "They've always taken their complaints to a Warden."

The situations that hurt the most were the times the Wardens would tell me that "some of the parishioners are concerned about the way you talk to them."

Thinking I must have slipped and said something crude, I asked, "What did I say?"

As usual, I was told, "Well, I can't say exactly but you just need to watch how you talk." I was completely befuddled – how could I possibly "watch what I say," if I don't know what it is that offends people.

Finally, I discovered that some of the things I said that they found offensive were "Southern" phrases that were foreign to most New Yorkers. Consequently, they were misunderstood as negative and offensive. Even though I never found out who complained, I did finally manage to get out of them a specific example. What was upsetting to the person was a phrase that I had been using my whole life. I knew what it meant and it was not offensive, but they did not know the meaning and therefore took it in a totally different way.

This misunderstood phrase was one that my father used all the time. "Pea turkey" meant something very small or insignificant. He would say something like, "that didn't mean pea turkey to me." What he meant was, "that didn't mean much to me because I didn't understand it, or it wasn't important." This phrase was part of my vocabulary and I often used it without thinking. Several people got upset when I said it, thinking I must be insulting them somehow.

Of course, if they had asked me what it meant, I would have explained it and the problem would have been solved or there wouldn't even have been a problem; but these folks were ingrained with their method of dealing with their complaints about the clergy. With the former Rector, they complained to the Wardens or the Vestry and that was the end of it. He was not confronted by people he was just accepted as he was, even though many times that included fits of anger and language I had never used in front of anyone at church.

Most of the people in this parish were never able to bring themselves to say to me, "I was offended by what you said," although I did train a few to be upfront with me about issues.

Mostly, though, any negative thoughts and feelings about me just piled up, souring many relationships and making it difficult for me to know where I stood with the people around me.

DIFFICULT DAYS

I had been the Rector for about six years when several Vestry members attended a conference on parish finances. They learned some things that led them to be concerned about whether our accounting practices followed IRS requirements for clergy compensation and parish finances. I had established an Accountable Plan for my professional expenses on the advice of my father, a tax accountant for 40 years, and it had worked for almost ten years. The course they took raised questions about the plan and they insisted that we had to change it to a system where I was required to turn in my expenses and be paid out of an expense account set aside for that purpose. The main thing that it accomplished was to add another duty to the Treasurer's already complex job. It also complicated my record-keeping as I now had to submit information to get a reimbursement instead of just adding the amount to a list of expenses allowed under my Accountable Plan. I had been handling my professional expenses successfully and according to the rules ever since I was ordained, but now I felt mistrusted and a lot like a dishonest child who had to be watched.

Then they decided to re-work our ministry agreement. They proposed to reduce my vacation from a full month to four weeks and to eliminate the payment of the "other half" of my Social Security, which was a sizable amount of money – one I could scarcely afford to lose. I read the Diocesan policy on Social Security payments to the committee, that the payments were not part of the salary amount but a benefit offered to the clergy separately; but they continued to question my interpretation and finally they called the new Bishop for clarification.

They did this often, and then would report back to me that the Bishop had either disagreed with me or had offered his own explanation. This view always seemed to be just different enough from my decision or explanation that they would reject what I had said as either a lie or just my attempt to make the system work to my benefit. I never knew whether what they reported and what the Bishop actually said were even close to being the same. After a number of these confrontations, I finally requested that a member of the Bishop's staff come and be an advocate for me in this process. The person who came out to meet with us asked what he could do to help, but when I began the discussion around my salary package, he stopped the conversation by saying, "Oh I don't deal with those issues." I was so shocked that I couldn't even respond to him. I just sat there while they whittled away at my benefit package in the interest of making sure that our financial dealings were "legal."

Things went from bad to worse during these discussions until one night when I was accosted in the Narthex of the church by two male leaders who came after me at the close of one such meeting. One of them was waving a receipt at me and yelling, "I can't believe you turned in this receipt!"

I turned around to face him and couldn't believe how angry he looked. The receipt was for food and supplies that I had purchased for a New Year's Eve party I had hosted for members of the parish. I said calmly, "That is a legitimate entertainment expense for clergy."

He continued yelling, "Other people have hosted this party in the past and they never asked for reimbursement!"

I was getting angry now, but I managed to control myself and said, "They are lay members of the parish; this is not their job. It is my job and so if I entertain members of the parish, it is considered a business expense." I tried to continue, "I offered them reimbursement every year and …."

I was interrupted and the yelling was really loud now, "No you didn't and this is not a legitimate expense. This is why the people in this parish think you are trying to steal money from the church."

I felt like I had been slapped down like a bad child. I was devastated. I had been operating under the assumption that we had a good working relationship; in fact, one of them had been a Warden and a friend for six years, but this whole process had shown me the extreme level of distrust and misunderstanding there was toward me. This distrust seemed to run throughout the parish and, not only with the newer crop of Vestry members and Wardens, but with those I had worked with for so long and who knew me so well.

Some of the more long-term members of the parish seemed to also have issues that I knew nothing about until they would come out in angry "dump sessions." Those are when someone has stacked up negative feelings about another person without letting that person know about it. The feelings begin to take root and get in the way, so they inevitably have to be "dumped" right in the lap of the poor unsuspecting and usually innocent "dumpee."

We had hired a "consultant" to help us deal with some of these issues as a parish; he was a native of the parish and a very successful and well-respected clergy in the diocese. Everyone knew him and responded well to his attempts to get us talking. He met with us one night and he began the meeting with a question: "What was your moment closest to Christ this week?" Some of the group had attended Cursillo (a renewal retreat weekend) and so were familiar with this basic question that was a part of every weekly support meeting. However, most of the faces around the table had a panicky look, as this was not something they were accustomed to doing. Things still went fairly well, until about half way around the large table, one man said, "Well I'm really angry with Susan Bowman." We were all surprised and I remember the consultant asking, "And that would be your moment closest to Christ – how?" The man ignored him and zeroed in on me as he began to tell the story.

The incident that he was describing had taken place in my living room some three months earlier. A group of parishioners had gathered for a fun night and there were two tables of Pinochle in the living room, with a very rowdy bunch playing some raucous game at the dining room table. Everyone was having a good time. My phone rang and someone handed it over to me, since I was sitting at a card table in a corner from which it would have taken way too long for me to extricate myself. I answered it and found an old friend on the line whom I had not talked to for a long time. I started to get out and leave the room but she said she couldn't really talk long, she just wanted to see how I was doing, so I decided to stay where I was. Just as she began to speak again, there was a loud roar from the dining room table group and I waved at them and asked if they could keep it down as I was on the phone. There was no acknowledgement from the group, but I was sure they had heard me.

I was trying to hear what she was saying when again came the loud laughter and hooting from the across the room. This time I raised my voice to be sure that I was being heard and said, "Hey guys, can you hold it down? I'm on the phone long distance." There was relative quiet after that, I finished my phone call and hung up. The evening progressed with everyone having a grand time as was

quite evident from the loud laughter that still drowned out our quiet
little card games.

   Now, at this public meeting some three months later, this
man was relating this story and he ended it with, "and I'm angry at
her for yelling at us." I was dumbfounded. I just couldn't believe that
this man had been offended by what I had said (he told the group
that I had "shrieked" at them although none of the other people who
had been present agreed with that description). He had kept it to
himself and had stewed on it for three months while he got angrier
and angrier. The whole thing could have been resolved by a simple
"I was offended when you yelled at us" and an "I'm sorry that I
offended you."

   When I found my voice, I managed to keep it low but firm
as I responded to this outrageous story. In a previous meeting, we
had been trying to understand each other and I had tried to describe
to them what it's like to always be "on."I had explained to them,
"We clergy never get to just 'be ourselves.' We are either around
parishioners, who are constantly watching and judging our behavior
or are with non-church people who think that every off-color word
they utter will get them a one-way ticket straight to hell because they
dared to say it in front of a member of the clergy."

   Some people had understood and even felt some compassion
for me but one woman was quite emotional about it. She struggled
to speak through her tears and what she said was, "So when you and
I go to the movies, you are working?"

   I tried to explain what I meant by "being on" but she
couldn't grasp it through her hurt from what she had heard as an
insinuation that I only spent time with her as a part of my job.

   So, here was my response. "Now I hope you all can
understand what I was trying to describe to you at the last meeting. **I**
was in my **own home** at an informal gathering that I didn't consider
to be a 'working' event; I raised my voice in order to be heard over
the loud bursts of laughter so I could hear someone on **my** phone. If I
wasn't the priest, do you think anyone would have been offended?"
I took a breath to continue but it wasn't necessary as the woman who
had been so incensed by my previous comments was now in tears
again.

   This time she said, "I am so sorry, so sorry! Now I know
what you meant and you are exactly right. We have unfair
expectations and **you** – she stopped and looked over at the man

who had started this whole conversation – **you** are out of line." We were both in tears by then and I got up and went over to her and we hugged right there in front of the whole group while she apologized again and I forgave her.

There was no further mention of the incident as the rest of the group shared their responses. Then we went on to some exercises to try and build better communication between all of us around the table. When the meeting ended, the usual "hanging out" was abandoned and the room cleared out in record time.

THE BEGINNING OF ANOTHER END

I had begun to think that it was time to leave; I had started looking at other parishes in the Diocese, and in neighboring Dioceses. After that meeting, I stepped up my efforts. I called clergy I knew in neighboring dioceses and continued conversations with my close clergy friends in the area; I was counseled by every one of them to get out. My former Bishop said that I had done all I could do there and that I needed to move on for my own sake.

I was looking but I was also quickly losing ground in my constant battle with chronic depression. I had been on anti-depressants since before I left Virginia. I had stopped taking them briefly, and then suffered an acute depressive episode and had to be medicated again. I was beginning to spiral down again, as is often the case with depression, you don't realize the downturn has begun and, if you do, you usually don't have the energy or capability to deal with it. I was losing the ability to deal with the depression and the added stress from the parish was exacerbating the problem. My doctor was adjusting my medication but it was a slow process and I had to deal with this crisis immediately. Things had been deteriorating almost daily, so we had scheduled a Vestry retreat for a weekend in November of 2000 to get to the bottom of what was ailing us as a parish and as a Vestry/Wardens/Rector entity.

About a week before the scheduled retreat I received a call from a member of the Vestry. I was somewhat surprised since this person rarely called me. There were no pleasantries. He just said, "Susan, you need to know that this Vestry retreat is really a 'get-rid-of-Susan' session. Why don't you save yourself a lot of pain and just resign now? Take three months. Find another position and we'll all be happier." I was stunned. First he had spoken to me like I was a child that deserved to be punished. Second, he had said that they actually wanted me to leave and that they had been actively working at getting rid of me. "There have been secret meetings," he said and, he went on to say, "Even people you think are your friends have been at those meetings."

Somehow I managed to ask, "Have you talked to the consultant about this change in plans?"

He said, "The consultant is not in charge of this meeting. We are."I couldn't speak at that moment, so he said, "Think about it Susan. This weekend won't be fun." And, with that, he hung up. I sat there holding the phone like I thought someone would be there to tell me that it had been a bad joke. But there was nothing there but the dial tone. Finally, I hung up. After a few agonizing minutes, I knew there would not be any Vestry retreat because I was not going to submit myself to whatever they had in mind. I called the consultant and left a message for him; then I called my best friend, also a member of the Vestry and my strongest support in the parish. As soon as she answered the phone, I began to cry.

She was aghast at my story and said she'd be right over. When she arrived I was still sitting in the same chair with my hand on the phone. I couldn't move. I was totally and completely devastated. I was drowning in hurt, anger, and disbelief. All I could do was cry. My friend held me and tried to comfort me but it took a long time for me to get myself under even a modicum of control. It was tenuous at best. After my friend left, thinking she had succeeded in calming me down, I began to cry again. When she arrived at my door to check on me the next morning, I was still crying, so she called my therapist only to find that he was out of town. She said, "Susan, you need to talk to someone." All I wanted to do was crawl in my bed and never come out again, so it took awhile for her to convince me. Finally, I agreed to go and she took me to see her therapist, a woman I knew and respected.

After a little bit of conversation on her part and a lot of my tears, she finally said, "Susan, I think you need to go to the hospital." I jumped up! "No way," I yelled. "I'm not that bad off! I won't let them do this to me!" I collapsed in the chair and started to cry again.

"Susan," she said, "what have you done since yesterday afternoon?" I said nothing. "Have you slept at all?" I hadn't but I refused to give in. "I promise you, this will not just go away. You will not get better on your own. You really need to be in a hospital where you can get help with this."

"Can't you help me," I asked.

She looked at me with great compassion and said, "No. I can't. I'm concerned for your safety and you need round-the-clock care that I can't give you."

Through the fog, I heard the words "acute depressive episode"; from some far distant corner of my brain, I heard my psychiatrist's words after my last one, "if this happens again, it will be worse and then the next one will be even worse...." I closed my eyes and said, "OK, I'll go."

Through my sobs, I could hear her making the arrangements with the hospital and then my friend was calling Scott. Somehow he and my friend managed to convince me to go with her and get lunch, and he would meet us at the Rectory later. By the time we left the therapist's office she had arranged for me to be admitted to Four Winds Psychiatric Hospital in Saratoga Springs, NY. By 6:00 pm, Scott and my friend were driving me northward to the hospital.

I was so far past devastated that I could hardly function, even in the hospital. My roommate was a snorer of mammoth proportions and I couldn't even close my eyes without seeing visions of parishioners talking about kicking me out and I'd start to cry again. I felt like I would never be able to stop crying and I couldn't even imagine what I was going to do after this was all over. Just the thought of my future threw me into racking sobs, which brought the nurses and the blessed medication that finally put me to sleep.

The next morning, I literally couldn't get out of the bed and the nursing staff brought me my medication in bed. I looked up at the nurse, and said, "You didn't have to do that." She said, "Can you get up for me then, and we'll go up to the nurses' station?" I tried, oh how I tried but my legs would not move; I could not even move my arm enough to throw the covers off. Finally, I gave in, took the medication and fell asleep again. After waking several times with a staff member speaking to me in a soft voice and gently encouraging me, I was finally able to get up and get dressed.

It was already lunchtime. I wasn't allowed to leave the building to go to the dining room so my lunch was brought to me in my room. However, I couldn't eat (there was a first!) so I wandered around near the nursing station until I got tired and sat down in a corner. A very kind nurse came over, sat down beside me and asked me, "How are you feeling?"

I started to say something like "Oh just ducky," but I didn't have the energy to talk, much less make jokes. I said, "OK, I guess," and the tears started.

She got up and said, "I'll be right back. Don't go away."

I remember thinking, "How ridiculous! Where would I go and HOW would I go?" I waited until she came back and by that time, I had stopped crying.

She handed me a cookie. "I know you didn't eat your lunch so you've got to be hungry."

I looked at it and thought, "I love cookies; why don't I want that?"

She put it in my hand and said, "Just take a bite – for me." So I did and then I took another bite. She said, "Good girl. Can you finish it for me?" I took another bite and thought how much I felt like a child, but suddenly that was OK. It was a lot less hazardous feeling than being an adult right now, so I relaxed and finished my cookie.

She was very easy to talk to and she actually got me to talk some by asking me about my son, my grandson, and my brand new granddaughter. I could talk about them without crying, and after a few minutes, she asked me if I would be willing to try and do a little written exercise.

I said, "Sure" before I thought about what kind of exercise she meant. Before I could wonder for long, she was back with a stapled sheaf of papers, and handed them to me.

"See if you can do this for me. Don't worry if you can't or if you don't feel like it right now. Anytime is fine." I took the papers and the pen she handed me and she was gone. I looked down at the papers and saw that it was a worksheet on dealing with criticism. I couldn't figure out how she knew that was a big issue for me so I figured maybe God was in this after all. I went off with my assignment and thus began the process of getting well.

I finished my assignment and delivered it to the nurses' station where I was given my medication and informed that there was a class for new patients going on if I felt like attending. I figured that I might as well go, and I took a seat in the back of the room. It was mainly about rules and limitations as well as some pep-talking about the treatment program. We were encouraged to participate as much as we were able, and to try and to attend every activity, including all meals. By the time it was over, I really wanted to go back to bed, but it was time for dinner and mine was waiting in my

room again. It would be the next day before I was allowed to go to
dinner with the group.

The next day, I started my treatment program with a session
that encouraged new patients to "tell their stories." I have never
been one to hang back in groups; in fact I was usually the first to
volunteer in such situations. Not this time. I was the last one, and
they had to push me to get me to talk about why I was there. Finally,
I figured that I had to tell it sometime, so I said, "Well I guess I'll get
it over with."

One of the patients said, "Don't do it for that reason – that's
not good enough. Do it for you." I was so shocked that I just started
talking and didn't stop for about 15 minutes. By then, I was in tears
and the entire group was up in arms! I was so surprised at their
responses. "What's wrong with those people?" "Why didn't you
slap those guys?" "I can't believe you put up with that!"They were
saying all the things that I had wanted to say and was unable to; I
felt like someone had dragged the dark, heavy blanket off of me and
let me out of the deep pit that I had plunged into just two days ago.
Suddenly, it was lunchtime and we all took off together with them
still asking me incredulous questions like, "How could they talk to
a priest like that?" "What did they want you to do?" "Why didn't
somebody help you with all of this?" I felt like I was being heard for
the first time in many years and I was actually laughing for the first
time in months.

The next day, there were more classes and I remember
talking to the group about how I felt about myself and my ministry.
At one point I said, "I wasn't very good at the administrative stuff
and I didn't run meetings very well. I just don't think I'm very good
at this."

Suddenly, one member of my group turned to me and said,
with blazing eyes and a firm voice, "Wait just a minute! This isn't
about how good a priest you are. You ARE a good priest and you
know it. I don't know you very well and I know it!" Everything
you've told us is proof. You ARE good at this." The rest of the group
was agreeing and echoing what she said and I felt like someone had
opened a jar of pure essence of joy and poured it over me. It was
the first time in a long time that I had felt good about myself and
my ministry. I knew I was a good priest but that knowledge had
been overshadowed by the negativity and almost obliterated by the
betrayal I felt. For the first time since I had arrived, I felt like I was

actually doing better, and that I might just be OK.

That night, I was surprised to receive visitors. My good friend and a few members of the church, with whom I had been very close, had driven up to see me; they were very supportive and upbeat. I was touched by their visit but, the whole time they were there, I felt an undercurrent of something I couldn't identify and I was glad when they finally left. I later found out that they were the instigators of the secret meetings that had been held to discuss "what to do with me." I discovered that these were the folks who were pushing for a sabbatical for me; apparently, they had some fairly solid plans in place but they were outvoted. While this was somewhat comforting, I was still stunned at the betrayal of these people who I had thought were my friends.

The real bombs came later when I found out about the meetings that had taken place on the Sunday after I went into the hospital. There were people who stood up and lied about me, called me a racist, a child abuser, and aired other complaints that I had never heard anyone mention. These were people that I had worked closely with for almost ten years and they had never expressed any kind of concerns about any of those issues. It was this constant and consistent refusal to communicate with me that had laid a foundation of negativism and unfavorable comparisons that had finally succeeded in destroying our common ministry.

The racist accusation was actually a racist comment in itself. An African-American woman announced that I had never stopped at her pew during Baptism services when I introduced the babies up and down the aisles, that I didn't ever speak to her after church, and that I hadn't ever let her do anything. Of course, none of her claims were true. I remember distinctly stopping to show her babies just as often as anyone else. I had grabbed her hand many times as she tried to sneak past me after services and wished her a warm "Good morning," and I had invited and trained her to be an usher, which she was currently doing on a regular basis. The lies were bad enough, but her claim that I had treated her that way because I was a Southerner was abominable.

I was also accused of abusing the children in youth group, a statement that was shouted down instantly as unfair and dangerous in this day and age, but the damage was done. It wasn't until several months later that I found out that this accusation stemmed from a youth retreat when, he said, "She called Annie a slut." When I heard this, I was outraged! At the first opportunity, I confronted him privately, which was a courtesy that he had refused me. I didn't waste a minute on greetings or anything polite, I just said to him, "You told the entire congregation that I abused the children in youth group. What were you talking about?"

He admitted to me that it was because "You called Annie a slut." I had thought long and hard about this and thought I knew when this had taken place.

I asked him, "So when did I do this?"

He said vaguely, "Oh I don't remember exactly. It was at some youth group meeting." I was furious! He had destroyed my reputation and my good name and he couldn't even remember when this had happened."

I asked him, with a cold fury, "Would this have been at the retreat where we did the Biblical simulation putting the Virgin Mary on trial for adultery?"

He said, "Maybe."

I could barely control myself but managed to ask him, "Would that have been the Annie who was playing the part of Mary Magdalene?" I didn't let him answer. "And what was Mary Magdalene?"

He said, "A prostitute."

I said, "So this would have been the same girl who was dressed as a prostitute and strutting around playing up her role to the hilt? It was this girl that I called a slut?" No answer. "Well, duh!" I said. "As I remember, she was rather pleased that she was so convincing! Did you, by any chance, ask her how she felt about this?"

He said, "She didn't remember it," and I finally lost it.

"How dare you? How dare you say such a horrendous thing about me, and she didn't even remember it? And this was two years ago!" With that, I stomped out.

The other accusations that were circulating at these meetings were petty and it was utterly ridiculous that these people had allowed such minor annoyances to destroy their relationship with me as their priest. To say that I was unaware of all of these "issues" is an understatement. I had been talked about and criticized and judged behind my back for almost ten years, and I knew that there was no going back.

THE END - AGAIN

I resigned immediately and even intended never to set foot in that church again. However, the Bishop agreed to be there with me at a final service. In the end, I was glad that I had agreed to it. The Bishop preached and I think helped to restore my good name, or at least my good intentions, publicly. There was a huge covered dish supper in my honor. They had prepared a scrapbook of pictures and letters of tribute, which I read once, put away in a box and finally discarded when I moved some nine years later. One of the now-grown-up youth group members sang "You are the Wind Beneath My Wings" to me as a stunned audience watched. There was hardly a dry eye in the room.

One woman stopped me at the kitchen door and asked to speak to me. I had vowed not to get into any conversations about the issues with anybody, but she looked so stricken that my pastoral side took over, and I agreed to listen. She then looked me right in the eye and said, "We were wrong. We treated you wrong and I'm very sorry to have been part of it." And she asked for my forgiveness. I forgave her, we hugged, and I've never seen her or most members of that parish since that day.

I moved out the next day and took up residence in an apartment in a neighboring town, thanks to the Bishop's successful negotiation for the church to pay me severance with all benefits for six months. He also sent me off to a wonderful place for "wounded clergy" in Pensacola, Florida for two weeks; when I returned, refreshed and beginning to heal, I began doing some Sunday morning supply in local parishes. Back in the pulpit and at the Altar, I regained my footing. By May, I was ready to find something more permanent. My severance package was due to run out in July, so I needed to get started with a search.

One of the places where I supplied was a small church in a small town about 35 miles away. It is a beautiful church and I was quite taken with the whole area. They were looking for a part-time priest and suddenly I was looking at the possibility of becoming a Vicar again. I sat down and prayed for the first time in months, asking God for guidance and felt a solid sense of rightness. I was back!

CHAPTER FIFTEEN

Diocese of Albany

THE NEW VICAR

I had been asked to supply for this church earlier in the
year before going to Florida and again when I returned. I liked the
church – it's old and when you walk in, it's so rich and so traditional,
that it just breathes "church" at you. The people were enthusiastic
about me and my preaching and the way I did the service, so they
asked me if I would consider a permanent position. I thought about
the fact that it was a part-time parish, which would mean that I
would have to get a part-time job somewhere in the area. There was
a Rehabilitation/Nursing Home close by, and I thought, maybe
I could pick up a part-time job as a Chaplain. I inquired and sure
enough, they were looking for someone.

I took that as a positive sign and decided that maybe this was
where God wanted me right then. So, I accepted their offer, applied
for and was hired as the Chaplain at the Nursing Home, and I started
packing. The big problem was where to live. Rents in this small town
were high and there weren't too many places available. George, the
Warden who encouraged me (begged might be a better way to put it),
said not to worry. He said that the church would help out with some
funds until I got settled and found permanent housing.

A member of the parish with an extra room in her home
offered it to me for as long as I needed a place to live, and I thought,
"Can't ask for better than that." On a very hot August day, we
all pitched in, packed up my apartment, moved the big stuff and
anything I could live without to a storage garage, and the rest to my
new temporary "digs."

The following day we enjoyed a wonderful first Sunday
together and then sat down to a little business meeting in the church.
I brought up the housing issue and innocently asked how much
I could expect from the church to help out until I got more extra
income than the nine hours a week at the Nursing Home.

OH NO! NOT AGAIN!

Suddenly, George jumped to his feet, yelled at me that he had never said such a thing, that I was a liar and it was no wonder that the other church had gotten rid of me. With that he stomped out of the church. I was stunned, to put it mildly. For a split second, I was speechless. Then I got up, began to gather up my belongings, and said, "I'm not doing this again. I told you that I would not tolerate such treatment and I meant it." The other Vestry members instantly stood and pressed around me so that I could not get out of the pew. They were one voice and they said clearly, "We don't agree with him. We don't think that you're a liar. We are not going to do things like he does."

"What if he comes back," I asked? They responded that they would make it clear that what he said and did was inappropriate, and that it would not happen again. They were so sincere, and I know to this day that most of them really tried to do that. However, when a group of people is operating under a cloud of distrust and disrespect, it's impossible to keep that promise.

THE BATTLE FOR AUTHORITY

For a few years, most things went well. Some members were eager for new activities and growth, while others seemed to be content with "the way things were." There were some growing pains but we settled into a life together that seemed to be working, except for two large issues. One was that a long-time member of the church had once been told by the Bishop that, when they were without a regular priest in charge, it was appropriate for lay people to take charge of certain areas of parish life in the interim. He took him at his word, and since they were in an interim situation, he assumed responsibility for some parts of the liturgy which are traditionally reserved to the clergy.

When I arrived, he wanted and tried to continue his position of authority. He was not interested in the Church canons, which stated that the Rector, Vicar, or Priest-in-Charge has absolute authority over all things liturgical, period. Needless to say, there was a serious disconnect when I made it abundantly clear to him that I was taking on the authority as all clergy did, I also was clear that I considered this to be a team effort, and that I welcomed his input. In fact, for the first months, I bowed to his wishes as I tried to get acquainted with the wishes of the people about our worship.

Our relationship was never more than barely cordial, as he did not like many of my worship practices, and he was highly resistant to the "new" music sweeping the church in those days. So there was an undercurrent of mistrust and dislike between us that permeated the entire parish and, unbeknownst to me, was already hard at work destroying any chance of a successful ministry for us.

There were others who shared my frustrations but, of course, there were some who completely supported Wayne and his claims to authority. I struggled to keep the peace, to still try to move us forward, and to fulfill the needs of as many people as possible. Once again, people in the parish complained about things they didn't like to each other, the Vestry, and the Wardens, but never to me. I encouraged them over and over again to talk to me, promised that I would never raise my voice (I did not), that I would listen to them (I did) and, while I might not always agree with them (I sometimes did and sometimes did not), I would do my best to honor their points of view (I always did).

A small group of people who had been very open about their opposition to hiring a woman, finally got themselves organized over a letter that was written to me by an elderly and long-time parishioner, Fred, whose wife had recently been ill and in the hospital. She was not a member of the church and, in fact had made it very clear to me that she didn't believe "any of that stuff," and that I didn't need to waste my time visiting her. I visited her anyway and one time, we actually had a very nice conversation and I left knowing exactly where she stood on matters religious and that I could visit if I wanted to, but it wasn't necessary.

She was chronically ill so it wasn't long before she was back in the hospital, and I went up to see her but she was asleep. I left word with the nurse that I had been there; so, I was quite surprised when I received her husband's letter complaining because I had **not** visited her. I called him and calmly explained that I had been there and that she was asleep; that seemed to placate him. I wrote him a letter, thanking him for his direct communication with me and assured him that I would continue to visit his wife whenever she needed it, even though she had made it clear that she didn't want me to visit.

THE TROUBLE JUST KEPT COMING

Some months after this exchange, a few other minor issues had surfaced. This small group decided that it was time to air their grievances in a public forum, and they asked the Vestry to schedule a meeting for the parish. We knew some of their issues, as they had been making a lot of noise about things they didn't like, and the Vestry wanted to refuse their request. They did not want to set me up as a target. I told them I appreciated that but I felt that a refusal would only convince them that I was hiding something.

So we planned the meeting, invited a local Pastor to moderate the meeting so there would be a cool head calling the shots and on the appointed night, the following people showed up:

- Fred, the author of the letter – one of the oldest members of the church
- Wayne, who had his visions of authority and who was old friends with Fred
- Ethel, a woman who had been negative about my ministry there from the beginning and who was also a long-time member and good friends with Fred and Wayne
- June, a member of the choir and sometime Vestry member who was very close to Wayne
- Jerry and Marilyn, a couple who had been members of the church for a long time and had a young daughter who was active as an acolyte and youth group member, and who attended church and Sunday School regularly.
- Philip and Mary Beth, the Wardens of the Vestry
- Several Vestry members (not all were present, as we later discovered, because they didn't want to "be involved in such doings")
- Several youth group members, whose parents were present at the meeting
- Pastor Mike from the church across the street who was the moderator, and
- me.

The meeting was an unmitigated disaster. After Ethel insulted and offended the moderator, she and the others jumped right into their complaints. I was accused of lying by Fred, which was quickly followed by an emotional statement by Jerry and Marilyn, who "just couldn't imagine a priest who lied." Jerry was very emotional and left after a time, in tears. The meeting went from bad to worse, with more accusations until I finally could not take any more. As the moderator was saying that we didn't seem to have anything new to say, I interrupted him politely and informed them all that I did have something to say.

I was literally shaking as I stood there trying to keep the tears at bay. I said, "First of all, I am not a liar. I did go to see Fred's wife, she was asleep and I left word for her that she obviously didn't get. Still," I reminded them, "I apologized to him for not visiting with his wife when I did." I had to hurry as I could feel the loss of control working its way into my voice. "What is needed now is not name-calling and meetings, but forgiveness. If you remember, we are Christians and we are called to forgive. As far as I can tell, you don't know anything about that and I will not be a part of this conversation for another minute." With that, I walked out. I did it with grace and my head held high. I went into the dark church, sat in the entryway, and cried.

I couldn't hear anything for a little while, and I figured they were talking about me but I didn't care. Then I heard people in the front yard, and I looked out the window of the front door and I saw Marilyn, Wayne, and Ethel standing on the sidewalk talking and gesturing. While I watched, the two young people who had been in the room walked by on their way to the drug store down the street. Then Ethel looked up and saw me in the window. They stopped talking, moved away, and left for their cars.

It took the Vestry and Wardens another 10 minutes to find me, and we quietly talked about how to handle the next step. Later, before we left, the two young people told me that, when they walked past the group on the sidewalk, they had heard the two women calling me names using curse words. They were appalled. I was sick.

I told the Vestry the next day that there was no next step for me. I was done. I had been accused of the worst things a priest can be accused of, castigated for trying to move the church forward, and it was obvious to me that I was not trusted, and there could be no further progress with me at the helm. They asked me not to do anything rash, and we parted for the evening.

MY SUPPORT GROUP

During my tenure there I was fortunate to have a huge support group of local clergy. There was a very active organization in place when I arrived, which for years, had organized Lenten Services/Luncheons, Baccalaureate Services for the local High

School, prayer walks, community activities, and it managed a very successful food pantry. I loved it. I had been involved in the local clergy/church group in South Hill, and I had started a Lenten Services/Luncheons program there, which was very popular. There were no such groups available in the area of my former parish, so I had missed this relationship badly.

The clergy of the area churches were a diverse group, and we started meeting weekly for prayer. The relationships we formed were strong and prayerful. We prayed for each other, we met every week for support and corporate prayer for the community and ourselves, and we took great care to encourage and uphold each other in our individual ministries.

These people were my salvation during this time. I shared openly my frustrations, my failures, and the many issues that seemed to plague us as a parish. I used this group shamelessly, not only for support, but for feedback. Every time I had a "story" to tell, I led with what I thought I had done to cause it or make it worse, and asked them to honestly tell me what I had done wrong and what I could do better, and how I could fix the situation. I have to honestly say that there were very, very few instances when the group found me responsible for the problems that were constantly presenting themselves.

They were mostly horrified at the way I was treated and at the non-communication that was typical of everyday life in our parish. They were sometimes critical of something I had said or done, but I don't remember a time when anyone said, "Boy you sure messed that up; no wonder they're so hard on you." It seemed that every week, we'd hash and re-hash some situation, and they'd all leave with profound gratitude for their own congregations. They were my entire support, as my requests for help from the Diocese were mostly ignored. It was a bleak time.

THE LULL BEFORE . . .

Things calmed down, somehow, the whole meeting sort of "went away," and life went on for a time. Then several members of the Vestry and I got the idea for creating a parking lot next to the parish hall for the handicapped members of the parish, including myself. One long-time member, Ursula, agreed to provide the money for the project, and we put a lot of thought into plans that would make it aesthetically pleasing as well as useful to those who found it difficult walking down the driveway from the parking lot. This was especially hazardous in the winter, when the accumulated snow and ice, the sun, and the black-topped driveway made for a downhill skating venue that was treacherous on many a Sunday morning.

. . . THE STORM

The same small group was up in arms again, and the plans were rejected and ridiculed. I was accused of using the church's money for my own purposes. Ursula had agreed with the original parking lot plan, and the Vestry had appointed a committee to finalize the plans we had agreed upon, when we found that a meeting had been scheduled by Wayne, who was solidly against the project. This meeting included everyone with an interest in the parking area, as well as all of the elderly members who had told me they thought it was a grand idea. At this meeting, when they were asked how they felt about it, they said they didn't think it was necessary.

The writing was on the wall – I needed to get out, as my effectiveness had dwindled away to nothing at this point, and everyone was miserable, including me. It wasn't as easy as it sounds, though. I had a part-time job as a Police Department Dispatcher in the Town Hall that helped to pay my bills, but it was not enough to support me without my income from the church. I had purchased a house at the end of my first year, because I was able to get a first-time mortgage with a lower payment than most of the rental property rates in town. If I was going to leave the town, which was preferable, I had to sell my house, find other employment and/or another church, and this would take time. I did not want to be there any more than they wanted me to be there, but we had to press on for a while anyway.

TIME TO MOVE ON

We were still struggling along, and I found myself alone again with a parish that didn't trust me, didn't want me, and, for some reason, thought they could treat me with little or no respect. Those members who trusted me, and really wanted me to stay, were appalled at the way I had been treated. More than one of them told me that none of these people had ever spoken to any Vicar (all males) the way they had spoken to me. Pastor Mike even called them on it at one point during the meeting when he chastised them for the way they were talking to me – without love, without charity, without grace.

Several months later, I was surprised at a Vestry meeting when the Warden informed me that they had talked together (even though a meeting without the Rector or Vicar is not allowed under Canon law), and they had decided that we should part company. I hadn't expected it this soon, and I was hoping to be the one to instigate the resignation. However, I was again being rejected because I didn't meet expectations which were impossible for me to meet. I know that I was not perfect in either parish situation, and I share the responsibility for my eventual downfall. I know that I could have done some things differently, but one thing I could not change was their refusal or inability to communicate with me about things I could have changed. Then there was the proverbial "elephant in the living room." That's the one thing that most people would have denied was an issue and so it was never discussed. It was also the one thing I couldn't change – I was not a male.

I do not mean to blame any of these difficulties on any person, or group of people, and I certainly don't mean to imply that, if I had been a man, there would have been no problems in my ministry. I acknowledge my lack of administrative gifts and I know that there were times when I could have done a better job. I could have preached shorter and/or better sermons, I could have chosen better hymns, I could have visited more, prayed more, and I could have been better organized. I also acknowledge the many gifts that I did use freely. I was a good preacher, a caring and compassionate pastor, and I was kind and polite to everyone, even those who mistreated me. Even in the most heated conversations, I tried not to raise my voice or to discount the opinions of others, even those with whom I disagreed. In most of the situations where I was spoken to rudely or with disrespect, I can honestly say that I did not deserve such treatment and in most cases, I don't believe that a male priest would have been treated the same way.

I left the parish after a low-key "last Sunday" worship service and a reception/lunch during which I was presented with a lovely gift and a lot of hugs from the children and many of the adults. I moved on auto-pilot that day, trying to keep my true feelings at bay so that we were able to end our relationship without too much discomfort. I had made myself almost numb on the outside, but on the inside I was hurting and dangerously close to the edge of an inner pit where I knew I would not be able to function without being cynical, sarcastic, and even rude. This was not a place I wanted to be, but I had lost my spiritual center and my ability to connect with God. The only way that I could hope to exit with grace was by losing my pain in that deep hole where it could do no harm. It was a difficult place to be and I was glad when it was over and I could go home to again lick my wounds and find some peace.

CHAPTER SIXTEEN

"Meanwhile" Again

TRYING TO FIND THE PEACE

I am convinced that for most of the people involved in these two parishes, there were only a few who were malicious and intentionally unkind. The vast majority of the members of these churches didn't have a clue that they were treating me in a way that undermined my authority as the priest in charge of the parish. I didn't even realize it for a long time, but I now believe that I unwittingly set it up, at least partially, by insisting on being called by my given name.

I never wanted to be called "Mother" because I felt like it placed a gender issue squarely in front of people, and for me, my priesthood was not a gender issue. I was a priest, not a woman priest, any more than a male would be called a "man priest." I wanted to NOT bring up the issue so I opted for the simpler, more casual address. It was more "me" anyway, as I have never been a formal person. I'm afraid that might have been part of my downfall – I didn't demand the authority and respect of a "title," and so I didn't get much.

This was a big issue in the church in the 1980's when I was ordained. Everywhere I went, I was asked, "What do we call women priests?" Of course, the first answer I wanted to give was "NOT women priests – just priests" but I knew what they meant. "Father" seemed hardly appropriate, although there were many hard-boiled Anglo-Catholic Episcopalians in the Diocese of Albany who just could not call me "Susan," and who insisted on calling me "Father." I knew that the title meant "Priest" to them and so it was fine with me, but it was very offputting to many people.

When I was a new priest in Southern Virginia, the new Presiding Bishop, Edmund Browning was scheduled to be the keynoter at our Annual Council Meeting – his first "appearance" at a Diocesan convention since his consecration. Bishop Vaché had called me one day saying that he needed his "Token Priest." That's what he called me – I was female and I was from the West so I filled both slots that he was always careful to fill so that members of the clergy in the far reaches of the Diocese as well as those in the minority felt represented. I knew that he really respected my skills and that he meant it in a positive way. I quickly agreed to be his "token" on a panel of clergy who would take pre-submitted questions for the Presiding Bishop, sort through them, and come up with a slate of Q&A's for an open session.

We got a ton of questions but many of them were similar. By the end of the allotted time, we had run out of written questions, and I could feel the Bishop getting ready to call the meeting to a close. I touched his arm and asked, "Bishop, could I ask Bishop Browning one last question?" He looked at me with eyes that said, "Don't make me sorry for this," and handed me the microphone. I stood and said, "Bishop Browning, there is one burning question that I have taken to the highest ecclesiastical authority in this Diocese and have gotten no answer." I could feel the Bishop glaring at me, but I pressed on. I had the whole room's attention at this point. My conversation with the Presiding Bishop continued:

> Me: "So would you answer this one question?"
> PB: "Sure"
> Me: "What do you call a woman priest?"

I brought the house down! Everyone, including my Bishop, was roaring with laughter. With perfect comedic timing, we continued:

> PB: "What do *you* want to be called?"
> Me: "Susan."
> PB: "Me too!"
> Me: "You want to be called 'Susan'?"

By now everyone was howling; we had done some serious ecclesiastical "schtick." My Bishop grabbed the microphone at that point to allow Bishop Browning to make some anti-climatic statement about women being called whatever they wanted to be called. The session ended, Bishop Browning came over, hugged me, and said, "Thank you! I haven't laughed that hard in a year!"

Thinking about all that, maybe I'm off base – maybe I was just a rotten priest who didn't deserve the authority and respect necessary to run a parish, but I don't think so. I received too many accolades; too many members of my parishes said things like, "You have changed my life" and "You're the best priest I've ever had" and "I wish you had been around when I was growing up."

THE END – ALMOST

I had been a broken priest after the first bad experience; I was ready to leave the church completely after the second one. For the first few weeks, I holed up in my house but then I missed being in church on Sunday morning, so I decided to go to church. I picked a church some distance away, because I wanted to worship where I would be anonymous. I was tempted to ditch the whole idea when I arrived and discovered that there was a baptism, but I decided I'd look pretty stupid if I turned around and left; so I found a seat in a pew near the side door and sat down.

The service was fine and I actually enjoyed the sermon and the baptism, but, during the announcements, the strangest thing happened. I began to hear these voices in my head that sounded suspiciously like the negative thoughts that I knew had been rampant in both of my last churches. In my head, while I was sitting in this nice church listening to their nice priest and her parishioners, announce upcoming events, I heard things like, "That's really a stupid idea – nobody will come to that" and "Why does she keep talking about Jesus being the head of the church – that's crazy." I wanted to jump up and run out of that place, but I managed to last through communion, which I needed desperately. Then I walked straight out of the church, went to my car, climbed in, and cried for 20 minutes, until people started coming out of the church. Then I went shopping.

Usually that soothes my savage beast, but not that day. I was in a deep spiritual funk, which just got deeper following the abject failure of a good shopping spree to restore my poor soul. I decided that, not only was I *not* going to take on another parish ministry, I was determined to quit the priesthood, the church, and Christianity in general. I was tired of being beat up by a ministry that was supposed to be fulfilling, enjoyable, and productive. I was living in what I called a spiritual limbo but in actuality, it was just hell. I couldn't find any peace, any job, or any grace in my situation. I couldn't see God's hand in it, and quite frankly, I was hoping God would keep out of it since it had all been one huge mess from day one.

TRINITY MARKETPLACE

Meanwhile, I was still stuck in town since I didn't have a buyer for my house. I had recently opened an online gift shop, called Trinity Marketplace, which wasn't really going anywhere, but I was convinced that I could make a go of it if I reactivated the website and did some serious marketing. I began looking at other online retailers' classified ads, so I could get some ideas as to how to go about my own advertising campaign. I was checking out ads one day and a large ad jumped off the page at me: "For Rent – Share space with local newspaper - $150 month."

My mind jerked into action. If I had a "bricks and mortar" store as well as the online store, I just knew I could make Trinity Marketplace a household word. Besides, I had always wanted to own a gift shop, and what a deal this was! I knew the newspaper reporter that worked in that office, and she only had office hours on two days a week. I liked her and knew we could work together. I thought, "If I'm ever going to try this, now is the time!"

WHITE CREEK

I was excited but I was also broke. I *had* to have some income soon, or I would be unable to pay my bills, much less open a store. Christmas came and went, and I really didn't get into it as usual. It was the second time in my life that I hadn't been to a midnight service on Christmas Eve and I missed it. It was the first time in years that I hadn't celebrated the Eucharist for Christmas, but I had managed to put that out of my mind.

A few days after Christmas, I was in my Physical Therapist's office, in which I spent way too much time and money. When I was checking out, the receptionist looked up at me and asked, "Can you do services in a Methodist Church?"

Before I thought about it, I replied, "I can do services anywhere; the question is 'Would the Methodist Church allow me to do services in your congregation?'" She assured me that the leader of this little congregation out in the country had asked the UMC Bishop and had been assured that it was fine.

I have no idea why I even gave this a passing thought, but for some reason, I thought it might be a good idea. When I figured out my finances, I could see that I definitely needed a better cash flow and **soon;** so I knew I'd better look into this opportunity. She had given me the phone number for the President, a woman named

Margaret. I thought long and hard about this little congregation. All I knew about it I had gotten from my PT receptionist. It was in the serious "boonies" of upstate New York; it was called Jermain United Methodist Church, and it was in White Creek, NY, better known by those who live there as "the Crik"; and they said that all they wanted was someone to do services for them.

So I called Margaret and, after a brief hello, she jumped right in and asked me if I could do services for them on the first Sunday in January. I swear I didn't even hesitate. I don't know if it was her sweet, soft voice (she was 90 at the time), or if I just needed the money, but I found myself agreeing to do their service on that Sunday. I got directions and other pertinent information, and hung up the phone, wondering, "What am I thinking!"

As it turned out, I wasn't thinking at all. I was moving on autopilot, which was still operating after 20 years of being the one at the front of the church on Sunday morning with the stole and the sermon. For that moment, I wasn't thinking about how much I wanted to chuck all of this. I just said, "Yes."

CHAPTER SEVENTEEN

The Beginning

BACK TO LIFE

Well, I am convinced that God brought me to this tiny little church in the boonies of Upstate New York not only so that I could minister to them, but so that they could minister to me. I had been a broken priest after the first disastrous church; I was destroyed after the second one. I needed healing and God had found the healer.

Of course, I didn't know that at the time. I just needed the money, and they needed me so I showed up at the picturesque white clapboard church, figuring I would do my

Jermain United Methodist Church
White Creek, New York

thing, collect my money, and go home. It was a good gig with no extraneous responsibilities to take time away from my new venture – setting up my brand new gift shop in the front office of the local weekly newspaper. I had decided that the opportunity to open a shop with such low overhead must have been some kind of sign, and when everything just fell together – insurance, phone, internet access, even an air conditioner! – I just knew it was right, so I jumped at it. On February 1st, I opened The Trinity Marketplace right on the main drag.

      Scott, now married with children, brought the whole family up on opening day and we actually had customers and made a few sales, which I rang up on my brand new cash register they gave me for my birthday! I was off and running. I had parted with the church in town on relatively friendly terms with a gracious parting celebration and gift, so I fully expected many of them to hurry over and check out my store. I was disappointed. In fact, I was disappointed in the entire community. I had been living there for almost five years and I was known by many, thanks to my high-visibility positions at the church and as a Police Dispatcher. For the first weeks, I sat there thinking about all the people that I was certain would come to the store, at least to satisfy their curiosity, if not as a show of support. I figured many of them would make at least a small purchase, if for no other reason than to be kind and supportive, but most of them never even darkened the doorway.

      I was already concerned about how I would pay the next month's rent, so when Margaret had asked me to do their services for the whole month of February, I had thought, "Why not?" They were nice, the church was sweet, and I was in that enviable position that makes all supply clergy happy – I got to preach and then go home. I wouldn't have to deal with the fallout or anything else. It was like being a grandmother – you know, when you take the grandchildren for the day, spoil them, have fun with them, and then deposit them in their parents' arms and go home. And then there was the rent to pay.

ANOTHER NEW AND UNEXPECTED ROLE

      I found that I really enjoyed leading the services at Jermain UMC. It was winter and they had closed the main sanctuary (which was huge and prohibitively expensive to heat just for a few hours a week), and set up a small worship space in the meeting area, which was closed off from the sanctuary by huge roll-down doors. It was a cozy arrangement which made sense for this small community of worshipers. On a good Sunday, there were 8-10 in attendance; with their portable organ moved into the space beside the podium, we all fit rather nicely.

      Toward the end of February, Margaret had booked me for the month of March as well, so I figured they must like me. I certainly liked them. They were responsive to my sermons and

funny stories, and they were beginning to talk about wanting me
to teach a Bible Study before church. I was flattered but I was now
very protective of my time and of my well-being. I shied away from
anything that smacked of "full-time ministry," and was still on the
look-out for the telltale signs of disapproval and unrest. So when
Margaret and Maurice, the new President, approached me to ask if
I would consider being their permanent pastor, I immediately felt a
huge "No way," working its way to my lips.

I was enjoying this limited ministry with them and I was
feeling somewhat less hostile about church; but I was still leery, so I
told them I would think about it. I went home and made two calls:
one to Scott who said, "Mom don't do this to yourself again" and
the other to my dear friend, Darius, who was less suspicious but still
advised me to be very up-front about exactly what I would do and
exactly what I expected.

"If they can't deal with it," he said, "you know what to do."
That would be the "Biblical boogie-on" prescribed by Jesus himself
to the disciples in the Gospel of Matthew (10:14): "If anyone will not
welcome you or listen to your words, leave that home or town and
shake the dust off your feet."

So the next Sunday, I told them that if they were serious,
I would preach a specific sermon the following Sunday about the
ministry of the church, and if they liked what they heard, we could
talk. They agreed and the following Sunday I preached a blistering
sermon on what I believed the Church is and should be, making it
very clear that I believed that Jesus was the head of the Church, and
that we were his arms and feet in the world. I made it abundantly
clear that I believed in the ministry of all believers and that I would
expect them to take their responsibilities seriously. I was in fine form
that day and my sermon was a barn-burner! When the service was
over, I stood at the podium while they all looked at me in silence. I
figured it was over so I just blurted out, "So, anybody want to talk?"

The organist spoke up first. Actually, spoke *out* would be
more like it because she actually banged her hand on the organ
bench and said, "That's exactly what I believe!" Nobody had ever
preached like that in their church and she loved it! Others spoke
up and said that they agreed with my theology of the church and
would be happy to have me preaching to them every Sunday. Then
someone said how excited she was about the prospects of the church
growing with my leadership. I felt the hair prickling on the back

of my neck so I quickly repeated the #1 rule: "I will *not* run your church." They could only pay me enough to do services on Sundays, preach, and pastor, and that was all I was going to do. If there was going to be any serious leadership, it would have to come from them. If they really wanted their church to grow, they would have to work at it.

I again reminded them that this also meant that I would not be involved in the finances or the business decisions. I asked them, "Do you want me to continue preparing the bulletins?"

Maurice immediately said, "Absolutely, we love them."

I remember thinking, "Am I dreaming? Is this guy for real?"

Then he added, "If you're going to do that, then this is not enough money. How much more will you need for ink and paper and stuff like that?"

I thought, "I'm in a parallel universe or something!" No one, in any church, in any town, had ever said those words or anything even close in my presence. However, I knew what negotiating could look like in the church and here's where I figured the conversation would go south. I began, "Well, I only print a dozen...."

Maurice interrupted me, "How about if we give you another $200 a month; would that be enough? I was really in shock now! Not only had they totally bought my theology of the Church and had agreed right then and there to try their best to live by it, they had also offered me a reasonable amount of money without being browbeat into it. Then they voluntarily added a more than generous amount for the printing. Could this be real? I was on the verge of saying "yes," but there was one more thing. I was almost there.

I said, "OK, this sounds good, but I have one more requirement." They didn't bat even one eye, so I continued, "If I ever, ever, ever find out that you are talking about me behind my back and if you ever, ever, ever crab about something you don't like to everybody but me, I will not only quit, I will walk out on the spot and you'll never see me again. I was almost destroyed by that kind of deceit and disrespect and I will not tolerate it."

There was silence – for one nanosecond – and then Margaret, the matriarch extraordinaire – said in a loud and clear voice, "I promise you, that if there's anything we don't like, you'll be the first to know about it." They all laughed but I could tell that they agreed with her. We all laughed and hugged and the deal was done. On the way home, I felt a twinge of "O God, what have I done?" but I immediately heard that peaceful divine sigh deep in my soul that said, "I approve," and it has been the best thing I ever did in parish ministry.

"LADY FATHER" – ALIVE AND WELL

I officially became their permanent supply pastor retroactive to March 1, 2006 and by this time I was well on the road to recovery. These wonderful Christians with their tiny little congregation of faithful folks who loved God, their church, and each other, opened their arms and raked me into their circle of love and acceptance. They didn't care what kind of problems I had dealt with; they didn't care what my former parishes thought of me. They listened to my sermons, begged for Bible Study, and listened to what I had to teach them, and they loved me.

No matter what, they still wanted me back every Sunday. And they have come faithfully to a half-hour Bible Study before worship (at 8:30 am, believe it or not) for the past five years. For a half-hour every week, they have asked questions and just soaked up everything I could teach them about the Bible, about God, about Jesus, and even about the Methodist Church. We have learned many things together and when we've gotten bogged down, one of them has always spoken up and said, "Can we move on to something new?" and we do.

To my knowledge, there have been no major issues, and you can believe that I have kept every ear I have to the ground. I talk regularly with the Organist and others about how things are going. Every time, I'm told, "We're all happy; everything is great." Once, one of the board members asked if we could not sing such long hymns on hot summer Sundays and once he asked if I could print more bulletins. And that's the way it's been. It's not perfect – nothing is this side of heaven; but it is a beautiful niche in God's church where there is no discrimination, no bias, no anger, no accusations, no back-biting, and "no fussing over nothing."

THE STRUGGLE TO SURVIVE

In the meantime, life went on for me and my new business. The shop had a decent amount of traffic for awhile and I was able to add a few new products. I now had some books, gifts (religious and secular), wall and other decorations, and lots of jewelry. That was the biggest seller so I kept getting new and different styles and types of jewelry; word began to spread that I had a dynamite selection of affordable jewelry, and traffic picked up some. During the summer, I took my shop on the road to the village park on Wednesday evenings where most of the people in the area gathered for the Community Orchestra concerts. There were other booths, one with hamburgers, hot dogs, and homemade desserts; the Boy Scouts sold popcorn; there were some organic farmers and other local growers with a farmers market, a few miscellaneous booths, and *me*.

I dragged so much of my inventory out to the park every week that I had to beg and cajole some teenagers I had met through the Youth Center where I served on the Board to help me set up and take it down. I made a decent amount off the concert-goers and I paid the kids with inventory so I didn't feel it too much. Several of them hired on to help me in the shop in the afternoons and on weekends. It really felt like things would pick up. At least I had all the right elements in place. All I had to do was get some of the local people to shop with me for Christmas.

Alas! Such is not the nature of small towns in upstate New York where there is a Wal-Mart close by. They just don't shop locally and support their neighbors! Even after I added the very popular Willow Tree line of statues to my inventory, I still wasn't making ends meet each month. There didn't seem to be much hope of any kind of profit in the foreseeable future, but I kept at it. I made signs and postcards and online ads and newspaper ads and I ran sales and tried in vain to set up home parties.

BACK TO THE GRIND

By November, it was obvious that I needed some serious additional income if I was going to be able to keep my house so I went online looking for something I could do part-time, still keep the shop open, and try to make it work. I found a part-time job some 40 minutes from home that just barely enabled me to pay the bills. The company was a business telemarketing company that refused to call themselves telemarketers; but what we did was call businesses that had previously purchased the business and financial books we sold for major publishers, and asked if they would like to take advantage of a sale or a new product. It gave a whole new meaning to the saying, "Back to the grind," and every morning that's where I had to go. I hated it so much that I began to be sick at my stomach during much of every day. When I was assigned the "Renewals,"

I was so relieved since these businesses almost all renewed their subscriptions. This meant less "pushy sales talk," an increase in my sales, and even a raise. I still dreaded it every morning, but at least I could stomach the job.

But the handwriting was on the wall. The drive was killing me with the cost of gas, and I was adding expensive mileage to my leased car. I needed to be closer to the Capital District where my son and his family lived. I was getting too old for the "midnight" shift at the Police Department, which I was still doing once a week but I figured that if I moved back to Albany, I could make up for the loss of that income by eliminating the 66 miles a day I was driving to a stressful job that I detested.

I continued to push the website and the shop but finally, after a so-so Christmas season, I had to face the awful truth. This town was not small-business friendly. In fact, three other businesses had closed their doors as the village continued to shoot itself and its small businesses in the foot, and it was becoming clear that I was next. I was going belly-up.

I closed the shop in February and continued to work at the hated job until one day in August, I was searching Craigslist for the hundredth time and finally, I hit pay dirt. I found an ad for a Travel Counselor with AAA in Albany, interviewed, got the job, and in August 2007, I became an Auto Travel Counselor for AAA. Suddenly, I was getting paid for taking people's money and telling them where to go! It was an amazingly low starting salary, not even as much as I was making on the phone lines, but I couldn't get out of there fast enough.

Although I liked the work at AAA, I really didn't want to work at a clock-punching job anywhere, but since I had joined the Church Pension Fund at the ripe "old" age of 38, my monthly pension amount was not enough to live on, making a supplemental job a necessary evil. At least this one was bearable – it was still a "grind," but a tolerable one. As I learned the ropes and became quite adept at making Trip-Tiks, I decided that it was a sweet retirement job for me. I loved maps and traveling and I especially loved people; talking to them all day long about their travel plans was nothing short of a miracle job for me. However, I was now driving 75 miles a day and the price of gas was soaring; I really had to get moving.

That's what I did. I sold the house and made enough for a nice nest egg, which I added to my smaller one giving me a comfortable cushion until I hit the magic age which would bring me the same amount of money I was making at AAA and the "mother of all reasons to be 66 years old" – Medicare!

THE BEGINNING

The parishioners at Jermain were panicky when I announced that I was moving back to Albany, but I quickly assured them that I would still be their Pastor. While this sweet little congregation hadn't grown as much as we all had hoped, we had managed to strike just the right chord for us as pastor and people. God had brought me full-circle once again – from the innocence of the Episcopal Church of the 1950's and 1960's where I learned about God, to the innocence of a tiny little United Methodist congregation where once again I learned about God. I began in a place where the church was engrained in me, only to return to a simple, country church that matched my soul's memories. I'm happy to report that my love for my church of origin has resurfaced, as I have shared some of the worship and music of my beloved Episcopal Church with these Methodist/Episcopal-turned-Methodists. I do miss the pomp and ceremony of the Episcopal Eucharist service but the Methodists put up with my signs of the cross and manual acts and Anglican vestments, which I wear for special occasions.

These simple, but loving folks have learned that I don't have all the answers, as I readily confess to them that I don't know the "God Things," because God has not told me about them yet. These are things like "who goes to heaven and who doesn't," "how did God make Jesus," and "why does God let bad things happen to good people?" I give them my best shot, and we even go looking for answers together; then there were the very special times when we all learned from an unexpected source.

OUT OF THE MOUTHS OF BABES

Remember Art Linkletter? He used to do the program called "Kids Say the Darndest Things." There were four little kids sitting on chairs in a line on a platform, so that he could sit on the edge of it and be face-to-face with them. He asked the kids questions about everything from family life to the Bible, and the answers that I heard were, and still are, some of the funniest stuff on TV.

Well, his premise is still true today. Kids, with their innocence and literal thinking process, absolutely say "the darndest things," and we adults continue to laugh at them. During my three years assisting Rick in the Lawrenceville churches, I had learned many things, the best of which was what he called "The Wonder Box." This was his children's sermon and it worked like this. He had a metal file box that was entrusted to a different child every week, with the instructions that they were to place an object (nothing live or that had ever been alive) in the box. At the appointed time in the service, he would gather all the children around him at the front of the church and, with great ceremony, accept the Wonder Box. It was called the Wonder Box because "he wondered what was in it." He would proceed to use that object to teach the children some profound truth about God. I have used the Wonder Box in many churches and they love it at Jermain.

One Sunday, I had asked a little girl to bring in an object for the Wonder Box and this precious 5-year-old came, with her mother, to the front of the church. Together they handed me a crucifix, which did not have a body on it. It was just a cross with holes in the two ends of the cross-beam and in the bottom of the cross. Her mother explained to me that when they had moved, the body of Jesus had come off of the cross, and they were hesitant to put it back on because they didn't know how they felt about nailing Jesus on the cross.

Wow! What a sermon opening! No preacher could get this one wrong. I always began by asking some questions to identify the object, like, "What is this?" and "What do we do with this?" This was to get the children involved, plus, it gave me time to gather my thoughts and plug into the Holy Spirit, who always gave me words at the right moment. Although, in this case, I already had the perfect lead-in, I stuck to my proven formula and said, "So, what is this?"

She looked at me like I was a dunderhead, and said, "It's a cross."

Then I asked her, "Why are there holes in the cross?" Again, I was following my outline and again she looked at me like she couldn't believe that I didn't know the answers to these obvious questions.

Then she leaned forward and whispered to me, "They were for the nails – to keep him on the cross." Before I could say a word, she turned to the congregation and said, in a loud voice, "I guess she doesn't know about Jesus and the nails."

Needless to say, she brought down the house! She didn't

know why everyone was laughing but she looked very proud that she had obviously said something very clever. She turned around and beamed at me and said, "I can tell you about him if you like."

Well, I was undone. I figured that it would be at least 10 minutes before I could speak more than a few intelligent words, but I did manage to say, "Great – tell me." And she did.

What a wonderful model for a Christian and for a preacher. That small child showed us all that it's not only OK to talk about our beliefs, but it's a necessary thing, if everyone is going to have the same information. She illustrated for us all how easy it can be to talk about what we believe, and how natural it is. My favorite thing about the whole encounter was her facial expression, which made it abundantly clear that she was appalled at how little I knew about someone as important as Jesus.

As someone once said, wisdom comes "Out of the mouths of babes" more often than it does from adults, and I believe that is because the children have not yet learned to be afraid of saying something stupid or wrong. They just say what they know. They have not yet become self-conscious about much of anything, which lets them speak their minds without all the qualifications we adults feel that we have to add in order to sound intelligent. Most adults would have answered my questions (if indeed they spoke up at all) as follows: "What is this?" "Uh, it looks like a cross." (God forbid they should be wrong so they hedge a little.) "Why are there holes in the cross?" "Uh, I'm not sure – maybe to hold it up on the wall or to hold a jewel or some other decoration. What do you think?" Another hedge….another effort to avoid making a mistake.

Thank God for kids who don't hesitate, hedge, or try to keep from sounding stupid. They just tell it like it is and the result is – they sound smart. Oh, that we adults could let loose and say the darnedest things again! From this little girl, I received a wonderful gift – a gift of trust and a gift of truth. She trusted me enough to share her treasured cross with me and she trusted me and the congregation enough to just be herself. From her, we not only learned about Jesus and the nails, but we also learned that truth is truth, even when comes "out of the mouths of babes." I will always treasure that little girl for her courage and her truth. I will also treasure the congregation of Jermain Church for trusting me to share God's truth with them.

In January 2011, we celebrated five years of basically

conflict-free ministry and God's plan to heal this wounded and hurting priest was a huge success. They brought me out of hell and back to life by giving me the experience of grace, even as I taught them its meaning. Early on in our ministry, I made them all memorize the definition of grace, and here's why. I didn't know what God's grace was until I was 32 years old, and I wanted them to know what I knew. I wanted them to teach their children and grandchildren, because no one should have to live without knowing and experiencing the free love of God.

That is grace – God loves us no matter who and what we are, no matter what we do or where we go, and no matter how many times we go away and then want to come back. God's love is simple, it's unconditional, and there are no strings attached. This is grace, and grace is what made me whole again.

POSTSCRIPT

As I write this, my Bishop who ordained me, and my spiritual director who helped me to find Jesus again, have both died. The Bishop of Albany is retired, and many of my friends from the early days in the Diocese of Albany have moved on. I received word, as I wrote this last section, that the former Rector of St. Paul's in Petersburg, the Rev. Sydney Swann, has also died. He was my first model of the priesthood, although he would have never called himself that. He was the one I watched and said to myself, "I wish I could be a man so I could do what he's doing."

Many of my heroes *are* gone now, but they live on in my heart, and I still have one left. I still have Jesus, who waited all those years for me to find him again in the attic of my soul, who will never leave me, and who was the one who made sure that I survived an outrageous and amazing journey so that I could be God's priest in God's Church for as long as God needs me. Hallelujah and Amen!

Disclaimer: This book is my honest recollection of the events of my life from 1975 to the present day. I have changed the names of some people, as it is not my desire to identify any-one who may have caused me pain. I have forgiven them and moved on and I sincerely pray that my words will not be a source of pain or embarrassment to anyone.

Betsy Hamlet Nichols

When Summer was in the Meadow

Author: Betsy Hamlet Nichols

ISBN-13: 978-0981472539
ISBN-10: 0981472532

Also Published by Aberdeen Bay

When Summer was in the Meadow records and preserves a time that is receding all too quickly into the lost pages of the last century. Based on actual events of the 20's and early 30's, the work is the real-life story of Evelyn Johnson, a child who in her own voice draws us into a magical world of backyard circuses, church picnics, and friendly neighbors. As she matures, her narration reveals with poignancy and humor life as it was lived by ordinary people during a critical period in American history. The story has historical appeal in its evocation of life in the South and in its recall of actual places, events, and persons of the time–from the talkies and Lindbergh to FDR and the Great Depression. In a larger sense, however, this is a story about ourselves and the power of remembrance to shape our lives and the lives of those who follow us.

""When Summer was in the Meadow" is a brilliant story told in such a way that one truly feels like they've stepped back in time. I think it will strike a chord in many people, and make real the stories heard from older members of a family. I highly recommend it."

-- J. Leverett

CPSIA information can be obtained
at www.ICGtesting.com
Printed in the USA
FFHW011354130919
54905280-60618FF